EAST ANGLIA
walking the ley lines and ancient tracks

EAST ANGLIA
walking the ley lines and ancient tracks

Shirley Toulson

Illustrated by Oliver Caldecott

Maps drawn by Sue Lawes

Wildwood House London

First published in Great Britain 1979

Wildwood House Limited
1 Prince of Wales Passage
117 Hampstead Road
London NW1 3EE

In Australia by Bookwise Australia Pty Ltd,
104 Sussex Street, Sydney, 2000.

ISBN 0 7045 3008 2

Designed by Fiona MacGregor

Typeset by Inforum Ltd, Portsmouth
Printed and bound in Britain by
Biddles Ltd, Guildford

Contents

For Ian and Mary Jane with love and
thanks

Acknowledgements

The people who helped me with this
book are almost all mentioned in its
pages. They include academic
archaeologists, whose patient attention
to detail makes them impatient of the
wide speculations on which my work is
based; and 'geomancers' whose beliefs I
have not always been able to share.
Members of both these groups have two
important qualities in common: a
genuine love of the countryside and its
history, and a willingness to give gener-
ously of their time to provide the
enquirer with topographical and historical information relating to it.

More specifically, I wish to acknow-
ledge my debt to Nigel Pennick and
Michael Burgess who discovered the
Nuthampstead and Bury St Edmunds
zodiacs respectively.

I also want to say thank you to the staff
of the Suffolk Record Office in Bury St
Edmunds, where much of my research
was done; to my friends Michael and
Anna Pollard who introduced me to
Peddars' Way, and who helped me seek
out Norfolk puddingstones; and most
especially to Joyce Rudderham who
shared her life-long interest and knowledge of Suffolk lanes with me.

These people are in no way connected
with the hypotheses put forward in this
book, nor do they bear any responsibil-
ity for any misinterpretations I may have
unwittingly put on the information they
so kindly gave me.

Introduction

One hot summer afternoon in 1921, Alfred Watkins, a gentleman in his mid-sixties, went riding on the Bredwardine Hills about 12 miles (19·3 km) to the west of Hereford. A local merchant used to making deliveries in the area, he knew the district well – and from several aspects, for, besides his business interests, he was an enthusiastic, amateur archaeologist and naturalist, and a keen photographer of rural landscapes. Yet that day, as he let his horse rest on a piece of high ground while he looked around at the familiar view, the countryside he knew so well suddenly switched into a new focus. He noticed that the salient landmarks – churches, burial mounds, mountain passes – were not randomly arranged but fell into patterns of straight lines, many of which coincided with roads, tracks or remains of old highways.

Five months later he published an account of this vision in a booklet entitled *Early British Trackways*; this was followed in 1925 by *The Old Straight Track*, the book that he is generally known by today, in which he elaborated the implications of his original deductions. His book was widely read from the start, and from 1933 when the first cheap edition was published, the phrase 'ley lines', which he used to define the old, straight tracks, became an accepted part of the language; although most dictionaries still ignore it, and refer the reader to the original meaning of the word 'ley' or 'lea' denoting a grassy field. The latter meaning accounts for the fact that the word is so often incorporated into English place names. Yet there is no conflict with Watkins' use of the word, and nothing absurd in his observation that 'ley' place names are often to be found at significant points on 'ley lines'. For a field denotes a settlement, and the most substantial part of Watkins' own definition of 'ley lines' was that they were straight lines running across country from one settlement to another.

Yet that is not the whole explanation either, and Watkins never thought it was; although in order to get his vision more easily accepted he stressed the final use of ley lines as trading routes above their more speculative origins as sources of earth energy coinciding with alignments drawn from sunrise or sunset at the equinoxes. This caution did not stop him from acknowledging the work on these alignments done at Stonehenge by Sir Norman Lockyer at the turn of the century; and throughout his book there are strong hints that he firmly believed that the Bronze and Iron Age surveyors,

7

whom he called Dod-men, were not simply concerned with matters of practical immediacy.

Not that I find it wise to make any sharp distinction between practical and mystical matters. For me the greatest mysteries are contained in the ways that individual human beings confront and attempt to solve the problems of existence in a seemingly impersonal universe. So I find a track that has been used as a trading route for thousands of years numinous for that reason, whether it aligns with a significant part of the heavens or not; and whether or not it coincides with lines which some people convincingly suggest carry energies and powers which, like electricity, cannot be completely accounted for by human reason.

Neolithic man needed three things which often had to be transported long distances. They were: flints for making weapons for hunting and for clearing the forests when he started farming; salt to preserve his food; and clay to make storage pots. Watkins found that the place names along many of his ley lines indicated that these commodities had once been carried along them. Flints are indicated by names incorporating 'knap' or 'chip'; 'white' denotes salt (although it can also simply refer to chalk); and 'red' is for potters' clay. Since Watkins' time the full significance that red ochre had for early man has been more fully understood. It is discussed in some detail in Lyall Watson's *Lifetides*. So I believe that the frequency of the word for 'red' in place names, particularly in Wales, must refer to that clay, rather than to the routes of potters. We now know from the red 'lady' of Gower, and other exhumed bodies from very early burial sites, which were in some way treated with this earth, that it must have had a deep religious significance for early man. Its considerable magical value must then have been greatly enhanced when it was discovered that red ochre is an active ingredient in the extraction of iron ore. So it is no wonder that any place at which it is concentrated in the ground, or over which it was transported, should be marked by its name.

Watkins did not stress, although he could well have done without attracting charges of supernatural mysticism, that his trading-route trackways also frequently coincide with the pilgrims' routes of mediaeval times. It seems to me that there is a very simple explanation as to how this came about. As Watkins noted, men marked the tracks with cairns, standing stones, henges (or sacred rings now often replaced by Christian churches), barrows and moats, so anyone moving along the track was bound to be walking from one holy place to another.

There are several explanations as to how these places came to be so holy, and first of all I want to consider a basic matter of secular convenience. Obviously one of the most heinous crimes one traveller can commit against another is to remove the 'mark stones' or alter their position in any way, as anyone who has been the victim of a twisted or demolished signpost will agree. Now

8

the most efficient way to enforce a taboo is to invest it with mystical potency. Folk tales about the disasters that happened to farmers who used stones from henge monuments to build their barns, as well as the commonly held belief that it is evil to tamper with burial places, could well have originated in the curses put upon people who interfered with the way marks.

The disturbance of these marking features would be even more serious if they were placed not only to mark trading routes, but also to serve as calendars, and as a way of marking out the course of the cycle of the seasons. Sir Frederick Hoyle's work at Stonehenge and Professor Alexander Thom's correlation of the orientation of stone circles and menhirs throughout the United Kingdom leave no room to doubt that the ley alignments radiating from these centres were deliberately drawn to mark the equinoctial sunrise and sunset; and to calculate the course of the phases of the moon.

The prehistoric astronomers who undertook this surveying, whose skill was so subtle that they could predict lunar eclipses, were naturally regarded with great awe by the common people, and it's easy to understand how their powers might have come to be regarded as having a supernatural origin. Watkins believed that the sighting staff with which the surveying was done was identical to all rods of office from the monarch's sceptre to the wizard's wand, and closely associated with the dowser's hazel twig.

There is one difference. It seemed to Watkins that the survey which resulted in marking out the lines of the seasonal alignments and the convenient trading routes was done with two staves; and that the Long Man of Wilmington, cut out in the chalk of the Sussex Downs to the north of Eastbourne, is holding two such staves in his hands to commemorate the meticulous surveying on which the religion and prosperity of Stone Age man was based. It is easy to understand why people believed that such a tremendous task must have been undertaken by giants.

To say that these surveyors, or Dodmen, were marking out paths aligned on the sun or other heavenly bodies is also partly to say that they were interpreting and making obvious paths already inherent in the earth's surface; and that this belief is central to an understanding of the power of ley lines. For many people believe them to be lines of power linked to the earth's magnetism, frequently following a geological flaw in the earth's surface. In this way they can serve as viaducts for the transmission of energy and even of telepathic communications.

The natural power of earth is closely linked with the element of water, which is why the rediscovery of ley lines in modern times is partly dependent on the skill of dowsers. For the route of a ley line often coincides with, or runs close to, the path of an underground stream; and standing stones, either on their own or as part of stone circles, usually stand over blind springs which, when tapped, are reported to have healing powers. In that sense the ley lines are a natural phenomenon, but the way marks which define their alignments are man-made. And whether you believe in the cosmic energy of the ley lines or not, as you walk through the countryside, the important matter, as Watkins wrote in 1925, is to decide whether the existence of the alignment of significant places throughout Britain is 'a humanly designed fact, an accidental coincidence or a "mare's nest" '.

Most academics have certainly treated Watkins' theories as a 'mare's nest', mainly by simply ignoring his publications, or by ridiculing any mention of ley lines without bothering to discover his true intentions. I think that this has come about partly through an accident of fashion in historical scholarship. For decades archaeology has concerned itself with minutiae, from which overall topographical patterns cannot easily be deduced. And although aerial photographs have been a pertinent tool for prehistorians for some years now, it is only very recently that they have been used to make any wide deductions about the lie of the land.

But scholars, with a few notable exceptions, have not just ignored Watkins' theories; they have treated his work with that quick scorn with which people often confront the disturbing. I have heard him rather oddly described as 'the man who bent straight lines' – or twisted the truth to suit his own ends. This is not to say that a ley hunter in a particular area should not beware of falling into a mare's nest. We are all prone to see what

we want to see, and in tracing alignments along ley lines throughout the country, it is all too easy to make significant landmarks out of what appear at closer inspection to be very recent or trivial disturbances of the top soil.

I do not agree though that an alignment point must automatically be discounted because it is modern. Water towers are likely to be situated at significant points over underground water, in the same way that holy wells were sunk there; and it has been pointed out that microwave towers can well be equated with megaliths (and as most of them stand on ley lines this could well be the case), if you believe that the standing stones were the focal points for energies travelling along the leys. Scoffers should beware of discounting the theory of ley lines by pointing to alignments of telephone boxes. As lines of communication their siting could be as relevant as that of Saxon churches to the ley alignments, although both the post office engineers and the church builders may well have thought they were simply complying with convenience in choosing the sites.

This is not to deny the possibility of chance. Watkins was constantly aware that an alignment of three or four churches, barrows or moats (for example) could be random, and he always urged ley hunters to be very cautious before making any quick deductions about a line. He advocated that at least five significant marks must be found before an alignment can be projected through them and that each of them must be carefully checked on the ground as well as noted on the map. So it is probably best to approach each ley hunting expedition with a certain amount of scepticism, and not to be too immediately convinced by the patterns the landscape presents and the coincidences in the place names that you'll come across.

It is important to remember that since Neolithic times, when the ley lines are generally believed to have been marked out by man, the British countryside has undergone at least three immense changes. These have been enumerated by O.G.S.Crawford (at one time archaeology officer to the Ordnance Survey). The first came with the setting up of numerous agricultural settlements in Iron Age times; the second with the Saxon invasions; and the third at the time of enclosures. I would like to add a fourth, for even in remote country areas the industrial revolution left its marks – in canals, railways and now motorway networks and the various sorts of power stations. These changes have obviously affected both the appearance and the accessibility of the alignments. You also have to remember that in most places, except where you have reason to believe that there has been considerable drying out of the peat, you will be walking several yards above the level of the land in the third and fourth millenia BC.

Nevertheless, it is along roads and trackways that have existed for thousands of years that you will follow the ley lines. Often these tracks will coincide with Roman roads, for the Romans were wise enough to make use of existing lines of communication. And it is in looking at the lie of Roman roads that we can get some clue as to whether the tracks were purely a matter of human construction, or whether they were ways of the earth itself, trodden by beasts, drawn along paths that exercised some sort of magnetic attraction, long before men tried to find their way across the country.

It is not always easy to understand why the old roads so often seem to take so little notice of the traveller's convenience. As Crawford points out, Roman roads hardly ever run along the bottom of a long valley, or if that was too wet, along the hillside. Instead they keep to the heights, going from hill-top to hill-top. And Watkins described how tracks on sited leys went straight up a mountainside over whatever 'seemingly improbable obstacles came in the way' rather than taking a winding, less strenuous path. There are a few exceptions, when a Roman road swerves to avoid an obstacle, and for our purposes the most notable of these occurs in Wiltshire, where the Roman road, now mostly covered by the A4, is deflected from its straight course by the prehistoric mystery of Silbury Hill.

So what we will expect to find in tracing out the relation between existing tracks and the ley alignments is some notion of how our ancestors co-operated with the forces of the earth in working out their routes. It is a sensitivity that we have lost in the building-up of motorway grids bearing their constant high-speed, impersonal flow of traffic, but in attempting to follow the course of the old alignments this feeling for the lie of the land may possibly be recaptured. The countryside Watkins knew was immensely quieter than ours; the secrets of the old trackways were more accessible to him than they can ever be to us. Nor was he by any means the first person to draw attention to the human design of way marks and their associated trackways along ley alignments. He quotes the work of R. Hippsley Cox, who wrote of the alignments of the Wiltshire countryside of 1912 in his book *The Green Roads of England*, and who noticed that barrows were 'often placed at the junction of a branch road, or on the conspicuous point of a hill, as if to serve as a guide or direction post'. From these barrows and underground chambers that are sited along ley alignments, some of which never appear to have been used as tombs, we can get some idea of when people started to move along these ways. However, we must remember that the ways were frequented and the important sites settled long before the great, stone or earth, long barrows were erected; and these are generally agreed to date from around 4000 BC and to have been in use for about a thousand years.

Many of the long barrows contain only a few human remains, and some scholars consider that these bones did not come there as part of a normal burial, but as the result of ritual sacrifice. So there are two main theories about the barrows. One is that they were great mausoleums for the very powerful; and the other that they were built as temples in which rites connected with the fertility of the earth were enacted. The fact that fossilized evidence of ploughing has been found beneath some barrows gives weight to the latter theory; and Paul Ashbee of the University of East Anglia points to the sad irony that sacrifices to ensure fertility should be perpetrated on land that was being systematically eroded by over-cultivation.

Ashbee touches on another mystery: the construction and orientation of long barrows throughout northern Europe show a remarkable similarity. He accounts for this by postulating some central policy governing their siting. Until I hear of a more convincing explanation I must assume that the knowledge of this policy was transmitted along the routes which the surveyors had marked on the earth's surface, or by telepathic communication along the ley lines on which the barrows themselves are aligned. If that was the case then it seems likely that the long barrows were a focus of strength, and that the people who met in them were vitalized by contact with the earth's magnetic forces.

This theory is strengthened by the fact that most long barrows are situated near springs or waterways; and that stone circles, now generally agreed to have been used both as temples and observatories, were built close to them. These were the original holy places, the nodules of the ley system, and the round barrows, which are simply burial places, were clustered round them in much the same way as graves in a churchyard. These barrows date from the Bronze Age and, together with mounds of all sorts, are frequently loosely described as 'tumuli'. They consist of small hillocks, originally encircled by the trenches (still sometimes discernible) from which the earth was removed to construct the burial mound. They can be either rounded or flat-topped, and it appears from the grave goods that have been discovered within them that the shape of the barrow was determined by whether the burial was that of a man or a woman. In either case, it is certain that these burials were reserved for people of some importance, usually the wealthy leaders of the tribe.

Today the sites of these tumuli are often commemorated by the term 'Giants' Graves'. Such 'graves' are frequently not in clusters of tumuli, but carefully sited on the skyline. In this way they served both as obelisks and way marks. You will find that they stand just beside the track, not directly on the alignment. In the epic poem *Beowulf* (generally supposed to have been written down around the seventh century AD but c mposed at a far earlier date) there is, as Watkins reminds us, a description of a barrow being constructed on a clifftop 'by wave-farers widely seen'.

Later, perhaps because one extreme always calls forth its opposite, important points on the tracks were often marked by the graves of outcasts; as by tradition suicides, heretics and criminals are buried at crossroads, which as we shall discover often cover the places where alignments converge. Another explanation for the burial of outcasts on the public highway and especially at busy crossroads is suggested to me by the old practice of burying diseased animals in gateways, in the belief that as the rest of the herd trampled over the corpse they would develop an immunity to the disease. But whether the significant sites are marked by Palaeolithic long barrows, Bronze Age round barrows, or a single stake marking an outcast burial at a crossroads, they are all part of the pattern of a landscape, which for millennia men have been shaping over the surface of the earth. The question we have to decide is whether the pattern is purely random, and has arisen by chance as man exploited the land to suit his immediate needs, in much the same way as ranch farmers grub out long-standing hedges regardless of the subsequent erosion of the soil; or whether our remote ancestors were guided by their knowledge of the earth's natural lines of force to sculpt more purposeful and vital shapes, linked by highways which for generations were considered sacred.

This is not a question that relates to Britain alone. One answer to our search for the methods and beliefs of the prehistoric surveyors comes from China, where until this century any addition to the landscape was done according to the practice of *feng-shui*. That is, the siting of the new building was considered in relation to the prevailing winds and the flow of water in its neighbourhood. For the good of both the land and the individual setting up the building, whether it was a house, place of business, or grave, the right orientation had to be mapped out before any construction could start.

Until the end of the nineteenth century, it was the accepted rule that those men whose professional studies had led them to realize the most auspicious lie of the land should be consulted by anybody planning any building project. These men took their title from their calling and were known as Mr Feng-Shui. Such a person was not only concerned with the prevailing winds and the flow of the surrounding rivers and underground streams, he also took into account the routes of the *lung-mei*, or dragon paths, which correspond to our ley lines.

The dragon is a universal symbol of power, frequently of positive creative power. Only in monotheist religions such as Judaism and Christianity are dragons linked solely with the forces of evil, and this is perhaps because they represent the continuing power of earlier beliefs. It is not only in China that dragons are linked with ley lines. In many legends dragons are thought of as the controllers of springs and rivers, and the guardians of the hoards of treasure that lie in the barrows. In Britain the great dragon-killing saints, St Michael and St George, are commemorated in church dedications along the major alignments. The piercing of the dragon symbolizes the capture of the earth's energy (possibly by erecting a standing stone) and its subsequent release through sacred places for the good of all mankind.

There is one other common tradition about dragons. They are fire-breathing. We have seen how the ley lines are linked with earth and water, and their connection with this third element can

be accounted for in two ways. If the energy that flowed through the uncluttered ley lines was akin to electricity, that would explain outbreaks of apparently spontaneous conflagrations, which are perhaps remembered in the ritual beacon fires that seem to have been lit along the ley alignments, if we judge by the numbers of place names containing the syllable 'Brent' – a word which Watkins claims to be 'an old English form of "burnt" '.

The fourth element is air. Dragons are thought of as flying creatures, and as such we may think of them perhaps as the missing link between dinosaurs, which trod the ancient paths of the earth's natural forces, and today's birds (into which they evolved), which use those same magnetic lines to guide their migratory paths. But there is another way in which the patterns of the earth are linked to the element of air, or rather to the heavens. This link is formed by the patterns on the land which have been drawn by men, making use of natural features such as streams and rivers, supplemented by hedges, woodland strips and trackways, to reflect the patterns seen in the sky. These earth patterns are known as terrestrial zodiacs, and in considering them we move some way out of the world of natural forces, to see how men have shaped the earth to their own ends, both sacred and profane.

The best known of these earth patterns are the lines in the desert of Nasca in Peru. For centuries these lines were regarded as quite meaningless until they were seen from the air; viewed from

14

above they took on clear shapes of men and beasts, including an eagle, the bird of Apollo (which in British zodiacs often stands for Aquarius), a humming bird, and a spider. But in the early 1920s, long before the Peruvian lines were understood, the first British zodiac was rediscovered and charted at Glastonbury by Katherine Maltwood. These figures had earlier been observed by John Dee, physician and astrologer to Queen Elizabeth I. Kate Maltwood made her discovery when she noticed that the River Cary flowed in a course resembling the underside of an animal's body; and when she investigated this further she discovered that it was possible to trace the outline of a lion, whose body stretched over 3 miles (4·8 km) in length .

They say that not everybody can see zodiacs, and I am one of those who can't. For this reason I remain agnostic about them, but not uninterested. It seems to me that, although no one can deny the reality of the Peruvian lines, people can easily be trapped into seeing the patterns they are subconsciously looking for in maps, in much the same way as one finds shapes and figures in clouds and flickering flames. But although I cannot see the patterns myself until they are carefully pointed out to me, any more than I can see the conventional shapes of constellations in the sky, I believe in the reality of other people's beliefs, and I am impressed by many coincidences in the place names associated with the zodiacal effigies, and in the strange but relevant histories and legends that are connected with many of the dominant features

within the effigies. And sometimes the course of a road, lane or ancient right of way seems to be shaped in a pattern that is almost inexplicable unless it was indeed being used to outline a terrestrial drawing. An example of this is the odd bend in the otherwise dead straight Fosse Way, where it forms part of the outline of the Glastonbury Virgo.

One argument against the existence of the zodiacs is the fact that it must have been enormously difficult to project complicated patterns on to a wide expanse of heavily wooded land; and almost impossible if it had to be done without the possibility of viewing the terrain from the air, or even, in the case of East Anglia, without the benefit of any high ground from which to make observations. The task would seem to present a far greater challenge than the carving of chalk figures on the hillsides, and prehistorians have long wondered how that was achieved. On the other hand, this very difficulty could be evidence that the ley system exists, for the only possible way men could have drawn these effigies on the ground would have been by means of some grid system of paths and alignments which had previously been laid out by comparatively straightforward surveying techniques. In many areas it seems certain that such a system exists for, as one walks in the countryside, it is immediately noticeable how many tracks follow almost parallel paths. On high ground this can sometimes be accounted for by the need for alternative routes for different weather conditions, but in the flat lands this is not usually the case.

As more and more people have become interested in the ancient tracks and ley lines, more zodiacs have been traced. In 1948, Lewis Edwards discovered one in the hills around Pumpsaint to the west of Llandovery; and in the mid-1970s Nigel Pennick, a Cambridge biophysicist, discovered one on the same latitude in the east of England, south of Royston. Now others are being reported almost annually, and some people believe that Britain was once divided into twelve sectors all focusing on the stone circle of Arbor Low in Derbyshire, and that each sector would have had its own zodiacs serving some sort of calendar purpose.

All the zodiacs so far discovered have notable individual features. The one in mid-Wales has a squirrel where the eagle representing Aquarius is usually found. But they are all mainly based on the classical zodiac with which we are all familiar. This would lead us to believe that if they exist, they were originally traced in Britain during the centuries when Romans and Celts worked together on the farms. In that case, these zodiacs might be a natural development and sophistication of the common mazes and spirals, which seem by their orientation to have served some sort of purpose connected with the seasonal fertility of the land, as well as providing initiation paths for men.

It would seem that the zodiacs must reflect known patterns in the heavens rather than the other way around. Rupert Gleadow in *The Origin of the Zodiac* stated his belief that the zodiac in the sky could have been used as a calendar device from the seventh century BC. However, he makes no reference in that work to terrestrial zodiacs; and Helen, his widow, cannot recall his ever having referred to them. Yet the many stories that we have of great men and giants being taken into the heavens suggest that people have always tried to draw a physical link between earthly and heavenly bodies.

The existence of terrestrial zodiacs could only be properly verified (or disproved) by painstaking research involving teams composed of professionals from various disciplines, whose members were prepared to trace the natural and human history of every footpath, hedge, woodland strip, stream and river. It will never happen for academics are, as a rule, unwilling to entertain speculations that are so unamenable to measurement. Nevertheless, it would be a good thing if they could at least give some respect to the wider hypotheses put forward by people who spend much of their leisure time working on their own or in small groups, trying to find a meaning in the lie of the land.

At least these people have a large popular following. The self-sufficiency movements and the cults of organic farming, which are largely a response to synthetic twentieth-century living, have led more and more people to take note of their natural surroundings, and in so doing to be aware of the elements which our prehistoric ancestors confronted. That leads them to become increasingly interested in the ways men worked with the forces of nature, both practically and spiritually.

I do not use that last word loosely. From within a stone circle, or on the grassy roof of a barrow, it is easy to journey back in time to an era when a phrase such as 'the spirit of the place' really indicated the existence of an actual being; and when the different characteristics of the prevailing winds could be given individual personalities. And looking at the sky on a clear night, from almost anywhere, it is hard to adhere to the pragmatic belief that the stars have no connection with the earth.

In these books, I have not attempted any detailed mathematical studies. Rather than try to follow Alfred Watkins' directions for drawing ley lines on maps, I have gone into the countryside and simply remained mindful of the old alignments; sometimes following the ley lines described by other people in the years before the last war and seeing how far one can still follow them, and sometimes walking along paths and tracks known to have a history going back several centuries (at least before enclosures) and seeing if alignments could be projected from them through sites of any importance. Very often this was the case; and I have especially noted where the projected alignment crosses a widely recorded ley line at some notable place such as a church, barrow or moat, or at a general junction of lines.

I find that one unexpected delight of walking in this way is an increased awareness of all aspects of nature, from the slowly changing geology of the rocks and composition of the top soil to the seasonal shifts of plant and animal life. It is on this dense surface that the palimpsest of human history waits to be decoded, through field patterns, churches, buried villages, castle mounds, standing stones, moats and earthworks. In following the ley lines your attention is focused on these things; and they reveal their individual history more readily when seen as part of a pattern than they do when each individual monument is studied on its own.

Looked at in this way, the landscape will frequently surprise you with coincidences of place names and strange juxtapositions between the local traditions of folklore and the observations that have been made by people who have carefully worked out the geometry of the ley alignments. The shock of recognition in response to the perception of a coincidence, what the psychologist Carl Jung called 'synchronicity', is partly a subjective matter. What strikes one person as being of the greatest significance may be trivial to another or to the same person in a different mood. This is not to say that the things observed are not objective facts, but that the feelings they engender will vary from time to time; and in following known ley lines, or in searching out new patterns, you will find that you have to become as aware of yourself as you are of the places through which you walk.

North is at the top of the page on all maps except those on pages on which a special indication is given of the orientation.

The maps 1–6 are sketch maps only, based on personal observation. They will help you to locate the walks in the book and pick out salient features on them, many of which cannot be found on other maps, but they are *not* accurate as to scale or topography.

If you are proposing to follow the walks we strongly urge you to equip yourself with Ordnance Survey maps – either 1:25000 or 1:50000 scale. They include contours, which our maps, since they are not the product of surveys, obviously cannot show.

KEY TO MAPS

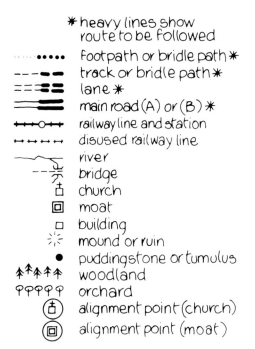

heavy lines show route to be followed

footpath or bridle path ✳

track or bridle path ✳

lane ✳

main road (A) or (B) ✳

railway line and station

disused railway line

river

bridge

church

moat

building

mound or ruin

puddingstone or tumulus

woodland

orchard

alignment point (church)

alignment point (moat)

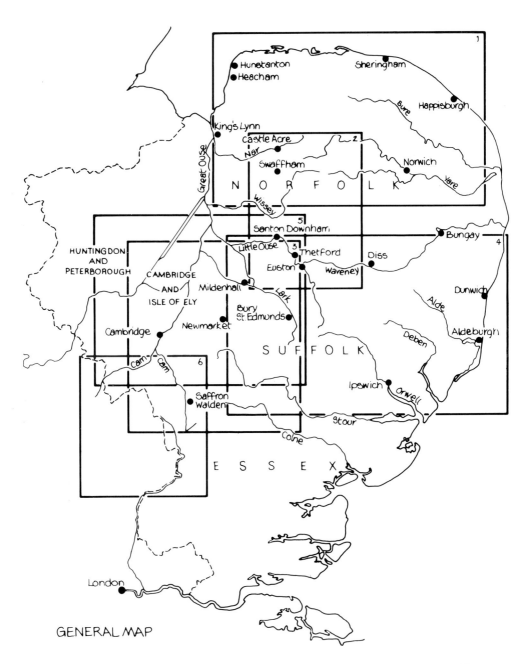

GENERAL MAP

19

East Anglian Introduction

In 984 AD, Oswald, Archbishop of York and Bishop of Worcester, anxious to strengthen the progress of monasticism in eastern England, presumably in an attempt to offset the effects of the invasions by the pagan Danes, invited the learned Abbon of Fleury to take charge of the Benedictine Abbey of Ramsey near Huntingdon for a two-year period. Abbon's interests extended to secular matters. He wrote treatises on prosody and pronunciation and, as the lands owned by the English abbey extended to the Norfolk coast, he was able to give us a fair picture of how East Anglia appeared to a foreign visitor at that time. For our purposes, the most important observation he made was that: 'From that part whereas the sun inclines to the westward, the province itself ajoyneth to the rest of the Island, and is therefore passable: but for feare of being overrun with many invasions and inrodes of enemies, it is fortified in the front with a bank or rampart like unto a huge wall, and with a trench or ditch below in the ground.'

Archaeologists working from aerial photographs are beginning to work on the supposition that the earthwork that Abbon was describing may have been a vast fortification built in early Neolithic times; but until quite recently his remark was taken to refer simply to the fragments of dykes which stand across the Icknield Way and are believed to have

been built by the Saxons against the Danes. It is now generally agreed that, although they were used as a defence against Danish invasion in the ninth and tenth centuries AD, they date from a much earlier time. We shall come across these dykes while following the routes in this book, which will give us a chance to speculate further about them.

What I want to do now is to look westwards along the chalk ridge, which as Abbon observed joined the flat lands and fens of East Anglia to the rest of Britain, and which takes us towards Avebury, along the course of the great alignment of ley lines which runs across the country from Land's End to the Norfolk coast.

The most obvious difference between the landscapes surrounding the western and eastern sections of these alignments is the fact that East Anglia is almost devoid of rock. Today you can see how the great churches were built of flint bonded with rubble. The sacred sites of prehistoric times had to be fashioned with oak posts, and although from the evidence of the post holes these were of enormous size, they leave only the faintest traces of the holy henges. And in central Suffolk especially we shall find that moats take the place of megaliths in marking the alignments. But the very lack of stones means that the few glacial erratics, sandstones and motherstones (or natural conglomerates, which are

Seven Hills Tumuli

popularly known as puddingstones and are most common in Hertfordshire) have a special significance, because being so rare they are only used to mark particularly important places.

There are other, less tangible differences and parallels between the lands to the east and west of Avebury. In folklore terms, these are expressed in the two great legendary heroes, Arthur and Beowulf, both of whom seem to have links with an actual leader or royal prince living some time between the

fourth and sixth centuries AD. Both their names, Arthur from its Celtic derivation, and Beowulf from its Anglo-Saxon, mean 'son of the bear'. And so they are linked with the early esoteric worship of the constellation pointing to the north star; as well as with a whole group of bear's son myths, of which the simplest and most popular version concerns the third or youngest disregarded son, who is miraculously elevated to heroic stature.

Arthur and Beowulf never seem to invade each other's territories, and in East Anglia we are concerned solely with the latter. Although his exploits are described as taking place in Scandinavia, the epic poem that comes down to us is believed to have been put together in eastern England some time in the seventh century AD; and has, among its general Christian orientation, several references that seem to me to refer to pagan East Anglia.

Two instances are particularly relevant to a study of the ley lines of the region. The first is the connection, which many scholars have noted, between the description of the great funeral rites of the hero of the poem and the excavation of the ship 'burial' at Sutton Hoo, whose treasures are permanently on display at the British Museum. The mystery of this indentation of a ship's hull that was found underneath a long barrow at Sutton Hoo in east Suffolk is that no human remains were found on the site. So it was not an inhumation, and now it is generally believed that the ship was ritually interred in the seventh century AD as a memorial to Anna, Christian King of East Anglia (and father of St Etheldreda, who founded the religious community of Ely), who lost his life in battle against the pagan Penda, King of Mercia.

The other aspect of the Beowulf story that interests us is that Beowulf was a dragon-slayer and the name of the dragon he killed was Grendel. Scholars who take the story as a nature myth believe that this treasure-guarding dragon represented the North Sea, and that Beowulf (who had previously triumphed in a swimming contest) symbolized man's struggle to reclaim the land. Could a vestige of that idea remain in the mysterious, deep, hollow paths that run between the moats of central Suffolk, and are known by the inexplicable name of grundles?

As the dragon-slaying hero, Beowulf is East Anglia's counterpart to King Arthur of the west; so is the traditional English dragon-slayer, St George, the counterpart to St Michael, the angel with the flaming sword, who is remembered in so many church dedications in the west country. You will find several churches dedicated to St George in connection with the East Anglian ley lines; but many more to St Andrew. In fact, I have been astounded by the number of times that ley lines converge at a church, often disused or in ruins, which has a St Andrew dedication.

I have not found the fact remarked on before; although T.C. Lethbridge does note that the dedication of the church at Whittlesford is shared between St Andrew and St Mary. He links St Andrew with that classical dragon-slayer, Apollo, and through him with Epona, the great horse goddess, known by various names throughout the Celtic world. In Ireland she is Macha, in Wales, Rhiannon, but she always has the triple characteristic of the female deity. She is mother, virgin, and destroyer. The Iceni knew her as Epona, and the Cambridge archaeologist Sir Cyril Fox identified her with the female horse-rider uncovered by T.C. Lethbridge on the Gog Magog Hills at Wandlebury (see p.180).

I cannot completely follow how Lethbridge makes the link with St Andrew, but I feel that the matter is significant enough to make it worth looking out for connections. These are the ones I find.

The first association with the name of St Andrew is automatically Scotland, and in terms of place names particularly with the north-east of Scotland. As the folklorist George Ewart Evans has discovered, there are many strong links between the customs of that part of Britain and those practised in some areas of Norfolk and Suffolk. These customs are all connected with the mysteries of the Horsemen's Society, which is discussed further in the introduction to the Suffolk section of this book. Another slight hint of a link between the two territories is the discovery of a Pictish inscription on a knife handle in the Norfolk village of Weeting.

Yet this connection does not help us to understand why St Andrew should be linked with Apollo the Sun God. Does the answer lie with the Celtic God Grannus, whom the Romans identified with Apollo? If that is so, it just might be that a certain similarity in the sound of the name caused early Christians to dedicate to St Andrew those churches used for the rituals of Grannus.

For Apollo's link with Epona, I have turned to Robert Graves' *The White Goddess*. He identifies Epona (sometimes worshipped in a triple form) with the more familiar classical Demeter, who disguised herself as a mare to escape the attentions of Poseidon. Apollo is linked with horses through his association with the horse-shoe-shaped well on Mount Helicon, which Pegasus ('Whose name means "the springs of water" ') caused to flow when he struck the rock with his hoof. Like a dragon-slaying, this story of the striking of a spring is a common interpretation of the channelling of the natural forces of the earth's energy at a particular place, which is then held to be sacred and have magical and healing powers. There is no doubt that to the British Celts generally, and especially to the East Anglian Iceni, the horse in its association with Epona was a sacred animal. The memory of this lingers in our present-day repulsion at the very thought of eating horse flesh. Archaeology has made it clear that the veneration of the later Iceni for the horse was somehow linked to the worship of Apollo, since coins of the first centuries BC and AD have been found which bear both inscriptions. It was these pagan symbols which the Church had somehow to Christianize; however this was achieved, it appears that in East Anglia the transformation took place by amalgamating

the sacred images of sun and horse into the figure of St Andrew.

In East Anglia, as everywhere else, the coming of Christianity did not coincide with any definite break with the pagan past, whatever the Church wished to believe. Obviously, people are driven by instinct to hedge their bets, to do all in their power to placate the old gods while they worship the new. So we shall find many early churches (as well as those dedicated to St Andrew) standing on sites that were holy places in Saxon times. When we visit these old churches, and hear the stories of the Old Religion which still cling to them, we shall do well to remember Pope Gregory's advice to St Augustine. When the Holy Father sent his emissary to set up the Christian Church in Britain according to the rites of Rome, he advised him that he should make use of pagan sites whenever it was convenient to do so, and this for the pragmatic reason that people would be more likely to come to worship at places which they already acknowledged to be holy.

Unlike Wales and the west of England, East Anglia was virtually untouched by the early Celtic Christianity that came from Ireland. Right through Roman times and in the early centuries of the dark ages, men and women who lived in these parts worshipped the same gods (tolerated by the Romans, though sometimes slightly affected or modified by the Classical Pantheon,) as their Bronze Age ancestors had done. The late R. Rainbird Clarke, a former director of the Castle Museum at Norwich, from

24

the evidence of archaeological finds in the southern Breckland and the eastern fens, believed that as late as the fourth century AD 'the bulk of the population was still pagan and doubtless flocked to rural shrines where the priests celebrated the rites wearing elaborate bronze and silver head-dresses.'

Christianity first came to East Anglia in the form of an established religion when Raedwald the King returned, early in the seventh century, from a visit to Kent which had been Christian since St Augustine's mission in 597. Raedwald probably became converted in order to gain some political advantage for his kingdom, for when he returned to Suffolk he set up a Christian altar (R. Rainbird Clarke thought that it might have been at Rendlesham) in which he retained another altar for the worship of the pagan gods. The Venerable Bede tries to excuse the king by saying that the pagan element was retained on the insistence of his wife and her false advisers, but if that was so they only set a pattern for many centuries to come. Right up to mediaeval times some corner of the church was always given up to the devil, even if he was attenuated into the figure of a gargoyle.

The spread of monasticism (for both men and women) dates in East Anglia from the middle of the seventh century when Etheldreda founded her religious community at Ely. Such communities also provided libraries and were the repositories of the written records of the time, the earliest to have survived being a seventh-century writing tablet from

Brandon Creek

Saxon church,
Cockley Cley

Blythburgh Priory in north-east Suffolk. Several of these foundations, notably Ely, seem to have continued as Christian centres throughout the Danish invasions; although for nearly a century there was no bishopric in an area which had previously boasted two: one at Dunwich on the Suffolk coast and one at North Elmham in south Norfolk.

Although the Church in East Anglia was established so late, and was so disrupted by the invasions of the pagan Danes from the mid-ninth century to the Norman Conquest, by the early Middle Ages this populous countryside supported many wealthy priories and abbeys. Our walks along the ley lines

will pass the ruins of many of them.

Dom Robert Petitpierre, an Anglican monk and exorcist, is keenly aware of the existence of ley lines running through places that are sacred to Christian worship. In his opinion they are channels of great force, which are not always used for good, and through them the demonic power of the Old Religion can be felt. In *Exorcising Devils*, he records a sensation of 'baleful influences' and a 'feeling of dreadness' in one East Anglian church, where the ley line ran north-west to south-east, going through the junction of the chancel into the lady chapel. He is also of the opinion that patterns drawn on the ground, which make constellations out of vital nodules of ley energy, could have been drawn as part of the pagan witch cults. He instances a diamond drawn from Castle Acre church, which shadows the one from Castle Acre earthworks, which Nigel Pennick discovered and which I have written about in Section 1, see p.46. I have discussed the implication of some of the other, more complex, patterns on the ground in the general introduction to this book, when I looked at the significance of terrestrial zodiacs.

In an agricultural region like East Anglia, the history of religion and folklore must be linked with the history of farming. Although people have made a living out of this land for millennia, I should like to start with the 'modern' farming, which has left its marks on the landscape we shall walk across. It started with the first agricultural revolution, which took place in the Bronze Age, when man began to supplement the energy of his own muscles with the technology of the wheel and the power of the draught horse. At that time, swords and ploughshares may not have been such distinct objects; and the Iceni's war chariots could well have doubled as farm carts.

During that period, and right through the Iron Age into Saxon times, the two great centres of population in East Anglia were in the Breckland (described in Section 2 of this book) and around Ipswich, which I have barely touched on, for unlike its northern counterpart it is densely populated still, and has become an industrial centre which offers little scope for following tracks in country areas. The effect that the Romans had on the agriculture of the region was mostly confined to the draining of the fens; and even this was only a temporary measure, for when the legions withdrew, the dykes they had caused to be dug, no doubt using Iceni slave labour for the purpose, were allowed to fall into disuse.

Agriculture in East Anglia has always had a particular character of its own. The open field system, so general throughout the Middle Ages in most of England, never seems to have pertained here. Twenty-five years ago the difference that made to the East Anglian landscape was still obvious. When Doris Mary Stenton revised *English Society in the Early Middle Ages* in 1954, she was still able to observe that the present aspect of East Anglia showed that the open field system had never flourished there for: 'The small compact farms that the traveller in those parts passes . . . remind the historian at least of the many grants of blocks of land in Norfolk and Suffolk villages which were made in the twelfth and thirteenth centuries.'

This is no longer the case. In the 'sixties, East Anglia pioneered the present trend towards ranch farming; so that the grubbing out of hedges and the amalgamation of farms has almost obliterated the traces of the course of agricultural developments over hundreds of acres of countryside. Yet elsewhere signs still remain of the way the land was used throughout the centuries; and these will be discovered by anyone interested in tracing the course of the old lanes and highways.

27

Many of the old ways which we shall be following in the course of these walks were drove ways which, from mediaeval times right up to the coming of the railways in the mid-nineteenth century, were packed with Scottish cattle being herded on to the Norfolk and Suffolk grazing lands. And then with these same fattened cattle, together with sheep, pigs and, in later years turkeys, being driven out of East Anglia to the London market at Smithfield.

The most important Norfolk market was at St Faith's just to the north of Norwich, near the present airport. There the graziers came to buy the cattle from the Scottish drovers. It was a busy trade in the early eighteenth century. Daniel Defoe reported that he had been told by informants whom he trusted that: 'there are above 40,000 of these Scots cattle fed in this country every year, and most of them in the said marshes between Norwich, Beccles and Yarmouth.' I have not included walks along the roads around St Faith's in this book, but we shall be following part of the course of one of the most ancient drove roads in the country. Still known as the Harling Drove, it runs eastwards from the fens across the southern part of the Breckland.

Changes in methods of arable farming, as well as the great industries that were built around the livestock, helped to fashion the East Anglian landscape of the eighteenth century and still leave traces that can be seen today. Perhaps it was because there was no tradition of linking the rotation of crops to the administration of an open field system that Coke of Holkham was able to get his revolutionary four-crop rotation accepted so readily. The 'Norfolk' method did away with the necessity of leaving any stretch of land lying fallow for a year, by alternating crops of wheat and barley with root crops and clover, which naturally improved the fertility of the soil, as well as providing concentrated fodder for livestock.

In the eighteenth century the soil was further enriched by a revival of the practice of marling, a system of spreading chalk over the heavy clay soils of the central and eastern parts of the area, which had been used to a limited extent at various periods from prehistoric times. At this later date some of the chalk was even brought along the coast by boat from the Kent quarries; and according to Defoe it was so prized that farmers would give 'two shillings and sixpence to four shillings a load for it'. That was as much as most agricultural workers could expect to earn in a month. But often marl was available closer to home, and one thing that the ley hunter has to be on guard against is mistaking an old marl pit for a piece of prehistoric track marking.

The improvements in agriculture that were going on throughout the eighteenth century were closely tied to the rapid increase in the amount of land that was privately enclosed (a trend which began spasmodically in the sixteenth century to facilitate the grazing of sheep). This movement affected the course of some of the old roads; as in other parts of Britain, the enclosure of

near Norwich

large stretches of land, and the creation of great parklands such as the one around Holkham estate itself, resulted in the removal or abandonment of many villages. This accounts for many of the isolated, ruined churches that we shall find along the ley alignments.

Yet these ruined churches, and the very many still standing rivalling cathedrals in size, which punctuate the landscape of Norfolk and Suffolk, indicate what a wealthy and densely-populated area this was, from the early Middle Ages through to the agricultural depressions of the nineteenth century. Much of that wealth came from wool and the cloth trade, in which the Flemish weavers, first invited into East Anglia by Edward III, played such a vital part.

This trade has left its mark on the villages, many of which still boast a row of weavers' cottages, which were actually primitive factories, with the loom sheds extending the whole length of the ground floor of the terrace. As for the Flemish weavers, they left their architectural signature on the 'Dutch' gable ends of many of the houses.

The great wealth that the land of East Anglia produced for its monastic and secular owners is only one side of the history of the agriculture of the region. The other side is not so pleasant, for often that wealth was produced at the expense of the mass of people who, having no land of their own, had to get their food by working for other people. Yet the region in which Thomas Paine

29

(author of *The Rights of Man*) was born and educated (in his home town of Thetford) has always produced men who were as diligent for social reform as the landowners were for scientific and technological improvements.

It was in Norfolk that the sixteenth-century Robert Kett preached a militant socialism, which drew such crowds of adherents that for a few days Norwich was held by the revolutionaries who are reported to have killed and eaten twenty thousand of the sheep whose enclosed pasture lands were depriving men of both homes and livelihoods.

Three hundred years later, Joseph Arch, a Midlands man who became a radical member of parliament for a Norfolk constituency, founded the Agricultural Labourers' Trade Union and won enfranchisement for the farm workers: a reform which Sankey, the evangelist, greeted as the best piece of good news since the Gospels.

Yet the struggle for the rights and responsibilities of the land will never be completely settled, and anyone walking in this area immediately becomes part of it. For the walker will find that in some places it needs courage, tact and assurance to assert one's legal rights. It is almost a public duty to do so. One old man, who has worked on the farms all his life, and who has watched the footpaths he knew as a child gradually disappearing, told me: 'The people are destroying their birth rights by letting the public ways fall out of use.' However, there are stretches of land which no one disputes, and in each section of this book

Ixworth

you will find long walks based upon these.

Many of the farm workers who benefited from the reforms that Joseph Arch worked for lived in the nineteenth-century, tied cottages, built by the wealthy and patriarchal large landowners. Some of these twin cottages, or 'double dwellings', and notably those in Walsham le Willows in central Suffolk, have lintels engraved with paternalistic and Biblical exhortations to the good and simple life. Although there was no open field system in East Anglia, the feudal system is not entirely dead even yet; you will be aware of it in the East Anglian villages, and when walking along the well-established rights of way that run across land used for the rearing and shooting of game birds.

Wherever you go you will notice the siting of the churches and the management of agricultural land; but in some areas you also have to cope with two government agencies, the Ministry of Defence and the Forestry Commission.

Although East Anglia has always been cut off from the west by the fens, it is still thought to be vulnerable to attack across the sea from the east. You won't be there long before you realize that this has always been so, and is never likely to alter. The country has always been a battle-ground, and sadly still is. Every few miles you will find Celtic or Saxon defensive earthworks, Roman forts, Norman castles and the disused airfields of World War II. Among these relics are the ones we pay our taxes to maintain today: the still-lively military air bases

and the Breckland battle zone. These make it impossible to follow the natural course of several alignments.

As for the conifers of the Forestry Commission, they don't usually render the land impassable, but they do change the landscape considerably from what the map leads you to expect. The trees grow quickly and the paths are always changing as new roads are made through the forests or old ones are planted over. I have tried to use only those which are not likely to be altered in this way. Indeed, because walking along forest paths can often be as tedious as motor-way driving, I have avoided them as much as possible or at least indicated alternative routes. When you can't avoid the forest you can at least remember that for centuries this area, which produced the story of *The Babes in the Wood*, has been covered with deciduous trees; and that although conifers may be duller they don't screen the summer light any more effectively, or make the way much more confusing than broad-leaf woodlands.

This is how our ancestors had to cross the land, and at least you should have the benefit of a compass. It is sensible to take one, but if you don't you won't need breadcrumbs. The forestry paths are all numbered, but you should make a note of them. They all look alike.

I have avoided the tracks that run across those areas of the region, such as the Norfolk Broads, that are particularly congested with traffic in the summer months; and I have obviously not tried to follow the alignments that are now

31

covered by busy main roads. But several of the walks do make extensive use of lanes and sometimes include short stretches of minor roads. I have indicated those that are likely to be busy; but the lanes on the whole are quiet and, apart from the occasional farm tractor, excellent for cycling along. If you are thinking of basing any of your excursions on two wheels, you might like to do it in proper East Anglian fashion. Mr and Mrs Dearnley (Sudbury 75007) hire out Black Suffolk vintage bikes by the day or the week.

Norwich Cathedral

Section 1

Important alignment points

Arminghall	134:239060
Castle Acre	
(castle earthworks)	132:818152
Cowell Stone	143:766098
Egmere Church	132:896375
Gayton	132:731194
Great Massingham	132:798230
Grimston	132:723219
Godwick Tower	132:905223
Happisburgh	133:370311
Heacham	132:682380
Litcham, Pilgrims'	
Rest House	132:889174
Narborough Fort	132:752131
North Elmham	
Cathedral ruins	132:988218
Peddars' Way	
Crossing of A148	132:771257
Snettisham	132:691344
Tasburgh Hill Fort	134:201962
Walsingham Abbey	132:935367
Wymondham Abbey	144:113009

Note: Grid references in this book are frequently written in a way which is not normal practice: e.g. 134:252043. This means grid reference 252043 number 134. I hope this style may be more convenient for readers than using the official 100 km squares.

33

Section 1: Norfolk

Long distance paths – traders, farmers and pilgrims

This is the county of East Anglia with the greatest extent of coastline, a large part of which is covered by the Countryside Commission's new Long Distance Coastal Path. However, the main tracks that concern us do not go round the coast, but run across the country, either going south from the old northern ports on the Wash, opposite the coast of Lincolnshire, or running directly west from the cliff-battering waves of the North Sea.

These are the trade routes which from earliest times were used to carry imports inland and to distribute the harvest of the sea (whether in terms of salt or shell fish). We shall follow the route of one of these salt tracks, though taking it in the reverse direction, going from the south of the county at Castle Acre to Salthouse on the north coast. There, until the eleventh century, a warehouse served as a depot for the salt dried out along the coast, on which generations of inland folk depended for the preservation of their winter food.

At that time, most of the mud flats and salt marshes were part of the North Sea, and the inland escarpment running west along this stretch of coast, surmounted by churches and tumuli standing on sandy heathland, once marked the cliff. It is the reverse story along the east

coast, where the cliffs are continually crumbling into the sea.

Going west along the salt marshes are the villages where, within living memory, people made their livelihoods by gathering whelks and cockles. When W. A. Dutt (a traveller who shared many of Watkins' beliefs) passed that way at the turn of the century, he found that the women of Stiffkey were engaged in whelk-gathering, an 'occupation which soon undermines their health and is as hard and wearisome as any work well can be'.

At that time the great market of the neighbourhood was King's Lynn; the shell fish were taken there and sent on to their new destinations by the railway, which is itself passing into history. But long before the railways came, the goods brought into the north Norfolk ports were taken to market along the ancient track of the Peddars' Way, and the less clearly defined ones that run to the east and west of it. Some of these goods no doubt found their way to the fair at Great Massingham, just north of Castle Acre.

To this inland fair, as to many others in Norfolk, most notably to St Faith's to the north of Norwich, farmers would bring their produce; cattle driven down from Scotland in their thousands were bought by the graziers to be fattened for the Michaelmas markets, and Norfolk turkeys started from it on the first stage of their journey to London.

In this farming county, the notion that tracks are sometimes formed by animals following the natural ley lines takes a new perspective. The salt marshes of the north coast have long been favoured grazing grounds, and they still are. It was the fore-runners of these cattle who, according to W.G.Hoskins, were responsible for the winding roads between the villages, and the meandering lanes from villages to marsh. 'The cattle on this coastland are still driven to and from the marshes every day,' he wrote, in the book which accompanied his television programmes on the English landscape. 'But cattle do not walk in straight lines, they mooch from side to side, eating as they go, and they trample out a path which naturally human beings follow. So the cattle track became a small mediaeval roadway from village to marsh and eventually village to village.'

The history of Norfolk is in so many ways also the history of agriculture; farmers, like sailors, or anyone dependent on the elements for their livelihood, are a superstitious people, and cattle are part of the folklore. George Ewart Evans tells how even the old tradition that the beasts kneel on Christmas Eve to mark the manger birth is given a new, sinister twist by the information which one Norfolk woman gave him: 'You mustn't enter the *nethus* at midnight on Christmas Eve. The beasts are on their knees at that time and if you disturb them you'll die before the end of the year.' The word *nethus* is almost pure Anglo-Saxon; it stands for neat house or cattle byre. But, in common with the rest of East Anglia, the best of the folk tales and wonders centre on the great mysteries by which the men who worked with horses guarded their skills.

Like any other countryside made up of small isolated communities, Norfolk boasted a number of witches. Accounts of some of these are given in *Arcady*, a collection of rural tales compiled by Canon Augustus Jessop, whose fifteenth-century parish church of Scarning we shall pass on one of the ley alignments. Many of the tales he recounts concern white magic and evil spells performed by 'cunning men' and witches; and the fears of mothers who were convinced that their children might fall sick from being 'ill-wished'. As late as 1882, Canon Jessop knew of an elementary school teacher in the neighbourhood who, as a young man, had furiously scratched an old woman's arm, because he was brought up in the belief that the only way to cancel out an evil spell was to shed the witch's blood.

Farming is luck and hard work. When the luck (good or bad) has been accounted for by witchcraft or any other means, there remains the human drudgery and ingenuity needed to actually get a living from the land. Sometimes this struggle degenerates into exploitation of one group of people by another, as happened in Norfolk in the mid-sixteenth century, when the landowners turned poor men out of their homes and livings; so that Robert Kett, the Wymondham tanner, was roused to preach his practical socialism. Sometimes whole villages have disappeared as groups of people suddenly lost their livelihood through enclosures; this accounts for the ruined, isolated churches we shall encounter on some of the alignments. But, on the credit side, we also find the eighteenth-century Coke of Holkham and his neighbour 'Turnip' Townshend, who brought new prosperity to the people by their courage and imagination in trying out new farming methods. And best of all, in the nineteenth century, we see the work of Joseph Arch, who started agricultural workers on the way to a proper realization of their worth, by organizing them into a union.

The evidence of Norfolk's great wealth from trade and agriculture, and the manufacture of cloth in mediaeval times, can be seen in the county's great numbers of churches, nearly all made of the only available building materials: flint and rubble. Of the earlier ones, 119 have distinctive round towers; and many of the larger ones that were built later are decorated with elaborate patterns of knapped flints. At one time these churches served large congregations, for attendance was obligatory; and the great landowners, abetted by the priests, found that donations to church building and church furniture was a good way of impressing the Joneses – as well as providing an insurance policy for the afterlife. But the motives that sent hundreds of people on pilgrimages (especially to

the shrine of Our Lady at Walsingham) cannot be so cynically written off.

Walsingham Abbey stands in the north-east corner of the county; the shrine at its centre was founded in the eleventh century. At one time this holy place was as important a goal for pilgrimages as St Thomas's shrine in Canterbury. People came to Walsingham from the cathedrals of Ely in the west and Norwich in the south, and from many of the abbeys throughout East Anglia. So we will find that many of the old tracks coincide with 'Walsingham Way', and are still marked by remnants of the crosses which were the pilgrims' way marks.

What made – or makes – people go on pilgrimages? In the Middle Ages, as Chaucer tells us, a pilgrimage was a sort of package holiday and a good justification for the desire to travel. The ultimate destination, the holy shrine, seems less important than the journey. And yet persistent laws against vagrancy have always insisted that a traveller must have a goal. I cannot help but link the power which is supposed to run along ley lines with the human urge to walk along them on one pretext or another; even joggers could as well go round and round the backyard if exercise were all they wanted.

The story of St Walstan, whose shrine at Bawburgh church – some 4 miles (6·4 km) west of Norwich – was itself a place of pilgrimage, is a beautiful illustration of how the old ways are linked both to the beasts and the gods, and of how they often culminate in holy wells with healing properties.

Walstan was born in Bawburgh, and at the age of twelve went to work as a farm-hand at nearby Taverham. I have his story from W.A.Dutt's *Highways and Byways in East Anglia*. Dutt got it from the eighteenth-century Francis Blomefield, Rector of Fersfield near Diss who he suspects had it from Capgrave's legends. This is how it goes. The young lad greatly impressed his employers by giving his food and shoes to the poor, and by being completely unscathed by thorns and sharp stones when as a result of his generosity he was forced to work barefoot. The farmer and his wife, taking this as a sign of divine grace, wanted to adopt the boy; but Walstan refused the offer, asking only that when a certain cow calved he should be given the creature. In time the cow gave birth to twin bulls and at the command of an angel, who told him that the creatures would conduct him to his place of burial, Walstan reared the animals.

He went on working as a farm-hand until one day, when he was mowing with a gang of workers in the meadows, an angel came to him again and told him his death was near, giving him the exact hour at which he would die. When the time drew close he called everybody together and asked them to promise that, as soon as his spirit had left his body, the corpse would be put in a cart, and his two oxen allowed to draw it wherever they pleased. His final prayer was that God should help any labourer who was sick or whose cattle suffered from murrain, provided that the help

was asked at his grave. His prayer was answered by a voice from heaven calling out: 'Oh, holy Walstan, that which you have asked is granted. Come from your labour to rest.' At that Walstan died; with his last breath a dove flew out of his mouth and soared into the sky.

His body was then put on to a cart, and the oxen drew it first to Costessy Wood, where it passed over a stream as though it were solid ground. On the crest of a hill (which now stands in Costessy Park) the oxen stopped briefly, and as they paused a spring of water broke through the earth, and was channelled into a well, that was later found to have healing powers. Then the oxen drew Walstan back to his birthplace at Bawburgh, where they stopped and would move no further. Another spring gushed through the ground at this point, and in Dutt's day it was marked by 'an old circular well, apparently only a few feet deep, and containing only a few inches of greenish water' standing in the middle of an orchard. The farmer told him that although there was so little water in the well, he had never managed to draw it dry. As for Walstan, the church that bears his name was erected over his tomb, and was served by six chantry priests; for the two wells, renowned for their healing powers, attracted pilgrims from all corners of England and even from across the sea.

Another story about the 'pilgrimage' of a corpse concerns the body of St With-burga, daughter of Anna, a king of East Anglia, and sister of Etheldreda who founded the religious community at Ely.

Withburga founded a nunnery at East Dereham in 654; when she died her body was buried in the usual way in the nuns' graveyard, but after many years it was decided that it should be moved into the church. When the grave was opened the body was found to be uncorrupted; and when it was moved into the church, so many miracles and cures took place at the shrine that, for over three hundred

East Dereham.
Tomb of Withburga,
AD 774

years, it drew thousands of pilgrims to worship there.

Then, in 974, the Abbot of Ely, jealous of the prestige and renown that the relic was bringing to East Dereham, arranged to have the body of the saint secretly taken to Ely, and buried beside her holy sisters, Etheldreda and Sexburgh. The people of East Dereham were naturally incensed at the loss, but had no alternative but to submit to the abbot's action, for he was their territorial lord, as well as their spiritual father. However, when the saint's body was taken from the church, a spring of water suddenly gushed from the earth at the site of the old grave in the churchyard, and its waters were found to possess such miraculous powers that pilgrims continued to flock to the town.

And as for animals in this story? The legend is that the name 'Dereham' comes from two deer, who in St Withburga's lifetime came regularly to the nunnery to be milked; until the devil inspired one of the townspeople to shoot the beasts. They died, and so did the man, of a sudden fatal illness he contracted as he killed the deer.

Like the pilgrims, the farmers and the traders, we shall be visiting such sacred places throughout the county, following tracks that run from the high ridge of chalk on its western side to the fluctuating coastline of the north and east. The walks are divided into three groups. Part A follows the course of the two main north/south tracks: the clearly marked Peddars' Way; and the much more elusive line to the west of it, which some people describe as the northern part of the Icknield Way, and which Dr W.R. Rudge, a former principal of West Ham technical college, reckoned was an alignment marked out by a series of puddingstones or motherstones. The southerly parts of both tracks are described in the next two sections of this book. In Part B, I have concentrated on some of the alignments which run horizontally or diagonally across the county, and which are linked with specific trading routes or pilgrims' ways; and in Part C I have looked at some of the old paths which run inland from the coast. This is by no means a comprehensive guide to the ancient tracks of Norfolk, but my hope is that in following some of the walks outlined here, you will be drawn to work out your own alignments from some of the important sites we shall stop at on the way.

East Dereham

39

Part A

Norfolk: ancient tracks, alignments and coastal paths

One of the best known and best pre-served of all the old, straight tracks (it is indeed listed as an ancient monument) runs through Norfolk. It runs south-south-east from the north coast, and because it is so well known, so easy to trace, and so delightful to walk along, I want to make it the starting point for the grid of prehistoric tracks and Roman roads which cover this county, and the whole of East Anglia. This track, known as the Peddars' Way, was undoubtedly used throughout the Middle Ages and Tudor times as a market route and drove road, hence its present name. But it had an earlier name, the Palmers' Way, when it was important as part of the pilgrims' route between Ely and Walsingham. Yet both these names are comparatively modern, for the Romans who used the Peddars' Way as part of their communi-cations system were converting an already existing Bronze Age track to their own ends.

To the west of the Peddars' Way there are much fainter traces of an even older track. Some authorities claim that this is the northern end of the Icknield Way, which follows the ridge of chalk that curves through southern Britain from the south-west to the Wash. I am inclined to a rather different opinion about the course of the Icknield Way, as I hope to make clear in Section 3, and I

prefer to see this path as it was envisaged by Dr W.R. Rudge. He worked out his track by noting where puddingstones, or natural conglomerates, were to be found in significant places, from the north Norfolk coast to the west of Berkshire. His stones are a mass of pebbles held together in a natural concrete. They are common in Hertfordshire, although they can also be formed in the Norfolk dark brown carstone, which is used for many buildings along the coast. Cars-tone is a ferruginous sandstone, which is the west Norfolk equivalent of the lower greensand, which flanks the slopes of the same chalk ridge as it comes into south-ern England.

The Peddars' Way

O.S. map 132

On the beach to the east of Hunstanton, you will find strange, black mounds lying in the sand. Happily, as I write this, they are not pools of oil. They are strange because they look like pieces of blackened, sea-washed timber and tree trunks. You can even still see the grain of the wood, but when you take them into your hand they dissolve into mud or dust. These are the remains of the great forests that grew here over six thousand years ago, when East Anglia was joined to Scandinavia and the Low Countries and the Wash was a river. Even now you do not need a brilliantly clear day in order to look across the water to Lincolnshire and note how Boston Stump makes a good sighting point for anyone making this journey to the north.

It is very likely that a ferry ran from here to Lincolnshire in mediaeval times, though it seems to me more probable that the quay was a little to the east, near

Brancaster Bay,
near Hunstanton

Thornham with its deep harbour channel. R.Rainbird Clarke in *Archaeology of East Anglia* tells of the finding of a polished flint axe-head embedded in a tree trunk on Thornham beach. He takes this, together with the discovery of other tools along the shore, as proof that 'this once was dry land and still inhabitable during neolithic times.' In Roman times a signal station was set up here to contact the garrisons in Lincolnshire.

You must make up your own mind about the actual point where the Peddars' Way meets the sea. It's a pleasant thing to do, for over 400 acres (161·8 hectares) of this stretch of coast, which runs between Holme and Thornham, is owned by the Norfolk Naturalists' Trust; and, as a good omen for ley investigators, the Norfolk Ornithologists' Association has based an observation station here for bird migration.

There are various nature trails throughout this reserve, and if you want to start off your walks by following one of them, you must work out a way to finish either at the eastern end of Holme golf course, or on the edge of Thornham channel. If you take the former way, you will go along the footpath that runs due south to Holme village, leaving the beach car park on your right. You will then be on the route that lines up directly with the Peddars' Way, although unfortunately after a few yards, you have to walk along metalled lanes to the inland hill-top village of Ringstead, about 3 miles (4·8 km) away. The Holme footpath brings you to Holme village shop. From there you continue south, crossing

the main road and climbing up to Ringstead Mill. At the top of the hill, turn round for your last look at the sea and the coast of Lincolnshire, before walking on into Ringstead.

The village boasts the first of many churches dedicated to St Andrew that you will meet on your walks through East Anglia; a splendid baker's shop (open on Boxing Day if you're taking a Christmas walk); and a rather over-done pub, The Gin Trap. It's worth looking at though for the neglected village stocks and the puddingstone in the forecourt. After passing the pub turn left again, and where the lane divides by the signpost for Docking, you will see the Ancient Monument notice for Peddars' Way.

You start off along a wide lane which goes uphill past several houses, but very soon the Way becomes a field path following the headland of arable fields, and running past a strip of woodland. The farm track comes out at Littleport, by an old disused chapel. I have not yet been able to find out its exact date, but it's worth plunging through nettles to take a look at it, if only for the iron rings used for tethering horses during the service, which you will see by the west door.

The actual course of the Peddars' Way has been tampered with on its next stage. It should run straight across the road from the chapel, but it has been diverted and you must go a few yards to the west along the B1454, where you can pick it up again by the narrow footpath which runs by a small group of cottages and then goes east through a field of parsley, which also boasted a fine crop of

70741

71140.

723369

hagstaper when I walked it. This plant (a remote cousin of dock and sorrel) gets its name from its wide leaves, which can be rolled, dried and used as a primitive form of lighting – a poor man's candle, fit for a solitary creature driven to such expedients.

Once across that field you join the Way proper. It is still a headland field path which skirts a small wood, and then goes downhill, through a very stony field, to a bridge over the infant Heacham River. There is no sign indicating the Way going north at this point, but you will find one to the south directing you across the causeway, which can get quite deeply flooded in wet weather.

The Way goes quite steeply uphill on the other side of the valley, and runs beside a stretch of woodland lying to the east, which for some time blocks your view of the neat little village of Fring, with its spruce farm and fourteenth-century church with a faint St Christopher wall painting – a figure who often appears in churches passed by many travellers. Just over a mile (1·6 km) beyond Fring, there is a point where several lanes converge; it would be interesting to find out the history of that junction, and the importance of the two tracks which run beside the Peddars' Way to the east. On this part of the Way you will have walked beside a great field of lavender. Past that the track begins to close in on itself. High hedges, thick bracken and gnarled, wind-stunted trees prevent you looking at the surrounding countryside; but they also provide good shelter from the sudden squalls of rain

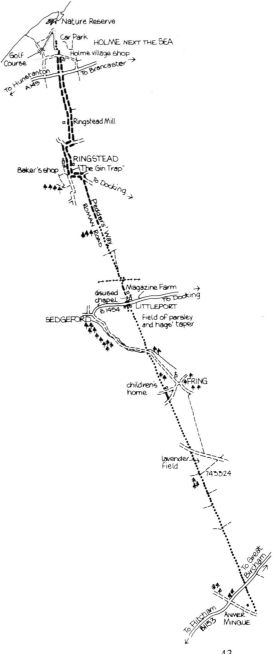

727356

43

Tumuli,
Harpley Common

and hail brought in from the sea by the prevailing north-east wind, heralded by deep purple clouds moving ominously across the sky.

Here the Way runs across high ground, and once you come up to the lane by Anmer Minque you will find it much clearer, and you can look eastwards over an extensive palimpsest of agricultural history: today's prairie farms, overlying the fields where Coke of Holkham tried out the Norfolk four-year rotations in the eighteenth century, and interspersed with shapely tumuli to bear witness to the prehistoric use of this land. We will consider the way Coke revolutionized the Norfolk landscape when we visit his birthplace at Mileham (p.60).

7627 The Way passes close to the tumuli (believed to date from the Bronze Age) and you can even make a slight detour over Harpley Common (north of Harpley) to examine them more closely. Shortly after that the Way descends

44

steeply towards the A148. Those strange prehistoric-looking mounds which you see lying across the road are made by a well-defended oil reserve. It was on the hill that lies to the north of the main road that, in the autumn of 1977, I had my first sad sight of the return of myxomatosis – half a dozen stupefied rabbits hardly able to stagger out of the way.

You cross over the A road to an old 771256 railway course now guarded by a cottage, which must once have belonged to a signalman. Just past that cottage, behind the oil pound and well sheltered from it, is a disused gravel working, smoothly grassed over, that makes an idyllic and sheltered picnic place. When you continue to follow the Way, you will meet a track which runs to the village of Congham. That is the one you 778237 must take if you want to make a circular walk, returning by the Puddingstone Track (see p.50).

If you want to continue along the Ped-

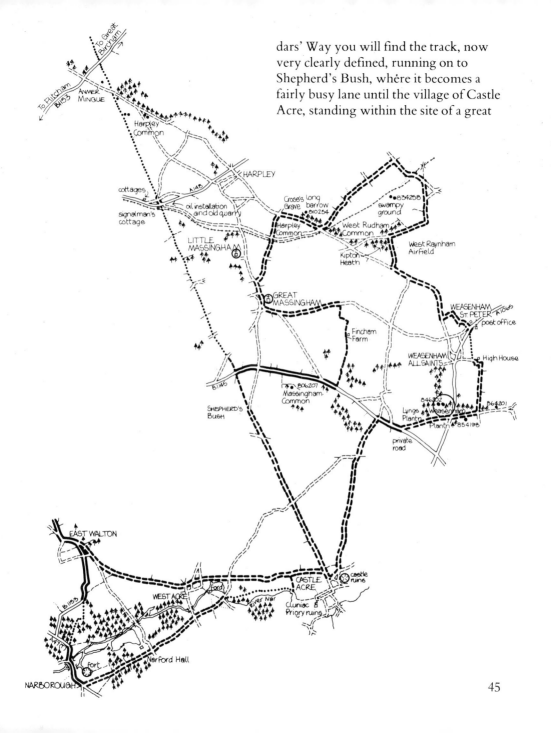

dars' Way you will find the track, now
very clearly defined, running on to
Shepherd's Bush, where it becomes a
fairly busy lane until the village of Castle
Acre, standing within the site of a great

Roman camp, which was once crowned by one of the largest castles in East Anglia. The village is actually better known for its priory than its castle, although both ruins are now in the hands of the Department of the Environment. If you wish to plan your walk to include an opportunity of visiting the priory, it is as well to bear in mind that it is closed promptly at 4 p.m. from November to February, at 7 p.m. from May to September, and at 5.30 p.m. during the other months,

It was a Cluniac priory built by the son of William de Warenne, who was granted this estate by William the Conqueror and built his great castle over the ancient earthworks. He had himself founded a priory at Lewes. In its day the Cluniac Priory of Castle Acre was one of the great religious houses in Norfolk, second only to the Franciscan Priory of Walsingham. Today you can still see the Tudor house which once served as a later prior's lodging and, going back in time to its origins, the Norman west front of the church and the skeleton of its perpendicular window. Otherwise most of the foundations are laid bare and clearly labelled, so that you can visualize the extent of the refectory, cloister, kitchen and infirmary halls. You will find more about the castle on p.55.

From Castle Acre, the Peddars' Way gets lost for a few miles under modern roads, and you will find the description of its course through the Breckland in the next section of this book. However, before you leave the area, either by car or on foot, you might like to make your own observations of the geomantic alignment observed by Nigel Pennick which he calls the Castle Acre diamond. It is an equilateral figure, and his discovery of it was first published in *East Anglian Geomancy*, a paper put out by IGR Publications, 142 Pheasant Rise, Bar Hill, Cambridge. To my mind, this figure provides further evidence that the land was once covered by a grid of alignments that could be used both for surveying a heavily wooded countryside and possibly for subsequently tracing on

Abbey ruins,
Castle Acre

to it figures of the heavens. Points on the western edge of this diamond coincide with the alignments from Tasburgh Hill Fort to Wymondham given on p.67.

According to Nigel Pennick's observations, the remains of the castle at Castle Acre (not the priory) form the bottom point of the diamond, whose apex is the tumulus to the north of Rudham Common, and whose western point is the tumulus on Massingham Common aligning with the eastern point, which is the tumuli in Weasenham Plantation.

18152

37257

06207

46202

If you want to make a walk visiting these four points and seeing some of the points enclosed by the diamond or connected with it, you could leave the Pedars' Way just before it reaches Shepherd's Bush, and go east over Massingham Common past the tumulus, which unfortunately cannot be reached. Then head for the northern apex of the diamond on West Rudham Common, passing through Great Massingham – now dominated by the airfield, but a centre for flint mining in Neolithic times.

791211

After turning at Cross's Grave you might wish to visit the long barrow. According to Helen Clarke's *East Anglia: Regional Archaeologies* it is one of only four long barrows to be found in East Anglia. Two of them are on West Rudham Common, and one of these has

803253

810253

Abbey ruins. Castle Acre.

Tumulus on Peddars Way

been excavated to show that 'the mound covered a platform cremation'. Helen Clarke elaborates on this: 'The body was first placed on an open wooden platform and cremated; the remains were then covered by a mound of turf sods, and finally the whole surmounted by a layer of earth which was dug from a ditch around the barrow. The final size of the mound appears to have been about 240 feet x 70 feet [73 m× 21·3 m].' The other two East Anglian long barrows are at Broome Heath, Ditchlingham, in Norfolk and near Worlington in Suffolk. The latter is described on p.126 in the section on the Icknield Way.

815249   Take the turn on the left at the crossroads past the barrow, and follow the lane going north of an old railway track;

48

at the second crossroads (the first is with a farm lane) turn right. The Rudham tumulus that marks the Castle Acre diamond lies in swampy ground to the south-west. Continue through the lanes until you reach Weasenham St Peter, where you can briefly take a footpath which runs opposite the post office across the A1065, going south to High House. From there the lane runs due south to Weasenham Plantation and several barrows lie around it. The ones on which Nigel Pennick bases his diamond are at 132:846202 and they lie in forestland in the north-west intersection of the crossroads. A more significant tumulus can just be seen in private land to the south of the lane at 853198. Richard Wainwright describes it in his *Guide to*

834261

85621

the Prehistoric Remains in Britain, South East as consisting of 'two saucer barrows, a bell barrow and a bowl barrow', and he gives the dimensions of the mound that can be seen from the road as 7 feet (2·1 m) high and 146 feet (44·5 m) in diameter. A further tumulus lies to the north of the lane just east of a second crossroads.

I have mentioned all these barrows because the Weasenham Plantation crossroads is a point in another alignment described on p.69, and if you want to follow some of those walks you should now take the lane running south-east from 865202 to Litcham.

If you want to make your way back to Castle Acre, take the lane running west through the plantation, turn right when you reach the B1145, and then take the first lane on your left. The farm track is on private property. Castle Acre lies just over 2·5 miles (4 km) to the south.

829199

From Castle Acre you can join the Puddingstone Track, and I shall describe that route below as it runs from north to south. However, if you want to make a circular walk you will find that it is possible to do by taking the lane running west from Castle Acre through West

Peddars Way. Ringstead

Acre to East Walton and then taking the road for Gayton to your north, where you can pick up the Puddingstone route.

If you want to join the Puddingstone Track further to the south, you can do so by walking westwards along the Happisburgh–Avebury ley line. West of Castle Acre, you may follow the farm track to the River Nar, and join the path going west, taking the lane to Narborough 752131 Fort, which is one of the alignment points on the ley line. It lies on private land. To reach Gayton from here, follow the A road through Narborough village, 746137 then go north on the footpath. It will bring you out on the B1153 just to the south of East Walton.

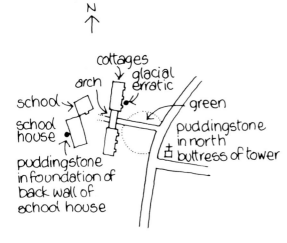

The Puddingstone Track

O.S. maps 132, 143

Dr Rudge started his Puddingstone Track at Heacham, where he located two stones, one in the foot of the north side of the church tower, the other in the 68238 back wall of the old school house, which is now a private dwelling. There is also a glacial boulder, which he does not mention. It stands outside the cottage door to the right of the arch leading to the school house (see diagram). The present occupant of that cottage, who has recently retired to the village, told me that he believed the stone to be Norwegian granite.

These three stones align, which is helpful for today's travellers, for as the old school house is now in private hands, you must take my word for it that the puddingstones are there. It is hardly fair to expect the occupants to have passers-by regularly scrabbling among the foundations of their house. The puddingstone in the church structure, although in a public place, is quite difficult to find. It is in fact only a small slither of conglomerate, and it lies in the very foot of the north buttress of the tower. The tower itself has a most unusual decoration of large and small carstones.

The next stone is reported to be at Snet- 6913 tisham, which was a very wealthy settlement in Iron Age times. In the last thirty years, eight hoards of objects made of bronze, tin and precious metals

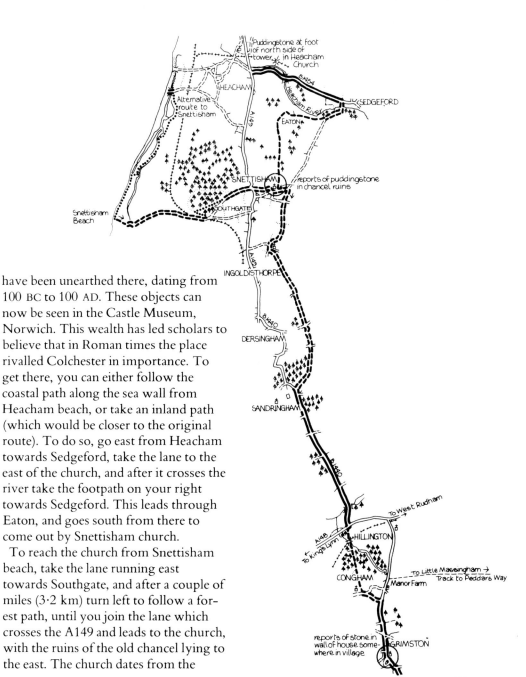

Puddingstone at foot of north side of tower, in Heacham Church

HEACHAM

B1454

Heacham River

SEDGEFORD

Alternative route to Snettisham

A149

EATON

SNETTISHAM

reports of puddingstone in chancel ruins

SOUTHGATE

Snettisham Beach

INGOLDISTHORPE

A149

B1440

DERSINGHAM

SANDRINGHAM

B1440

To West Rudham

A149

HILLINGTON

To Kings Lynn

CONGHAM

Manor Farm

To Little Massingham →
Track to Peddars Way

reports of stone in wall of house somewhere in village

GRIMSTON

have been unearthed there, dating from 100 BC to 100 AD. These objects can now be seen in the Castle Museum, Norwich. This wealth has led scholars to believe that in Roman times the place rivalled Colchester in importance. To get there, you can either follow the coastal path along the sea wall from Heacham beach, or take an inland path (which would be closer to the original route). To do so, go east from Heacham towards Sedgeford, take the lane to the east of the church, and after it crosses the river take the footpath on your right towards Sedgeford. This leads through Eaton, and goes south from there to come out by Snettisham church.

To reach the church from Snettisham beach, take the lane running east towards Southgate, and after a couple of miles (3·2 km) turn left to follow a forest path, until you join the lane which crosses the A149 and leads to the church, with the ruins of the old chancel lying to the east. The church dates from the

596363

673366

691344

mid-fourteenth century, and the puddingstone is reported to lie in the ruins
of the older chancel in the west of the
churchyard. But, although I have been
on my hands and knees dividing the
grasses around these ruins, I cannot find
any trace of it. However, I have not yet
given up hope of coming across Dr
Rudge's stone. Andrew Perssene, at present running the Norfolk Heritage Trust
from The Rural Life Museum at Gressenhall, near East Dereham, was the first
person to point out to me that puddingstones can be formed out of carstone,
although the ones at Heacham are not.
He also told me that no one knows
exactly what the binding agent in the
natural conglomerates is, although it is
probably connected with iron. So these
stones may be found in any area where
iron was known to have been worked
from the third century BC. In view of
what we know of the importance of
Snettisham as an Iron Age settlement, it
is very likely that carstone conglomerates would be found in that area.

I have also been unable to locate the
next three stones in Dr Rudge's track.
The first one is somewhat vaguely
reported to be in the wall of a house in
the village of Grimston, settled near the
site of a Roman villa, and the second is
said to be in the yard behind the Mill
stores in the village of Gayton, but I suspect that it has now been removed. The
road on which these two villages stand,
the B1153 south from Hillington, is

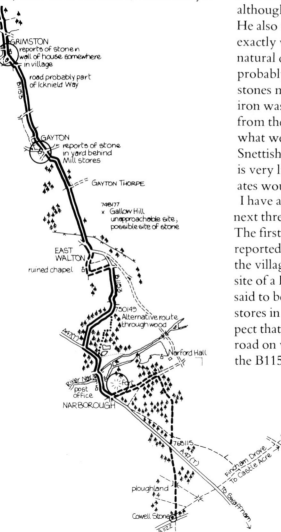

thought by some authorities to be part of the Icknield Way.

To reach these two villages from Snettisham, you have to follow the lanes which run almost parallel to the A149. The lane will take you first to Ingoldisthorpe church, and then runs east of Dersingham to Sandringham. You must follow the B road towards Hillington, but when you cross the A148 take the farm track running to Congham church. If you turn east from Congham for the B1153, and then go north to Manor Farm, you will find a track running east which joins the Peddars' Way just south of Little Massingham.

If you want to try your luck at finding Dr Rudge's stones, then you must continue south along the B1153, through Grimston to Gayton. The churches in those two villages align with those at Snettisham and Heacham, but the third stone, which I could not find because the site is unapproachable, is reported to be at Gallow Hill (132:748177). If there is a stone there it is well out of alignment; and I find that strange for the next stone, which lies about 3·5 miles (5·6 km) to the west of Swaffham at 143:766098, comes back into the original line. Yet Gallow Hill is not an impossible location. It aligns with the Saxon church at Gayton Thorpe to the north (near a tumulus and a Roman villa, excavated in 1822, believed to have been occupied from the middle of the second to the end of the third century AD) and with the fort to the east of Narborough to the south. Perhaps it was from Gallow Hill that the track turned westwards, the

situation now being changed by the altered course of the River Nar. But, as there are no public footpaths to Gallow Hill, you must go south from Gayton to East Walton, where a ruined chapel, off a side road to the south-west of that village, is on the Puddingstone alignment.

Now head for Narborough, which lies on the A47(T). You can reach it either by continuing along the B road from East Walton, which will bring you out about half a mile (804 m) north-east of Narborough; or you can take the footpath through the woods.

The most pleasant way to the Cowell Stone near Swaffham is through Narborough village, turning left at the first crossroads towards Narford Hall. You will find a forest road on your right. This track runs almost directly south crossing the A47(T) again at 132:767115. Just before you reach another main road, the A1122, which some people believe to be part of the Icknield Way and which is in any case a Roman road, you will find a belt of trees on either side of the track. Round the northern side of the belt on your left is the Fincham Drove, which goes towards Castle Acre. The Cowell Stone, a large flat boulder obscured by undergrowth in the summer, is on your right, lying to the west, at the side of the path, just south of the belt of trees.

This stone is not a puddingstone at all, but a glacial erratic, and it was once a boundary stone marking the old rural district boundary. It is not shown on the current O.S. maps, but does appear in the First Edition County Series 1:2500 scale map Norfolk 58/8 surveyed in 1883 and

591327
710253
713237

722239

745186

752131

743162

750127
763133

767096

53

published in 1884. It marks the junction of several important tracks; and for us it will serve as the boundary between the Norfolk paths and those which run through the Breckland, which will be dealt with in the next section. From Heacham church to the Cowell Stone is a matter of some 19 miles (30·4 km), and between those two points we have noted five aligning places – at three of which Dr Rudge discovered puddingstones. The five are Snettisham, Grimston, Gayton, East Walton and Narborough Hill Fort.

Peddars Way
nr. Little Massingham

Narborough to Happisburgh

I have divided this part into three groups of walks. In the first I will look at some remaining footpaths and places which lie along the main alignment to Happisburgh, which W. A. Dutt listed in Alfred Watkins' *The Ley Hunters' Handbook* (1927). The second includes the tracks of the Salters' Way, first pointed out to me by Ben Ripper, the Swaffham barber and local historian, which seems to run 767096 from the Cowell Stone (see the Puddingstone Track, Part A, p.53) to Salthouse on the coast at 133:077439. In the third I will trace out some of the fourteen ley lines which W. A. Dutt 201962 found radiating from Tasburgh Hill Fort to the south of Norwich.

The first two points on this alignment are the fort to the east of Narborough (132:752131) and the castle earthworks at Castle Acre. The line between these 818152 two points goes through the priory ruins, but there is no trace of any track remaining apart from a short section of lane which lies to the south of the fort. I described the best way to walk between these two points in Part A of this section, when I explained how to reach the Puddingstone Track from the Peddars' Way (see p.44).

At one time, one of the many mysterious East Anglian earthworks, severally known as Devil's Ditch (which are considered in more detail in the section on the Icknield Way), ran south from the fort at Narborough, but the only trace of it to be seen now is to the west of Swaffham a short way beyond the Cowell Stone. It crosses the A1122 at 143:746085 above Beechamwell Warren. There is no right of way along this dyke; it all lies on private land and some of it was recently ploughed up by a farmer, who was quite unaware of the significance of the raised hedge.

There is much more to see at the Celtic earthworks of Castle Acre. These were turned to good account by the Norman William de Warenne, who later built his own formidable castle on this site. It was abandoned to pasturage in 1347 and the earthworks are now in the hands of the Department of the Environment. You can walk freely along the southern parts of the battlements. To get there, go south through the bailey gate in the centre of the village, and then turn left along the lane on the north side of the Methodist chapel. For the best view of these earthworks as a whole, you need to go south-east on to the lay-by on the west side of the A1065 at 132:827148.

There are now only a few traces of footpaths left between Castle Acre and the earthworks around the ruins of the Saxon cathedral at North Elmham. The actual alignment, which was once also a

Lexham, a St Andrew's church with the oldest round tower in the county, built about 900 AD (the church stands on slightly raised ground among farm buildings, mostly used for pig fattening, and it is dwarfed by massive, handsome flint barns); West Lexham; and Great Dunham, which lies to the south of East Lexham. Great Dunham is another St

83115
86017

84317
87414

pilgrims' way, runs close to the course of the Nar, as it flows east to Mileham. To reach it, take the Rougham road out of Castle Acre, and turn right at the first crossroads. When this lane, which goes over Fiddler's Green, crosses the Nar, you have the choice of a lane to your right and a farm track to your left. Both ways bring you on to the A1065. From there you can go east to the villages of East Lexham and Litcham. The lane at East Lexham is a continuation of the farm track from the Nar.

There is an abundance of Saxon remains in this area, and these ancient churches may well have been built on sites chosen for their relation to the alignment. The four churches are Newton by Castle Acre (on the A1065); East

819157

831163

Andrew's church, with a pointed, filled-in Norman door at the west end, a central tower, and Saxon windows on the north side. For an explanation of the significance of dedications to St Andrew see p.120.

From East Lexham take the lane east through the woods to join the B1145 going to Litcham. By the River Nar, to the south of that village, you will find a rather trendy antique shop and restaurant on the site of the pilgrims' rest house. It is the meeting place of several ley alignments (see p.69).

The way now goes along the B road to Mileham. This will take you past the castle earthworks, now in private hands but quite visible from the road. They are on your right, and are surmounted by

91515

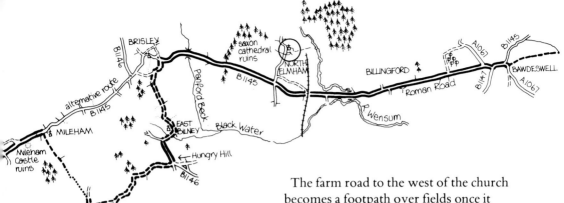

The following map labels appear: BRISLEY, saxon cathedral ruins, NORTH ELMHAM, BILLINGFORD, BAWDESWELL, B1145, B1146, Panford Beck, alternative route, B1145, MILEHAM, Mileham castle ruins, EAST BILNEY, Black Water, Hungry Hill, B1146, moat & chapel, BITTERING, Roman Road, Wensum, A1067, A147, A1067

the ruins of the stone keep of a Norman castle built by the FitzAlan family, who were granted the manor in the eleventh century; and who considered it important to defend this way, which was then a major thoroughfare running across the middle of Norfolk. This road runs just slightly to the north of the great alignment which started from Avebury.

It has been a busy highway all through the centuries. The Romans used it and it was much travelled right through the Middle Ages. Brisley church to the north-east has wall paintings of both St Christopher and St Andrew. However, the B1145 doesn't make very interesting walking today, so the best plan is to take the farm road which runs to the west of Mileham church. If you want to visit the church before leaving the village, you will find that it is approached along a drive-way from the road. The oldest part of this church, which is dedicated to St John the Baptist, is the fourteenth-century north door. An ancient cross of uncertain date is mounted on a fifteenth-century dais tomb in the churchyard.

921197

The farm road to the west of the church becomes a footpath over fields once it passes the farm buildings, and comes out on to a lane by a small patch of woodland. Continue past the moat and chapel of Bittering and head for the earthworks at Hungry Hill on the B1146, to the south of East Bilney. Here, in the early 1530s, the martyr Thomas Bilney may have preached during his progression to Norwich and the stake; for when he got there he was arrested for speaking out against the worship of relics and the mediation of saints between man and God. From Hungry Hill follow the lanes northwards to return to the B1145. If you prefer not to make this detour, you can follow the B road all the way from Mileham through Brisley, going east across Panford Beck to North Elmham.

932178

9317

956186

Here you will find signs directing you to the remains of the Saxon cathedral, which stands to the north of the town. In the eighth century, this cathedral ranked equal in importance with Dunwich. The interpretation of the ruins is given in an excellent little handbook, sold from a nearby cottage, and at 2p (the 1978 cost) very good value indeed, so it is unfair to complain that it makes no reference to the building materials that were used.

988218

57

But these are quite remarkable. Dominating the flints and rubble that make up the majority of all East Anglian buildings of any age, you will find great, dark carstones, embedded with an assortment of pebbles and forming impressive natural conglomerates. And when you look closely at the ruins you will find that a lot of use has been made of thin Roman bricks. Between the ruins of North Elmham Cathedral and the railway which runs by the river, there is a tree-topped earth bank of a much older date than the ruins. It rises from the clear outline of a causeway. It seems to me that these remaining earthworks, which

you can pick up one or two short, intermittent traces of it.

The best way is to follow the lane from Jordan Green round to Reepham. Continue past Booton to Eastgate, where 1423 you will get back on the course of the Roman road for a short distance until you come to the B1149. The path then crosses the heath to Little London, 18623 whose name indicates that it was once an important place to the drovers going south from Holt to the St Faith's Fair. After passing through Marsham, the

are well to the north of the alignment, may have formed part of a dyke protecting the central tracks of the Icknield Way, which some authorities believe ran along this alignment to the coast at Happisburgh (see Section 3, p.116).

The possibility is strengthened by the stretch of Roman road which, as the B1145, runs through Billingford towards Bawdeswell, and which continues as a footpath to the east of 072213 Bawdeswell going to Jordan Green. This road leads towards the site of the Roman 205246 buildings to the south of Aylsham, and as you follow the lanes to the north-east

58

lanes will bring you to a footpath running by a stream which is delightfully known as the Mermaid. This path and stream join the B1354 running south-east out of Aylsham, a spa town in the eighteenth century, whose spring is still commemorated by Spa Farm. The footpath continues across the B road, then 213245 goes across the railway line to come to a bridge across the River Bure, on the other side of which is the church of Burgh next Aylsham. W.A. Dutt's 21825 alignment went through the earthworks at Round Hill to the south of this village.

The next point on the line is marked by the crossroads at Skeyton, which you 245257 can reach by the lane running to the east. Unfortunately there are no footpaths on the next stretch of the line either, which

34300

63308

follows the lanes through Worstead and Honing to Crostwight church, which again has a St Christopher wall painting. To get to Walcott House, the last point on the alignment before Happisburgh itself, take the lane towards Ridlington where you will find a footpath going due east. It comes out on the lane just to

the north of Walcott House. Continue east by Walcott Hall, and then take the footpath that brings you to the B1159

370311

leading to Happisburgh church. Happis-burgh is pronounced Hazeboro, it being a common Norfolk habit to discard superfluous consonants. The village stands on the top of greensand cliffs, overgrown with tansy and the creeping Dunwich roses. However it is not as

North Elmham,
Saxon Cathedral

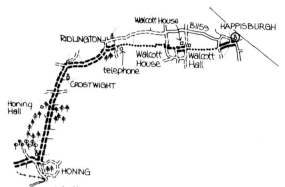

RIDLINGTON
Walcott House
B1159
HAPPISBURGH
Walcott House
Walcott Hall
telephone
CROSTWIGHT
Honing Hall
HONING

idyllic as that suggests, for the cliffs are also the site of a caravan camp. The church, which stands on high ground a little back from the cliffs, marks the end of the alignment. From Burgh next Aylsham, a distance of almost 11·5 miles (18·5 km), the line has passed over four stretches of high ground, Swanton Hill, Westwick Hill, Sandy Hill and Meeting House Hill, by the cross at 133:315287; and then beside three great houses, Honing Hall, Crostwight Hall and Walcott Hall. Around Happisburgh church are the graves of sailors, drowned in the treacherous seas below. Here lie thirty-two sailors drowned when H.M.S. *Peggy* was driven on to the cliffs in 1770; another 132 from H.M.S. *Invincible*, wrecked here in 1801 on her way to join Nelson's fleet at Copenhagen; the crew of H.M.S. *Hunter*, a Revenue cutter wrecked in 1804; and six sailors from the barque *Young England*, lost off Winterton in 1876. On such a coastline it is no wonder that there are many tales of smugglers and wreckers.

'Le Pedderysty, alias dicta Saltersty' was a name given to a branch off the Peddars' Way running through Beacham-well[1] to the west of Swaffham. R. Rainbird Clarke, who traced this name for the route to the fifteenth century, naturally claimed that it indicates 'one of the commodities transported along it in historic times'. Ben Ripper, of Swaffham, believes that it also indicates a much earlier route, and he has found an alignment leading from the Cowell Stone (see p. 53, which runs to the west of Salthouse on the north Norfolk coast.

A good place to start from is the Fincham Drove (also noted on p. 53) which goes across the main King's Lynn road, the A47, out of Swaffham towards Castle Acre . It comes to an end at the second lane it reaches to the north-east of that road, but the natural course would have been for it to continue to the place where seven ways once converged on Bartholomew's Hills. From there, the alignment would run over Hungry Hill towards Tittleshall.

It is from the church there, dedicated to St Mary the Virgin, that I want to follow the route to the coast. Tittleshall is near Mileham, the ancestral home of the Coke family, who built Holkham Hall on the north coast of Norfolk in the mid-eighteenth century. The actual founder of that estate, Thomas Coke,

77810

81813

895212

9219

first Earl of Leicester, was an ingenious and hard-working farmer; but it was his great-nephew, Thomas William, whose farming methods so revolutionized agriculture that he became known as Coke of Norfolk.

When he inherited the estate in 1776, the land was so poor that ten thousand quarters of wheat had to be imported into the area. Forty years later, he had farmed to such good effect that the same area was able to export eleven thousand quarters. There were other great yields besides wheat, for by introducing a four-course rotation of turnips, barley, clover and wheat, he was able to do away with the wasteful fallow year of the old three-course rotation. And he was as interested in livestock as he was in arable farming, so he was also famous for his improved strains of South Down sheep, Norfolk cattle and Suffolk pigs. These animals were all kept on land that

half a century before had been nothing but a sandy waste.

'Coke of Norfolk' did not get his affectionate title simply by working for his own gain. He instituted the 'Holkham Shearings', which are still a popular annual event, and which were the predecessors of the modern agricultural show. The purpose then as now was partly pleasure – Coke feasted his guests lavishly – but mostly educational. His idea was to provide a meeting place where farming problems could be discussed, and where he could demonstrate how his model farm was run. When he died in 1842, at the age of ninety, his fame was so great that the procession of mourners stretched for 2 miles (3·2 km) from Litcham to the family vault at Tittleshall.

There is a path to the north of Tittleshall church, running towards Whissonsett Hall, which could well be a continuation of the Fincham Drove. It runs for about 2 miles (3·2 km), and passes a moat and the tower of the ruined church

61

of All Saints, Godwick, which as long ago as 1603 was described as 'whollie ruynated and decaied longe since unknowne by whose negligence', as you can learn from the notes supplied by the church at Tittleshall. The church stands close to the site of Godwick Hall, which flourished until the sixteenth century, and was the centre of what must have been quite a prosperous village. When the public footpath was open along that way you could still trace the outlines of the streets and some of the houses in the raised earth, but now the only secular building remaining is the barn. Unfortunately, the path has recently been closed to the public on account of some unspecified dangerous work going on in the area. But if you take the lane going 896226 north from Tittleshall church, keeping to the right-hand fork when the road divides, you will be able to see the church tower and the barn to the south. This lane brings you into Whissonsett by The Swan, almost opposite the long drive through public grazing land (used by a goat and a donkey when I was last there) and so to the church. If you want to visit the church to see the Celtic wheel cross, dug up by a sexton in 1900 and now standing against the east wall of the nave, leave it by the west door and continue your journey by the lane running north to Colkirk.

From the church tower at Godwick, the next clear alignment goes past the 962275 moat at Great Ryburgh to the crossroads 993309 at Fulmodestone, which is reached by passing south-east of Colkirk and following the roads first to Great Ryburgh.

This is a fairly busy little town, and the moat is just to the east of the railway line. Walk through the village, across the River Wensum to Clay Hill, and on towards Stibbard. From there it is just 4 miles to Fulmodestone crossroads.

A short diversion will take you to the ruined chapel of Croxton. To make it, 9843(0 turn left past the Hastings Arms at Fulmodestone and then take a lane going south which leads to the big house in Croxton. In the southern corner of the intersection between two lanes, you will find the ruins of a chapel almost completely buried in ivy and hidden in the undergrowth of a small wood. Here you can make a short, circular walk by following the original lane to the southwest. It is now a wide, grassy track which curves round to Clipstone House, 9743(from which you can take the lane to the road and return to Fulmodestone.

The next point on this alignment is at Letheringsett church on the banks of the Glaven, and it can only be reached by 0603(lanes. When you take the farm track from Gunthorpe, if you follow the curve round the western edge of a wood you 0235 will be following part of the course of the original alignment. But unfortunately that is a dead end now.

To get to Letheringsett, you must retrace your steps, then follow the track to the National Trust property of Bullfer Grove, and from there make your way 0173 north-eastwards through Sharrington to Little Thornage.

At Little Thornage crossroads you can 0593(8 make a short, pleasant diversion by turning right and taking the footpath beside

62

a deep, unbridged ford where the River Glaven crosses the lane, and from there turning north to the village of Letheringsett. The church can be reached more directly by taking the northern lane from Little Thornage.

This is a St Andrew's church (the saint whom T.C.Lethbridge links with Apollo), and mainly dates from the thirteenth century, although its round tower is some two hundred years older. Anyone interested in the part that alignments played in measuring the course of the day and the months of the year, will be amused by the flowery epitaph for the village's most illustrious inhabitant, whose tombstone stands just opposite the lych gate. This was the nineteenth-century blacksmith turned clock-maker, one Johnson Jex, who 'lived and died a scientific anchorite'. Some of the watches he made and the tools he

worked with are preserved in the Castle Museum, Norwich.

From Letheringsett, the next point on the alignment is the church at Kelling. 088417 The old track still exists, but unfortunately it now goes through the private lands of Letheringsett Hall. So probably the best course here is to turn east to Holt, and then take the lanes to Salthouse Heath, whose name is a direct indication of the track we are tracing.

You have to reach Holt by the main road, which is not such a hardship as it

63

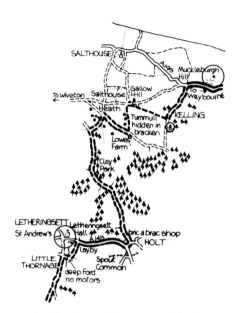

quished tribes (whose talk was gobble-degook or cuckoo to their conquerors) were imprisoned.

In more recent times the people of Holt again had to accustom themselves to an almost strange tongue, for this was a great centre for the Scottish drovers, who in the mid-eighteenth century brought over forty thousand Highland cattle a year into Norfolk. Many of these collected here in Holt for the last stage of their journey to the great St Faith's Fair on the outskirts of Norwich. They took the road to Horsford, avoiding the toll gate at the fork of the Holt and Aylsham roads.

Just as you get into the town of Holt, you will find a lane on your left, beside the delicately painted blue and white façade of an antique-cum-bric-à-brac shop. This lane leads to Cley. Follow it for about 2 miles (3·2 km), where you will find a turning on your right, which goes through a wood to Salthouse Heath. Here you will find many sandy tracks running across the heath to the north.   06741

Although many of these will take you in the right direction, the best course is to follow the lane to Lowes Farm, opposite which you will see a green lane going north across the heath, with a field hedge to the east. Follow it until you come to a clearing on your left, where in summer the tumuli, which Richard Wainwright believes may date from the early Bronze Age, are completely hidden by the bracken. Now continue north until you come to a place where five ways meet: the track you are on; the lane   07842

07841

sounds, for the road is not unduly busy and there are wide grass verges.

Just before the road bears right to climb the hill that leads into Holt, you will find a lay-by on your right. From here a path goes to Spout Common, where the citizens of Holt exercise their dogs. This common is mostly composed of small mounds round a central marshy area. On the western side of it there is a spring, now covered by brickwork, but which was originally surrounded by an enclosing wall. The story goes that a man once tried to pen an owl overnight. This apparently trivial anecdote was linked by John Edward Field, the author of *The Myth of the Pent Cuckoo*, with other stories of trapped birds throughout eastern and southern England. The Rev. Field believed that these marked places where slaves from recently vanquished tribes

64

directly ahead of it which runs to Salthouse church; a lane going west to Wiveton; a lane going north-east to Weybourne; and a grass lane, which later becomes a field track, on your immediate right. This is the path you want, but before you take it you may like to look at the tumulus on Gallow Hill, one of the many Bronze Age burials in the area. It lies just to the north of the lane on your left. The path will bring you out by the little thirteenth-century church of Kelling, with its bare interior, and tiny, pointed church door.

From Kelling church, go downhill towards Weybourne. Here Muckleburgh Hill lies between you and the sea, and on your left you will find many sandy paths leading up to its flat, circular summit and the tumulus to the north. The coast directly ahead of you has now been taken over by the Air Force, so you cannot now go down to Kelling Hard, where up to the Middle Ages salt imported from Gascony started its journey inland.

01430

The lines from Tasburgh Hill Fort

O.S. map 134.

The Iron Age hill fort at Tasburgh is best reached by taking the lanes south of Norwich. They run through an area which was, until the Roman Conquest, the most sacred and important part of East Anglia, for here a wooden henge, possibly of equal importance to Stonehenge, once stood. To get there, leave the city by the A146 and then turn away from the main road, down a lane, just after you have crossed the River Yare in the suburb of Trowse Newton.

This lane runs past Arminghall, the only henge in East Anglia of which we have visible traces; although there is an unexcavated site of one at Stratford St Mary near Ipswich, and rumours of another beneath the sea at Dunwich (described in Section 4, p.166). This henge has been thoroughly excavated.

The reason for the disappearance of the East Anglian henges is simply that, in this stoneless land, they had to be made of wood. The henge at Arminghall was first recognized in modern times by Wing Commander Insall V.C., who flew over the site in 1929. The subsequent excavations revealed eight post holes showing a horse-shoe arrangement of what must have been great oak posts, probably projecting about twenty or thirty feet (6-9·1 m) above ground level. for the socket holes were found to be

201962

246067

239060

65

seven-and-a-half feet (2·2 m) deep and three feet (0·9 m) in diameter. Most authrities agree with Evan Hadingham's estimate in *Circles and Standing Stones* and put the date for this henge around the middle of the third millennium BC. E.C. Axford in his chapter on stones and crosses in his book *Bodmin*

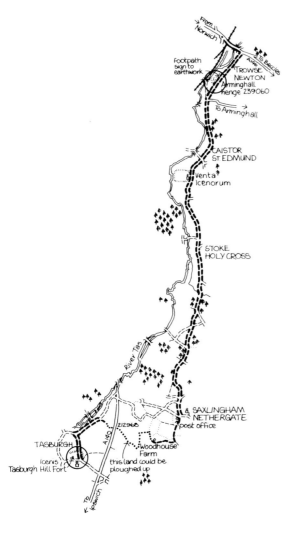

Moor believes that Arminghall was contemporaneous with the Bodmin stripple stones.

Interestingly enough, the site slightly to the east of Arminghall has been found suitable for a power station, and a network of overhead cables converge beside the remains of the henge. From the lane from Trowse Newton, a footpath sign on your right directs you across a field to the earthworks by the river that are now the only signs of this sacred place. The henge originally had a single entrance to an area ninety feet (27·4 m) in diameter, which was enclosed by an inner and an outer ditch. The ditches can be easily traced on the ground. Like all sacred circles, Arminghall is associated with water, and the River Yare runs close by.

From Arminghall carry on to the south-west past Caistor St Edmund, once the most important stronghold of the Iceni, which was known to the Romans as Venta Icenorum and was possibly one of the chief centres for woollen cloth in Roman Britain. That square city lies buried to the south of the modern village, whose church stands on the remains of the eastern part of the Roman wall, which is approached by a path that was once the east gate into the Roman city. Now there is little evidence that a flourishing city, with a temple in which both Roman and Celtic gods were worshipped, and a manufacturing town (there was a glass-making works and a pottery) existed here until the end fourth century AD. But from the air the air the grid of the streets of a Roman town, extending beyond the walls, is clearly discernible.

From Caistor St Edmund, the lane continues south for just over half a mile (804 m) through Stoke Holy Cross to Saxlingham Nethergate; which in its northern part covers the Roman road linking Venta Icenorum with Colchester.

222965   From Saxlingham Nethergate you can take a footpath past Woodhouse Farm, crossing the main road, to join the lane which climbs uphill. At the top of the hill, you will find on either side of the
201962   lane the traces of the Iceni's hill fort of Tasburgh. These earthworks now form a tree-topped bank, eight feet (2·4 m) high in places, outlining a field boundary. The lane then descends to a church
201958   with a round tower, probably built in Saxon times, which is thought to occupy a site that once marked the centre of the fort's enclosure. It is from here that I have taken the alignments, one of which goes north-east through Norwich Castle to Happisburgh.

For the purposes of this section, I am going to trace two other alignments in some detail. They both go to the coast, one through the abbey lands at Wymondham (pronounced Windham) and the other through the earthworks at North Elmham.

The Tasburgh – Wymondham line
O.S. maps 134, 144, 132

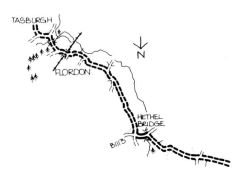

There are very few footpaths on this route, and this could now be one of the alignments that are best followed by bicycle or car. The lanes are quiet and pleasantly free from much traffic other than farm tractors. Leave Tasburgh by the lane that runs north-west through Flordon to join the B1113 at Hethel   174993
Bridge. From there it is nearly 4 miles (6·4 km) to Wymondham, which you enter to the north-east. The abbey lies to   106015
the south-west, on the banks of the River Tiffey. A Saxon church once stood in the abbey meadows, which run down to the river. That church was probably built on the sacred pagan site with which Tasburgh is aligned. The present abbey was completed about 1130, and dedicated first to St Mary and St Alban, the latter saint being shortly afterwards replaced by St Thomas of Canterbury.

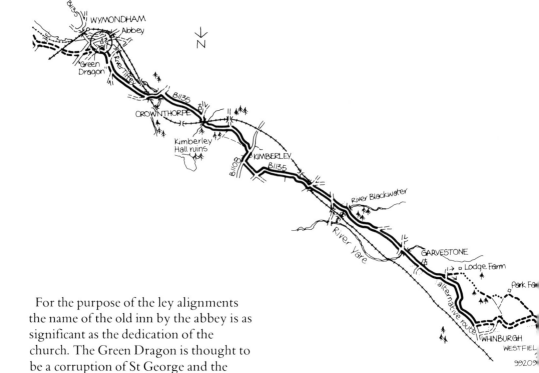

For the purpose of the ley alignments the name of the old inn by the abbey is as significant as the dedication of the church. The Green Dragon is thought to be a corruption of St George and the Dragon, and it could be that the original Saxon church was dedicated to St George. We shall notice in Suffolk especially (Section 4) that on the ley alignments of East Anglia our familiar dragon-slayer St George is much more predominant than the St Michael of south-west Britain.

From the abbey the line goes through Crownthorpe church to the crossroads at Westfield (144:992096). Take the B1135 out of Wymondham; it is a matter of about 5·5 miles (8·8 km) to Garvestone.

014075   Here, if you are on foot, you can go a short distance by footpath, past Lodge Farm and Park Farm, to join the lane

going north-west to Westfield cross-roads.   994087

If you are following the lanes, you will reach this point by going along the B1135 to Whinburgh, and then taking the lane for Westfield.

The next point on the alignment is at Scarning church, whose rector from   995123 1879-1911 was Canon Augustus Jessop, author of several books on Norfolk local history and folklore. The old way has

68

completely gone, although the lane follows it for about half a mile (804 m) to the south-east of Scarning village. To get there turn left at Westfield crossroads and make your way to Daffy Green, then pass Lawrence Farm and keep going north-west to Scarning church.

The next point from Scarning lies to the west of Litcham, where the line passes close to the old pilgrims' rest house on the banks of the Nar (see p.56. To get there from Scarning, follow the lane to Longham, where you turn left over Hulver Hill to the village of Litcham.

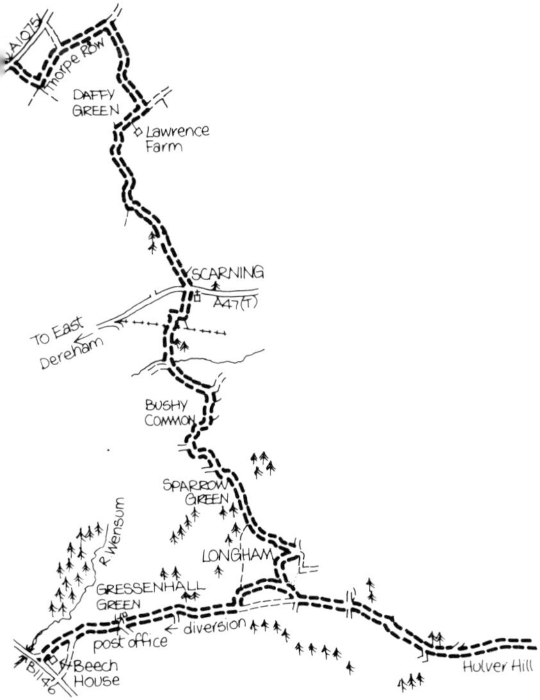

889174

941164

If you want to make a diversion before going to Litcham, turn right at Longham and go over Gressenhall Green and up the hill, to where the old Poor Law Union, Beech House, dominates the landscape. This building is now Norfolk's Rural Life Museum, and it is open during the summer months. The old workhouse dining hall is filled with relics from bygone methods of agriculture, among which stand two stuffed specimens of the extinct Norfolk Horn Sheep. Before Beech House became a museum it was an old people's home, but try as the authorities did to brighten the place up, the families in the local villages still regarded the place with dread. The large, brick building is set on high ground above the village, and for generations people regarded it as a place of bitter degradation which robbed its unfortunate inmates of all individuality and effectively separated them from their families. The present curator, Bridget Yates, is sensitive to this feeling and, in preserving memories of the past, she includes imaginative reminders of the daily lives of the people to whom the place must once have been an inhuman prison.

974171

To return to Litcham: the next point on the alignment is the crossroads in the middle of Weasenham Plantation. This brings it into conjunction with the diamond alignments from Castle Acre (see p.47). To get there, follow the lanes north-west to Litcham Heath. A tumulus lies beside the road to the north, and there is another to the south just after you have gone over the next cross-

849198

roads, which is described on p.49. The lane now brings you to the crossroads, the north-south road being covered by the A1065.

'93242 The next point on the alignment is Little Massingham church. To get there, carry on over the crossroads to the B1145, which you follow for about 1·5 miles (2·4 km) until you join the lane that takes you through to Great 314209 Massingham, and on to Little Massingham. There the church stands off the lane to your left.

From here the alignment crosses the Peddars' Way at the place where several 771257 roads meet, the most important by today's reckoning being the A148. Those who are interested in the way that the old alignments intersect with modern installations will note that in this instance the crossing is marked by the great oil store mentioned on p.44.

The last notable point on the alignment is Ingoldisthorpe church. If you are on foot you can walk north along the Peddars' Way to the tumuli on Harpley Common, and from there follow the lanes through Anmer to Ingoldisthorpe. The other way, if you are travelling by car, is to follow the road past Flitcham Abbey and Flitcham to rejoin the route south-east of Anmer.

From Ingoldisthorpe, the line reaches the sea at the long spit of Heacham Harbour at 658358. A footpath goes from the village to Southgate, from where you take the lane running to the coast. You can also get to this lane by following the A149 to Southgate. At the end of the lane to the coast, a footpath takes you over the marshes almost to the point where, on the land as it is now, the alignment ends.

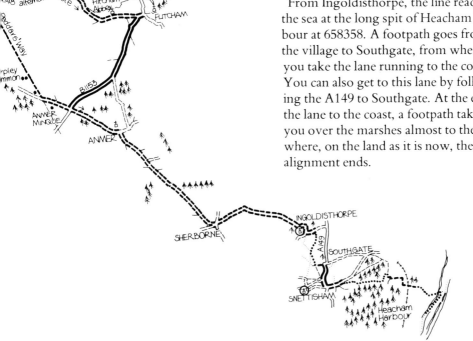

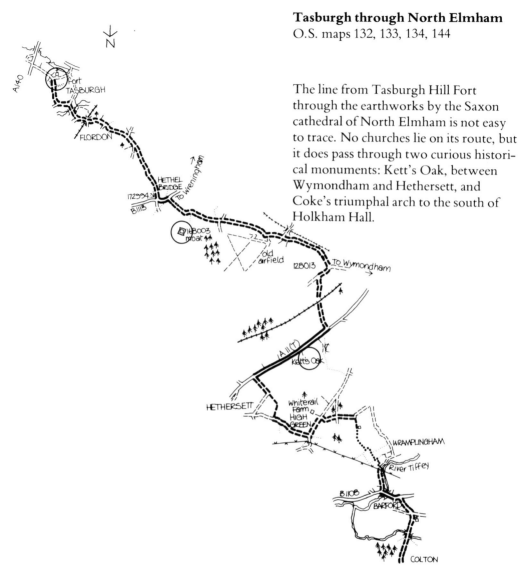

The line from Tasburgh Hill Fort
through the earthworks by the Saxon
cathedral of North Elmham is not easy
to trace. No churches lie on its route, but
it does pass through two curious historical monuments: Kett's Oak, between
Wymondham and Hethersett, and
Coke's triumphal arch to the south of
Holkham Hall.

The first point on the alignment from
Tasburgh is Hethel Bridge at
134:172993, which you reach by the
lanes to the south of Flordon. From
there the line goes past a moat to the

north of Wreningham church (144:168003) and then on to Kett's Oak, a memorial of the peasants' revolt, led by Robert Kett, a Wymondham tanner, in 1549, and brutally crushed by foreign mercenaries in the August of that year. The oak is fenced round, and stands in a lay-by to the north of the A11, about 1·9 miles (3 km) north-east of Wymondham Abbey. If you have already visited Wymondham, you can reach this point by leaving the Wymondham road from Hethel Bridge at 144:128013, and fol-

lowing the lane to the north, until you get to the main road, where you turn right.

There are no lanes past Kett's Oak, so to follow the course of the alignment you have to go east along the A11 towards Hethersett and take the first lane on the left for High Green and Barford. Turn left at High Green, and make for Wramplingham on the banks of the Tiffey. A stretch of this footpath follows the alignment to the south side of the river.

Kett's Oak,
near Norwich

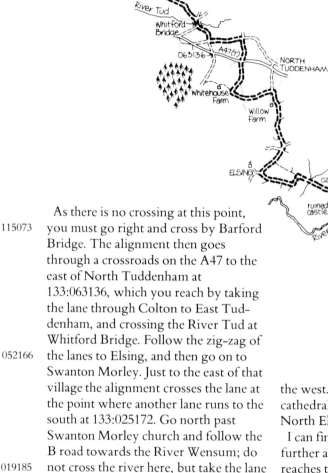

As there is no crossing at this point, you must go right and cross by Barford Bridge. The alignment then goes through a crossroads on the A47 to the east of North Tuddenham at 133:063136, which you reach by taking the lane through Colton to East Tuddenham, and crossing the River Tud at Whitford Bridge. Follow the zig-zag of the lanes to Elsing, and then go on to Swanton Morley. Just to the east of that village the alignment crosses the lane at the point where another lane runs to the south at 133:025172. Go north past Swanton Morley church and follow the B road towards the River Wensum; do not cross the river here, but take the lane on your left going north-west towards North Elmham. The alignment crosses the river at 133:002203, where the B road from Billingford now runs beside it. The present bridge, which goes across to North Elmham, lies a little further to

115073

052166

019185

the west. The remains of the Saxon cathedral and the pagan earthworks in North Elmham are described on p.57.

I can find no features of great interest further along the alignment until it reaches the dramatic ruins of Egmere church about 4 miles (6·4 km) from the sea. So I am going to incorporate the northern end of this ley into the next part of this section, which deals with the north Norfolk coast from Holkham to Kelling.

98821

89637

74

Part C
The North Norfolk Coast

O.S. maps 132, 133

Hill forts, barrows and tumuli abound all along the northern stretch of the Norfolk coast. There is a certain amount of debate about their origin, but I believe that they were most probably bridgeheads established by the Belgic Celts when they came westwards into the country from the continent. However, the forts were probably used for both attack and defence, while some of them may have been quite peaceful farming settlements, for we must always bear in mind the changeable nature of this coast.

To begin our explorations I want to jump forward in time, first to the Romans and then even later to Thomas Coke and the agricultural reforms of the eighteenth century. I am going to begin, incongruously enough, by the Garden Centre attached to Holkham Hall. This is only open at week-ends, but the path that covers the old Roman road runs just to the west of it and is always there for you to walk on.

In his study entitled *Norfolk*, W. A. Dutt tells us that when Thomas Coke came to build his great estate here in the eighteenth century, he declared that the place was so barren that 'two rabbits could be found fighting for one blade of grass'. It is salutary to realize how much good husbandry has changed this landscape in two hundred years; and it's a reflection that should stop us making any quick generalizations about the lie of the land in prehistoric times.

The old Roman road begins about 2 miles (3·2 km) to the east of Burnham Market. The road leading to the Garden Centre just before this point gives no indication that there is a right of way along the old Roman road which runs to the west of the estate, beginning to the right of the gates that lead into the Garden Centre. If you are planning to do the road part of the route by car, it's worth noting that it is strictly forbidden to park here. 867430

The Roman road, which is sometimes a wide sandy track and sometimes a narrow path along field headlands, runs straight to the south-east, with the Holkham woodlands on the left-hand side. The alignment which ran from Tasburgh Hill Fort through North Elmham, see p.72, crosses the Roman road at a point where a farm track runs south-west to Burnham Thorpe. From that intersection the alignment then continues north-west until it reaches the coast at Overy Staithe. 870416 845444

The Roman road takes you past a field to a gate, which brings you on to the lane going downhill to Burnham Thorpe. If you turn left here away from the village, you will face several miles of lane walking, but they are still pleasantly quiet enough to make it enjoyable to take some of the detours that are involved if you want to look at two more points on the Tasburgh-North Elmham alignment (the Holkham triumphal arch and the ruined church at Egmere), visit Little Walsingham, and 873401 882395 896375 9336

75

944408 walk round the hill fort at Warham St Mary.

887398 To get to the triumphal arch turn off the lane before New Holkham. Then at

883392 the next crossroads, you will see the lodge gates by the road, and the driveway leading through a massive arch, presumably quite unconsciously set up over the ancient alignment. If you continue to the south-west, you return to one of the last fragments of the Roman road from Holkham. Turn left at Hag-

878373 gard's Lodge if you wish to make the detour to the ruins of Egmere church –

896375 standing on a clearly defined, circular hillock to the south of the road. This church, which stands on private land, was already in ruins by the time of Elizabeth I. The village it served decayed as the land was given over to sheep farming, but from the road you can see irregularities in the grassland, which indicate where the cottages once stood.

The Tasburgh-North Elmham alignment runs through the church to the bridge over the River Stiffkey at East 917 Barsham. An extraordinary, massive and ornate, red, Tudor brick manor house dominates this part of the road. Henry VIII slept here the night before he made his barefoot pilgrimage to Walsingham. From the ruined church of Egmere, continue east along the lane which was once part of the way that linked the Roman road we have been following to the Peddars' Way. The lane leads to Little Walsingham, which you 933 happily enter across the disused railway

Hill Fort
Warham St. Mary

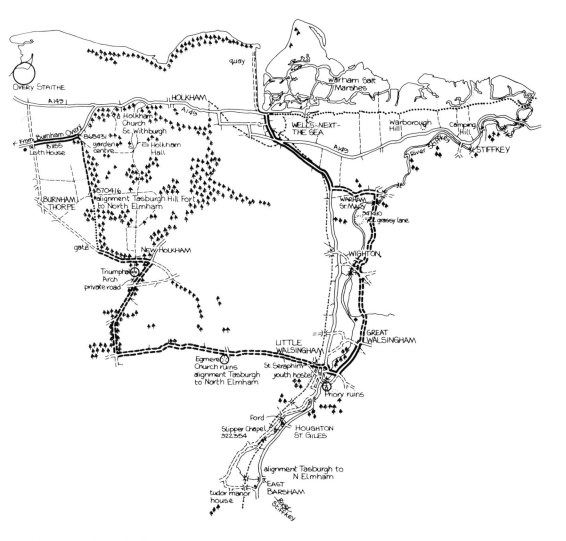

OVERY STAITHE

quay

Warham Salt Marshes

A149 HOLKHAM

A149

Holkham Church St.Withburgh

WELLS-NEXT-THE SEA

Warborough Hill

Camping Hill

From Burnham Overy

B1155
Leith House

garden centre

Holkham Hall

River Stiffkey

STIFFKEY

A149

870416
alignment Tasburgh Hill Fort to North Elmham

BURNHAM THORPE

WARHAM St.MARY

941410

grassey lane

gate

NEW HOLKHAM

WIGHTON

Triumphal Arch
private road

GREAT WALSINGHAM

LITTLE WALSINGHAM

Egmere Church ruins
alignment Tasburgh to North Elmham

St Seraphim youth hostel

Priory ruins

ford

Slipper Chapel
922354

HOUGHTON ST. GILES

alignment Tasburgh to N.Elmham

tudor manor house

EAST BARSHAM

River Stiffkey

line. I say 'happily' because to me the only living part of this holy place lies in the little Russian Orthodox church of St Seraphim, whose cupola stands above the waiting room of the old railway station. The church is now run by a non-monastic brotherhood of six, led by an orthodox priest; they are tenants of Norfolk County Council, who bought the land from British Rail in 1969.

According to a fifteenth-century ballad, the Holy Shrine of Walsingham was founded in 1061 and modelled as a replica of Our Lady's House in Nazareth. When the real house fell into the hands of the Mohammedans, it was put about that the Virgin deserted the Holy Land for Norfolk. In any case, her shrine here is believed to be the first in Britain to be dedicated to the Virgin Mary. Until the Reformation, Walsingham was almost as popular as Canterbury as a place of pilgrimage. Among its holy relics was a phial of the Virgin's milk, so the palmers' path across Norfolk from Ely was popularly known as the Milky Way. A secondary reason for the name was that the pilgrims were as numerous as the stars.

Robert the Bruce was one of the many monarchs who visited the shrine; later Henry VII came here, after the defeat of Lambert Simnel, and gratefully presented the Virgin with the upstart's banner. The most illustrious commoner to visit the abbey was the cynical Erasmus, who was able to write: 'Before the chapel is a shed, under which are two wells full to the brink: the water is wonderfully cold, and efficacious in curing pains in the head.'

To the south of the village is the Slipper Chapel, where pilgrims left their shoes before making the rest of the pilgrimage barefoot. It stands on the banks of the river by the hamlet of Houghton St Giles. In Walsingham itself, the site of the shrine lies among the ruins of the twelfth-century priory in the grounds of Walsingham Abbey. The actual shrine was destroyed at Henry VIII's command, some time after he had himself paid homage there.

78

In Walsingham, there is a small museum run by the County Museum Service. It closes at 4 p.m. Although much of the village is given up to accommodate the numbers of people of various denominations who visit Walsingham as a holy place, there is a Youth Hostel for the general visitors; and you may find this a convenient base for walks in the north Norfolk area, if you cannot face the one in the busy seaside town of Sheringham.

From Little Walsingham, follow the road to Great Walsingham. Although there is not much to be seen at Great Walsingham now, it must once have been a place of much more importance than the Holy Village. It was an urn excavated in the cemetery here that inspired Sir Thomas Browne, a Norwich doctor and author of *Religio Medici*, to compose his more famous *Urn Burial* in 1658. 943?

About 2·2 miles (3·8 km) to the north of Great Walsingham you will see a grassy lane on your left. There is no sign to indicate that this is the way to one of the most clearly defined forts in the whole of East Anglia. The green lane brings you to a small gate opening into a field. There you will see the outer ramparts of a circular riverside fort, whose double ramparts reach as high as thirty feet (9·1 m) in some places. It is known as Warham Camp, and it would be complete but for a partial destruction on its south-western side caused by the altered course of the River Stiffkey. The fort, which encloses an area of some 3·5 acres (1·4 hectares), is presumed to have 9474

944

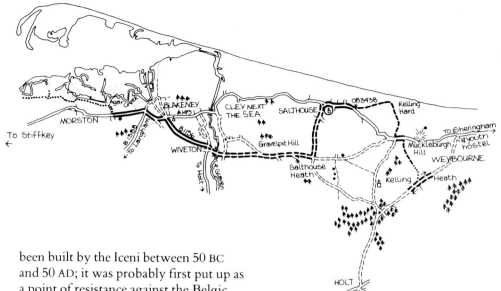

been built by the Iceni between 50 BC and 50 AD; it was probably first put up as a point of resistance against the Belgic invaders.

To the north-west, the alignment from the camp at Warham St Mary extends

78437 through Holkham church, which stands in private land to the north-west of Holkham Hall. The church once served the village that disappeared when the Coke family laid out the parkland. It is the only church dedicated to St Withburga, Etheldreda's sister, whose story I have mentioned in the introduction to this section. From Holkham church, the alignment extends to the point on the coast where the north-west alignment from Tasburgh through North Elmham reaches the sea, although we must remember that the changing outline of the coast may make that last point fortuitous. To the south-west, the alignment is more definite. It goes through the abbey in Little Walsingham to the hill-top church in Fakenham, and then to

19295 the ruined tower of the church by the lost village of Godwick between Tittleshall and Whissonsett (see p.62), where it crosses the Salters' Way. 905223

The lane to the east of the fort goes north through Warham St Mary to Wells-next-the-Sea, a noisy holiday resort for the brief summer season, and still a centre for whelks (locally pronounced wilks) all the year round.

From the quay of Wells-next-the-Sea you can follow the path (now part of the long distance coastal way) which runs alongside the southern edge of the salt marshes. It passes Warborough Hill and Camping Hill. On Warborough Hill is a 961435 round barrow surrounded by a ditch, which was found to contain remains from multiple cremations dating from the Iron Age. Helen Clarke points out that its importance was revived in the fourth century AD when, like other high points along the Norfolk coast, it was used as a signal station to give warning

79

of Danish invaders.

Carry on along the path until you come
017437 to Agar Creek, where you must join the
main road, and the tumulus to the east of
Morston. If you want to explore the
fresh water marshes, and watch the birds
for which they are so famous, turn off
the main road towards Blakeney quay.
Follow the road across the harbour inlet
and past the big hotel until you find the
path going across the marsh.

The coastal path comes to an end here
at Blakeney. So the best way to the east
is to take the B1156 past Blakeney
church with its slender second tower
(once used as a lighthouse) as far as
Wiveton. From there (unless you want
to visit the shell museum down the road
at Glandford), take the lane which goes
over Gravelpit Hill to Salthouse Heath
and then head for Salthouse. Salthouse
176437 church is dedicated, like so many
fishermen's churches, to St Nicholas.
The pews are marked with sailing ships
carved in bored moments by
Elizabethan choir boys. It is a sixteenth-
century church, standing on the eastern
side of the village, with a fine uncluttered interior, and the remains of a much
earlier church on its northern side. From
Salthouse, you can once again take a
path along the outskirts of the marshes.
It leaves the main road at 133:083438.
The coastal path makes a great loop
towards Kelling Hard, and then turns
inland just to the west of Muckleburgh
Hill (see p.65).
096429 You can then take a path going south-
east over Kelling Heath. When it reaches
the lane you can choose between

80

Weybourne and Holt.

If you decide to go further east, you
could stay overnight at the Youth Hostel 1534:
in Sheringham, for the sake of visiting
some of the places to the south-east of
this seaside town. The area, which is full
of prehistoric remains, has strange
stories attached to it, which may well be
pertinent to the ancient trackways. Most
of these tales are connected with the
famous 'shrieking pits' of Aylmerton. 1854:
These are small depressions in the
ground near the Roman camp, which
stands in wooded ground on Aylmerton
Heath, across the A148 from the church
and just under a mile (1·6 km) to the
north of it. There are nearly two
thousand of these pits, which are
believed to have been pre-Celtic cave
dwellings. They are now said to be
haunted by a wailing woman.

On Runton Heath to the north of the
pits one of East Anglia's black shucks, or
ghost dogs from the underworld,
prowls the cliffs between Sheringham
and Cromer. Some people say that this
one is headless, but the usual tales of the
black shuck credit him with one fiery
Cyclopean eye. The ghostly dog walks
silently, but the howl of his awful voice
can drown the noise of a gale. To meet
him is to be warned of your death within
the year, although you can escape that
destiny by closing your eyes and refusing to confront him. Folklorists will tell
you he has his origins in the Black
Hound of Odin, and that he was
brought to this coast by the Norsemen.
We shall meet him again in a more cor-
poreal form in Suffolk.

Section 2

Important alignment points

Breckles Church	144:958946
Grime's Graves	144:817897
Illington Church	144:947900
Knettishall ruined church	144:973802
Roudham ruined church	144:955872
Thetford Castle	144:875828
Weeting Castle	144:777892

Peddars Way,
Knettishall Heath

Section 2: Breckland

Celts and Saxons

O.S. map 144

Between them, the Iron Age Celts and the early Saxons made a dust bowl of south-west Norfolk. Yet they were only continuing the process of erosion which began when Neolithic men used axes, made from the flint which was mined in the area, to clear the original forests and start arable farming. That in its turn was only an extension of the primitive agriculture and herding which began when men first settled in the land to the east of the fens. For thousands of years, this area and the region around Ipswich were the main centres of population in East Anglia.

Several signs of this early occupation can be seen as we follow the ley lines, but unfortunately the meres, on which some lake villages were settled, are now unapproachable. They lie within the area of 25 square miles (6475 hectares) that the Army has taken over as a Battle Area, and are therefore absolutely inaccessible to the public. Only two of the historic meres, Lang Mere and Ring Mere, are now passed by a right of way. They are described on p.109. The forty-acre (16·2 hectares) stretch of Thompson Water, which lies to the east of the Peddars' Way, is an artificial mere made in the mid-nineteenth century.

Yet, despite the encroachments of the Army, there are still many signs of the very early occupation of the region. The most important are the extensive flint mines of Grime's Graves to the north of Thetford; but we will also find numerous Bronze Age barrows, and even one holy well, which could date from pre-Iron Age times. All these sites are linked by alignments, some of which were trading routes, two of them being extensions of the Peddars' Way and the Puddingstone Track described in Section 1.

By the first century BC, the region had been thoroughly settled by the Iceni, the Celtic tribe into which Boadicea was to be born. They were people with a fairly advanced technology, using iron for essential work and harnessing horses to pull their battle chariots. Their mobility is now ironically commemorated in the naming of the Iceni motor cycle shop in Swaffham. A little more seriously, just to the south of that town is the village of Cockley Cley, where a reconstruction of an Iron Age fort (looking a bit like an adventure playground) will give you some idea of how these people lived.

There are not many Roman remains in the area; but we shall find traces of very early Saxon settlements, some of which were set up before the Romans left Britain. They are concentrated on the northern banks of the Lark and at West Stow (see p.99), where authentic recon-

82

structions of their dwellings have been put up by a group of archaeologists. For over two centuries from approximately 400 AD, about eighty one-roomed houses built around large halls stood on this 5-acre (2 hectares) site. Although the original Saxon village was buried in a sand blow, people lived and farmed in this area until the seventeenth century, when the land seems finally to have given out, and a new community settled a couple of miles to the east – where West Stow village now stands. Right into mediaeval times most of the area was intensively farmed, although the light, loose topsoil covering the chalk was becoming increasingly dry and thin so that from time to time the region was subjected to sand blows, as it still is. When this happens, the sand can build up into great drifts blanketing acres of ground. Such a 'blow' took place on a great scale around 1300 AD, and it is that sand which preserved the already buried remains of the original Saxon settlement for the archaeologists who came to excavate it in 1965. In the following century, the erosion became almost complete. Rabbits were the only creatures that flourished in this sandy wasteland; and the mediaeval landowners throughout the Breckland exploited them. They had good reason, for at that time rabbits were a greater delicacy than chicken. It was due to the cultivation of warrens here that one phase in the long saga of the battles between gamekeepers and poachers began. You will see evidence of it in the fortified warrener's lodge on the Brandon road out of Thetford.

If we take cattle and deer as the heraldic animals of north Norfolk, then the rabbit must be the emblem of the south. From a commercial point of view not only was it a valuable source of food, but within living memory it provided the pelts for the making of top hats which, along with flint-knapping, was the great industry of Brandon.

Although as a general rule you won't find hares where rabbits abound, much of the folklore associated with those solitary, numinous animals does get transferred to the mundane, gregarious rabbit. This is particularly so of albino creatures. It is well known that it is very unlucky to see a white hare; and this may account for the stories of dire events heralded by a glimpse of the White Rabbit of Thetford Warren (see p.96). There is no way, though, that we can hope to make any observations about ley lines from the random scurryings of healthy rabbits, though the mysterious, deliberate jumps of the hares might be linked with patterns of earth energy.

What we do owe to the rabbits is the history of modern settlements in this desert area of south Norfolk. Rabbits were big business, and as the warrens could not be farmed in any ordinary way, they were taken over by the landowning families, who came to have enormous power in the region. It was they who later planted belts of broad leaf trees to counteract the erosion, and to give some screen to the game birds which they imported in large numbers. So for some decades the place was a rich man's playground. Then, soon after World War I, the land passed from private into public hands, but the pattern of great stretches of land being owned by one authority remained. First the Forestry Commission took over the region around Thetford. Then, at the beginning of the last war, the Army moved into the east of the region and, as we have noted, still hold it.

Yet the great, private landowners have not vanished without trace. In the west the belts of deciduous trees are, happily, interspersed with the Forestry Commission's conifers; and in the east good stories are still told about the families who once owned the wide parklands and lived in the great halls.

In *Frivola*, Canon Jessop of Scarning retells the ghost story of Breckles Hall (standing to the east of the B111), which he heard from one of his parishioners.

Iceni Village
reconstruction.
Cockley Cley

The story is connected with the legend of Sir Thomas Boleyn, father of the ill-fated Anne, who as an annual penance has to drive a team of headless horses from his home at Blickling in north Norfolk over forty county bridges. His coach is urged onwards by a pack of fiends screeching fearfully.

At Breckles, Sir Thomas's coach came for a notorious poacher, George Mace of Watton, on a night when he was leading an expedition of his fellows into Lord Walsingham's coverts at Merton. The party had agreed to meet at the back of Breckles Hall and all went well until, as they were about to set off together, Mace, the leader, could not be found. Suddenly the rumbling of wheels was heard and coach lamps, so bright that they shone from the front to the back of the hall, dazzled the petrified men. They heard the coach stop by the front door, the steps lowered, and the door opened and shut again with a slam. Then darkness, and the coach seemed to vanish without a sound. The men did not stop to investigate, but went quickly back to their homes. In the morning, 'Jarge Mace was found lying dead at the front door of Breckles Hall. Not a mark upon his body; not a stain upon his garments; his eyes staring glassily, stiff and cold!'

It would be an interesting venture to try and trace the stories of Sir Thomas's carriage with reference to what we know of the ley alignments of Norfolk; and to consider why it was drawn to Breckles Hall. We know that the Hall was a refuge for Roman Catholic priests in the sixteenth century; that the wife of

84

its first owner, Francis Wodehouse, was a lady of extreme religious views, who insisted on being buried in an upright position; and that, according to W.A. Dutt, two subsequent owners of the Hall (before the Mace story) committed suicide. The place is ominous. The Saxon church at Breckles, which stands on the road to the west of the Hall, aligns to the north-west through Great Ellingham church with Wymondham Abbey.

It was not until the late nineteenth century that the distinct character of the area we are considering, from Swaffham in the north to Bury St Edmunds in the south, and from Mildenhall in the west to Attleborough in the east, was recognized by being given a name. In an article in an issue of *The Naturalists' Journal* in 1894 W.G. Clarke, who lived in the area, called his home region 'the Breckland', taking the name from the term for an area of heathland which is intermittently cultivated. His designation has remained.

According to his son, the late R. Rainbird Clarke, who was director of the Castle Museum in Norwich for many years, he so loved the area that he had named that he was unwilling to spend a night away from it, and regularly shaved with a prehistoric flint implement which he found near Brandon. The best guides to the human and natural history of the district are the essays he wrote between 1909 and 1913, which were gathered together by his son, who added some supplementary articles, and published them in 1937 under the title *In Breckland Wilds*. A semi-fictional account of the

people who lived and worked in the Breckland during W.G. Clarke's lifetime can be found in the books by the novelist Michael Home. Although, unfortunately, he finds it expedient to give his places imaginary names, his villagers are clearly and authentically rooted in north-east Breckland, and it is more than likely that you will meet some of their descendants during your walks.

Walking in the Breckland you will sometimes have occasion to curse both the Forestry Commission and the Army, but at least you will not have to suffer the indignities that befell the Victorian walker who, according to W.G. Clarke, met with such underground ramifications of rabbit burrows that 'at times hardly a yard passed without a hurried and undignified descent into the depths sometimes up to the waist.'

For the routes that I have described in this section, it would be sensible to base yourself either at Swaffham or Thetford. The former is simply a large market town with an imposing butter cross. Its most famous citizen was John Chapman, the Pedlar of Swaffham, who set out to find wealth in London, but once there was led back home by a dream which promised him buried gold in his own Norfolk garden. When he dug under the tree which the dream had indicated, he found a pot of gold, and on that pot was an inscription which told him that if he dug deeper he would find even greater wealth. This he did, and the inscription proved true. He was thus a very rich man, and used some of his great wealth to build the north aisle of the church. And there he is remembered to this day by two bench-end carvings; one shows him and his wife in their shop; and the other depicts him on his travels, walking with his pack on his back and his muzzled dog at his side. Swaffham's historian today is Ben Ripper, who is responsible for preserving the 'Swaffham Stone'. This is a great boulder, which you'll find opposite the post office, which he thinks probably served as a Saxon settlement stone when the town was founded in the fifth century AD, although he agrees that the stone itself may well have had a much earlier significance than that.

Thetford is a much larger town than Swaffham. It has several industries and a population of sixteen thousand. Its most important citizen was the radical Thomas Paine, who was born in White Hart Street in 1737 and educated in the grammar school there. But, for our purposes, the most significant feature of the town is the mysterious castle mound described on p.96.

There are four main routes in this section: the southern part of the Puddingstone Track; part of the Peddars' Way from Castle Acre to Knettishall Heath in Suffolk; the Harling Drove, which we shall follow from east to west; and an easterly north-south track going through Roudham and Illington.

Part A
The Puddingstone Track (2)

O.S. maps 143, 144

It is in the Breckland that Dr Rudge's Puddingstone Track, much of which is coincidental with the suggested routes of the Icknield Way, really comes into its own. We left it at the Cowell Stone to the west of Swaffham, and the next stone is located at Cranwich church, just over 9 miles (14·4 km) to the south. It is best reached by taking the forest road that runs south from the other side of the A1122 from the Cowell Stone. This path goes through forestry land for most of its course, but after about 2 miles (3·2 km) it runs downhill across a stretch of arable farm land. 7660

After Swaffham Forest the track crosses a lane which is worth following for just a few yards to the east. Just outside the gate of the first house you come to, you will notice a large boulder. It is probably a glacial erratic, though local tradition holds that it is part of a meteorite. The wife of the farmer, whose house, gate and stone these are, told me that her husband came across the boulder when he was ploughing in one of their fields. It could, I suppose, be one of the intermittent stones on the long route between the Cowell Stone and Cranwich. 7800

The forest track brings you out by Cockley Cley. The most important building in this village, which many people, including W. G. Clarke, consider to lie on the Icknield Way, is the tiny, 7904

early seventh-century chapel dedicated
to St Mary. But do not head straight for
the chapel. As you turn left into the village, you will see the present village
church and a pub with the unlikely but
recent name of The Twenty Church-
wardens – arising from the current practice of grouping parishes so that they
work together under one vicar. The
steep lane from here not only takes you
into Cockley Cley, but also leads to the
reconstructed Iceni village. Although
this reconstruction is more popular than
authentic, and although it lies in a valley
rather than on a hill-top, it does go a
long way towards helping to envisage
the sort of buildings that stood in the
enclosures of the Iron Age hill forts,
from which the trackways running between important points in the countryside could be surveyed. From here it
is only a short walk to the tiny chapel,
which lies on the lane you must now
take towards Cranwich. There are
unfortunately no footpaths on this part
of the route.

769963   Follow the lanes to the River Wissey
where you can join a farm track and a
776952 footpath taking you on to the A134 just
west of Cranwich. You will find the lit-
783948 tle thatched church of Cranwich off a
lane on your left. It is approached by a
field path.

    I could find no puddingstone in the
structure or the churchyard of Cranwich
church, but it does have a round tower
whose base is oddly decorated with a
ring of rather gritty carstones. Perhaps
this is what Dr Rudge was referring to.
This old church, dedicated to St Mary

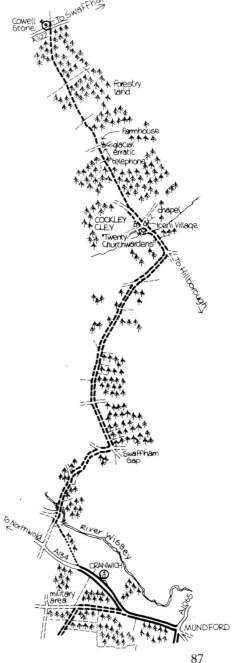

the Virgin, stands on raised ground close by the river, on a site which is generally agreed to be pre-Christian. Its builders must surely have made use of any available materials from an earlier building, and these could have included the gritty carstones. The base of the tower (with this decorative layer) could well have been built about 700 AD.

Anyone interested in general church oddities will appreciate another, more modern, aspect of Cranwich church, having no connection with ley lines and much to do with 'magic' of a more commercial sort. The makers of its Victorian harmonium boastfully marked its pedals as 'mouse-proof'.

817897 The next stone, which again I have been unable to discover, is supposed to be in one of the clay pits of Grime's Graves; if it is to align with the one after

that, on Blood Hill Tumulus, then it 84187 must be at the north-eastern end of the flint workings.

You can reach Grime's Graves, which lie about 3·5 miles (5·6 km) south-east from Cranwich, by taking the main road, A1065, south out of Mundford. You will find the B road leading to Grime's Graves well signposted.

There is another, more interesting, way to reach the flint mines, and although it involves a long detour from Dr Rudge's track, it takes you through the Saxon vil- 7788 lage of Weeting, which lies to the west, which lay on the pilgrims' route from Ely to Walsingham. To reach it, take the lane on your right running to the 78893 south-west from the main Mundford road. Although it now looks as though you are retracing your steps, you must take this lane – any short cut goes through War Department land. You can then take the forest lanes and paths southwards. This entails following, for a time, the eastern edge of the Fossditch, a low but quite distinguishable earthwork dating from about the fourth century AD, until you reach a forestry path on your left. Along the forestry path you are asked to keep your dogs on a lead to preserve wild life. As well as birds and small mammals, the place has an abundance of wild flowers, being particularly rich in scabeous and the brilliant, delicate musk mallow; others such as centaury, golden dock, sand sedge, yellow vetch and Spanish catch fly are survivors of the time when the land was under the sea.

To start with the track is clearly defined. There is a belt of trees known as the Wellington Plantation on your left, and to your right a newly-cleared stretch of land which may be replanted by the time this book is published, but which when I walked this way consisted of high mounds running north to south and completely obscuring the natural contours of the land. This makes it very hard for anyone trying to follow the paths as they are marked on the O.S. maps.

Everything is fairly clear until you round the corner of the Wellington Plantation and come to a place where five forestry roads join. To find the one you need to follow, consult the map closely.

The path you take runs through deep woodlands in which pines are interspersed with deciduous trees, and climbs slowly up the gentle hill to the north-east. When you reach the tumuli, you will see a path going due south to the village of Weeting, known as the Pilgrims' Walk or the Walsingham Way. R. Rainbird Clarke quotes the eighteenth-century topographer Blomefield's description of this path: 'In the fields of Weeting north of the town is a greenway called Walsingham Way, used (as it is said) by pilgrims on their way to the Lady of Walsingham, a madonna of such repute that the Galaxia or Milky Way was called by the people of those parts the Walsingham Way as pointing to that angle; here was formerly a stone cross, now broke into two pieces, commonly called the Stump Crosses.' There is another explanation for the path being known as the Milky Way (see p.77).

I have been unable to find any trace of Stump Crosses, which is reputed to have

Iceni village,
Cockley Cley

stood on the low hill or artificial bank known as Mount Ephraim, which runs across the path. From there the pilgrims must have gone north-east to cross the River Wissey at Ickburgh. The Rev. Leonard Whatmore, who has worked out various routes to Walsingham from all over south-east England, gives this route as running through Pickenham and North Barsham to the north, and south to Newmarket, Babraham, Whit-Whittlesford, Barley and Barkway (see p.119).

As you are coming south into Weeting, you will find an abrupt kink in the path at 144:775898, where it turns towards the east. You could now follow the path straight to the A1065 and then on to Grime's Graves. But it is much more interesting to take the track to the south. This will bring you out by the lane which runs past the present church to the ruins of the castle which William the Conqueror built during the siege of Ely. Although this castle dates from the eleventh century, it stands on raised ground which had probably been put to significant use many centuries before the Normans came. To the south of it are the remains of Weeting's old church of All Saints, which was demolished in the eighteenth century.

777892

Weeting is an important site in the history of East Anglia. In Norwich Castle Museum you can see a knife handle, made from a deer's antler, which was found in this village. The interesting thing about it is that it carries an ogam inscription (in which the letters are indicated by long or short horizontal or

90

diagonal lines cut into the horn) which is unrelated to any known Celtic language, but which shows a similarity to the Pictish inscriptions of North Uist and Orkney. The problem is to decide whether this indicates literate pre-Celtic occupation of the area, or whether it tells us something about the great distances covered by trading routes in prehistoric times.

Today Weeting is a rather ugly, over-grown village, full of suburban villas, but with one strong redeeming feature: a long terrace of farm cottages, facing the village green, which confront you as you come on·to the main road from the church lane. Follow that road past the post office towards Brandon, and turn on to a short stretch of lane which is part of the Harling Drove described later in this section. You will not have gone far along it before you notice a clearly-shaped tumulus on your left, and a path running to the north. That path runs past a patch of woodland known as Shadwell's Plantation, a name which commemorates the Shadwell family, whose main home was at Santon Downham to the east. Follow the track past Brickkiln Farm and on to Bromehill Cottage, where some claim that the dramatist and poet laureate Thomas Shadwell was born around 1640. The alternative birthplace is Santon House to the east.

782882

78588

805892

The track turns sharply to the north, and comes out opposite a pair of tumuli on the lane which leads to Grime's Graves.

Until 1870, these prehistoric flint mines

from Anglo-Saxon times, and shows that those superstitious people held the place in awe, and related it somehow to Woden or Odin. It is generally agreed that this was because Woden, as a hunter of men's souls, became linked with the

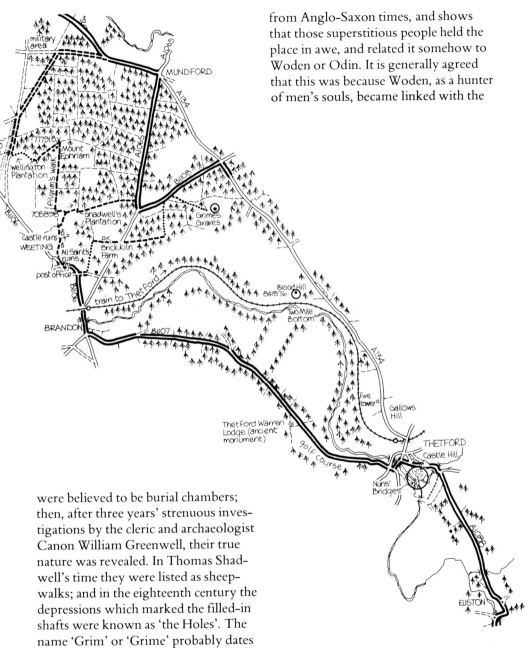

were believed to be burial chambers; then, after three years' strenuous investigations by the cleric and archaeologist Canon William Greenwell, their true nature was revealed. In Thomas Shadwell's time they were listed as sheepwalks; and in the eighteenth century the depressions which marked the filled-in shafts were known as 'the Holes'. The name 'Grim' or 'Grime' probably dates

Tumulus, near Weeting

Christian devil more than any other pagan god. The mines are now in the care of the Department of the Environment.

Very probably it was the Belgic Celts who introduced flint mining into East Anglia; although as similar mining operations have been recorded in Scandinavia, it could be that it was from there that the idea spread across the North Sea. On the other hand, the inspiration for the project could have come from the west, for although Grime's Graves is probably the best known flint mine in Britain, it is one of several; and some people believe that flint mining was a native British development, evolved by the Windmill Hill folk in Wiltshire, whose civilization centred on Avebury and Stonehenge. If that is so, the mining of flint may partly

have been an economic answer to the trade in stone axes from Cumbria.

In East Anglia, the flint mines provided the Neolithic farmer with the flint axes he needed to clear the forest, to make rich arable land by slashing and then burning the trees and undergrowth. What we do not know is how far or to where the Grime's Graves flints were exported, but it is likely that they were taken some way south-west along the Icknield Way. The mine appears to have been at the height of its activity between 2300 BC and 1800 BC, but the exact dates are uncertain, and the discovery of a bronze spearhead on the site suggests that there may have been intermittent activity here until the Bronze Age.

Today an aerial view of the 34-acre (13·7 hectares) site looks like the pockmarked surface of the moon. From the ground, the scrubby heathland is seen to be covered by numerous round hollows. These are the filled–in pits of the mine workings, numbering nearly eight hundred and 346 shafts have been explored. During the excavations, some have been cleared and two are usually accessible to the public.

Apart from a few pits which appear to have been used for open-cast mining, the depths vary from thirty to forty feet (9·1 m to 12·2 m), depending on the lie of the land. To sink a pit, the miners had first to remove the surface land, which is believed to have been done with wooden spades. Then deer antlers were used as picks to cut through the hard chalk until the floorstone, where the best flints lie, was reached. As they removed the chalk

and rubble the miners presumably threw it into a neighbouring worked-out pit.

The worst part of the whole operation must have been digging through the long galleries which link one pit with another. The main galleries are about 6·8 feet (2·1 m) wide and 4·9 feet (1·5 m) high, which allows a reasonable space for movement; but the smaller ones are only 1·9 feet (0·6 m) in width and 2·9 feet (0·9 m) high. In these, the miner would have had to lie prone to extract the flint and then crawl with it to the main pit. In order to see what he was doing he used some form of tallow taper burning in a chalk cup.

We cannot know what sort of men these miners were; not even whether they doubled up as farmers for part of the year or whether they made their

Weeting castle

homes on or near the site. But, because of the complex, technical and dangerous nature of the work, it is very likely that they were a group of élite craftsmen, living rather separately from the main community, and provided with food by the neighbouring hunters and farmers in exchange for flint. R. Rainbird Clarke, who wrote the H.M.S.O. guide to Grime's Graves in 1963, suggested that the discovery on the site of a skeleton of a girl aged about thirteen could indicate that the miners' families visited them there, even if their homes were elsewhere. But it could be unwise to base too much speculation upon such evidence; the girl could have been a single camp follower.

In any case we can only speculate as to how many men were involved at Grime's Graves at any one time. R. Rainbird Clarke surmised that the miners must have descended into the pits by rope ladders fastened to a beam placed

Grimes Graves

across the opening; and that the flint and chalk would then have been hauled to the surface in skin bags or baskets. From this, he calculated that it would take at least three people to work each pit: one quarrying, one carrying the material to the base of the shaft, and one on the surface hauling it up above ground. From the average extent of the pits, he calculated that each one would be used up in a little less than six months of continuous working. If these pits were opened up each year with a labour force of about nine to a dozen men, then the site would be exhausted in about three centuries. This estimate is, of course, based on the assumption that the work went smoothly; and in any case we have to allow for the fact that, although three people might be able to work a pit, it would take many more to do the original digging. Even so there can never have been very great numbers of people working here, and that adds weight to the belief that the Grime's Graves miners were an élite body of men.

They were also religiously inclined, or were as superstitious as miners, sailors and actors still are today, for they practised some sort of fertility rituals to increase the output of the mines. Canon Greenwell found phallic carvings in the mineshaft he excavated, and in 1939 a complete chalk phallus was found in one of the pits. Near to it was the chalk figure of a pregnant woman, standing 4·25 inches (108 mm) high. In front of her was a votive offering of mined flints, a chalk lamp and a pile of seven antler picks.

The next puddingstone is reported to 8487 be at Two Mile Bottom on the banks of the Little Ouse, about 2·5 miles (4 km) to the south-east of Grime's Graves. This area is now completely covered by Thetford Forest, and although the routes through and around it are included in the description of the Harling Drove (see p.109), I could find no sign of a puddingstone.

From Grime's Graves there is nothing for it but to make your way to Thetford, the chief town of the Breckland. You get there either by going north-east to join the A134, or by retracing your steps and going south to Brandon. 8678

For centuries Brandon kept its link with Grime's Graves through the traditional industry of flint-knapping; here gun flints were made in four sizes for muskets, carbines, horse pistols and single-barrelled pistols. And the making of flint-lock weapons continued here until 1948, for Olive Cook in *Breckland* commented on the constant sound of tapping which for centuries echoed through the Brandon streets. The memory of that time is now only kept alive by The Flintknappers Arms.

The other industry of Brandon has vanished completely without trace. It was the curing and preparation of rabbit skins in the manufacture of top hats. It was an industry that flourished during the nineteenth century, before the forests had replaced the warrens as the Breckland's greatest natural reserve.

You can take a train from Brandon to Thetford, or follow the B1107. If you choose the road, look out for the

Ancient Monument sign on your left at the western end of Thetford golf course. This points you to an old fortified building dating from mediaeval times, used by the owners of the warrens at a time when rabbits were considered a great delicacy. The whole area, on both sides of the road, is known as Thetford Warren. It is haunted by a spectre known as the White Rabbit – but it has nothing to do with Alice's genial busybody. This creature rushes by with enormous flaming eyes, portending disaster.

Dr Rudge located two groups of stones on the outskirts of Thetford. The northerly group is on Gallow Hill, where the fire tower now stands; the others he listed as being on either side of the ford across the Little Ouse, south-east of the town. That ford is now covered by the Nuns' Bridges in the park directly south of the castle. You can see one puddingstone on the second bridge, from the north-east bank.

864848

875825

Thetford Castle is a tall chalk mound of mysterious origin lying under a tangle of shrubs and bushes. It is ascribed to Norman times, but the site has produced evidence of much earlier use. R. Rainbird Clarke tells of two Iron Age weaving combs that were found there in the eighteenth century, when they were described as 'tattooing instruments used by the aboriginal inhabitants of this island'. There is no evidence of any stone building, and the Norman fortifications appear to have been dismantled by 1172. But the castle stands at such a strategic point on the Icknield Way that it seems most probable, even from a purely

military point of view, that there was a substantial earthwork here long before the Normans shaped their 81-foot (24·7 m) mound. The tradition which has it that the castle mound was formed by the devil scraping his shoes after he had dug his dyke on Newmarket Heath may reflect a folk memory of the extreme antiquity of the earthwork, although in fact it was probably built before the dyke.

It has one other connection with the devil. A hollow to the north-east of the northern rampart, which contains water, is generally known as Devil's Hole – and it is said that the devil will appear to anyone rash enough to walk around it seven times at midnight. This may link with the belief that when the priory was destroyed six silver bells were taken and buried beneath the hill. The same story is told of Santon, where three silver bells are supposed to be buried. This is significant, for, as T.C.Lethbridge pointed out in *Boats and Boatmen*, the burial of bells was meant to be a way of scaring off malignant forces.

Like many other places that are important in ley alignments, Thetford has a spring with healing properties, which was rediscovered in 1746. It bubbles up near the Paper Mills. Among the people who were cured by its waters when the town was a spa in the late eighteenth and nineteenth centuries was a Mr Matthews of Ixworth, who was relieved of fits, severe headaches and violent dreams. According to Dr Accum's *Guide to the Chalybeath Spring of Thetford* (1819), quoted by Olive Cook, to be efficacious

Castle mound, Thetford

the water had to be taken at the fountain-head between May and September.

From Thetford Castle Mound, Herbert Hudson traced a 40-mile (64 km) Beltane fire line, passing through at least four places named Bel (the Celto-British name for Belus, the Babylonian Sun God). It is a midsummer sunset alignment and goes through Wyverstone to Tuddenham (see p.126), Kesgrave, near Ipswich, and Walton, which are beyond the scope of this book. This alignment, and sunrise alignments parallel to the one running through Wyverstone, are given in the *Journal of Geomancy* (vol. 1, No. 2). Hudson could find no sunrise

lines through the mound itself. From the placing of the Heel Stone to the northeast of Stonehenge, we deduce that the main alignments from the henges were traced towards the point of the sunrise at the summer solstice. Sunset alignments are much rarer.

It does not necessarily follow that alignments based on projections from astronomical observations – whether of the sun, the moon, or the planets – necessarily coincide with the ley lines, on which the henges, mounds or wells are purposefully sited. From Thetford the Puddingstone Track breaks any connection it may have had with the Icknield Way, and starts to head towards the

Saxon village site,
West Stow

south-east. The next stone is reported to
be in the churchyard of Great Livermere,
about 7 miles (11·2 km) south-east of
Thetford Castle. The village can unfortunately only be reached by road. The
best way is to take the A1088 (Ipswich)
road, which goes through Euston. Here
there is a tree, which I have still been
unable to locate, which is reported to
have sprung from the stake with which
the body of the pirate Chunk Harvey
was pierced, when he was executed on
that spot.

It was at Euston that the eighteenth-
century rustic poet Robert Bloomfield
(author of 'The Farmer's Boy') found a
patron in the third Duke of Grafton. The
road then goes through the village of
Little Fakenham, which provided him

885714

8978

with copy for 'The Fakenham Ghost' in
which a benighted old lady mistook an
ass for a spectre, and so to Honington
where he was born. That village now
has an airfield obscuring most of the
countryside which Bloomfield would
have known. It all stands over an area
which in late Neolithic times was inhabited by a group of people, living in
tents, who practised a little husbandry,
but mostly kept themselves alive by
hunting and cut rushes from the Black
Bourn to weave into creels and baskets.

As you take the lane from Honington
towards Troston, you will pass the barrow of Troston Mound at 144:903742,
where some of these people lie buried.

There are two churches in the village of
Great Livermere, both stand on Saxon

foundations. The tower of the ruined one looks in almost better shape than the main church, on the high ground overlooking the lake in Livermere Park. Both churches are of much the same age. The one I have called 'the main church', which has a thatched roof, is kept locked, for the parishioners are making church history by taking the unusual step of refusing to use their church and bear the financial burden of its up-keep. The ruined church is reached by a road leading to Park Farm and stands in private grounds, but it is possible to obtain permission to go into the churchyard. I have not been able to find a puddingstone in the grounds or structure of either building.

The next stone at Thurston lies to the south of the Breckland, and that is the point at which I will continue the story of this route in Section 4. There are however two Breckland journeys to be made from Great Livermere. The simplest one goes east to Ixworth Priory, which you reach by taking a very muddy footpath across ploughed land, which was open heathland until the early nineteenth century.

The second is more complicated, but it is also the more interesting path. It leads

you to the reconstructed Anglo-Saxon village of West Stow. To get there, go through the park and carry on through Ampton, Ingham and Culford to the village of West Stow.

Continue past King's Walk (a twenty-three-mile [36·8 km] stretch of forest roads, which have no particular historical significance), and you will see a terrace of three cottages on your right. Opposite them is a gate leading to a field path. Follow it over the sandy heath until you come to a most scholarly and

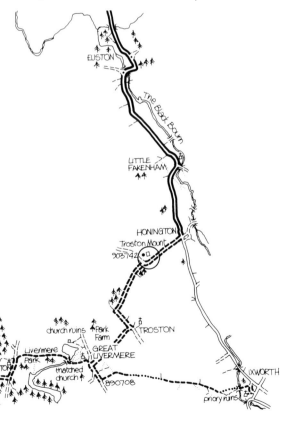

99

authentic reconstruction of one of the Anglo-Saxon settlements that are known to have stood in this area in the sixth and seventh centuries, and which we shall pass again in the next section which deals with the Icknield Way.

You will find a small leaflet in one of the three huts explaining the history of the reconstruction, the process by which the present huts have been built, and the plans for future development of the site, which include some attempts at Saxon arable farming. Already some Saxon crafts are being tried out; when I last visited the village, clay loom weights were hardening in the sun.

Saxon village
(reconstruction)
West Stow

Part B
The Peddars' Way (2)

O.S. maps 132, 144

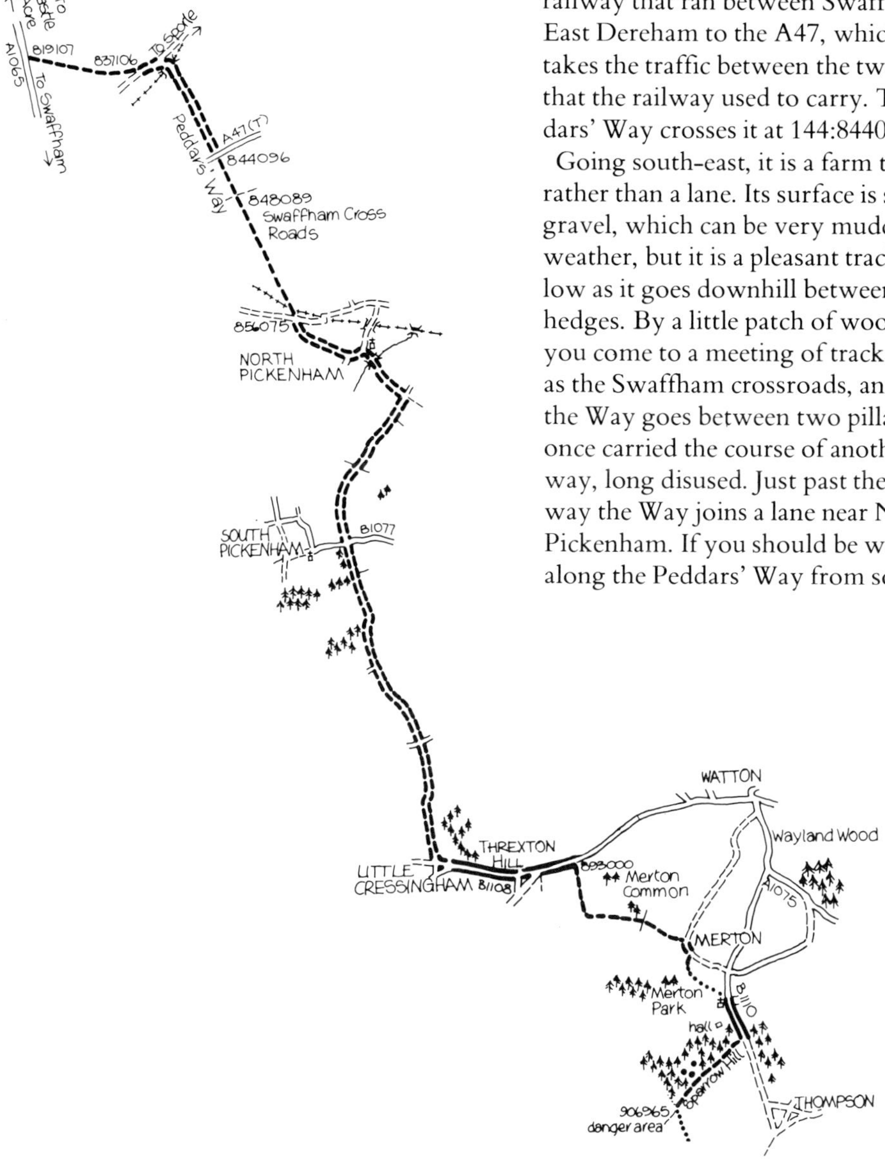

The direct route of the Peddars' Way comes to a temporary end at Castle Acre in north-west Norfolk. You pick it up again at 132:837106, where you follow the lane crossing the course of an old railway that ran between Swaffham and East Dereham to the A47, which now takes the traffic between the two towns that the railway used to carry. The Peddars' Way crosses it at 144:844096.

Going south-east, it is a farm track rather than a lane. Its surface is sandy gravel, which can be very muddy in wet weather, but it is a pleasant track to follow as it goes downhill between wide hedges. By a little patch of woodland you come to a meeting of tracks known as the Swaffham crossroads, and soon the Way goes between two pillars which once carried the course of another railway, long disused. Just past the old railway the Way joins a lane near North Pickenham. If you should be walking along the Peddars' Way from south to

855073

north you will find here no sign indicating the Way. Indeed, it once more seems to peter out at this point.

W.G. Clarke, who believed that the Breckland section of the Peddars' Way dated from Roman times, considered that the 'intervening sector was straight, linking up the Sporle-Swaffham boundary with the Threxton-Merton boundary'. And whether the Way was Roman or, as I believe from the barrows which lie on each side of it (and from the Celtic coins that have been found there), of a much earlier date, that was surely the way it went. All traces have long since disappeared under the plough.

The way to get to Threxton now, where the Peddars' Way re-emerges, is to take the lanes through North Pickenham and Little Cressingham.

East of Threxton crossroads, at 144:893000, you pick up the Way again. But you can only follow it for a short while as it skirts the west side of Merton Common. A little to the south, and probably well within Army territory is the Merton Stone, whose removal according to legend would cause the waters to 'rise and cover the whole earth'. However, there is no great danger, for no one now seems able to find the stone, for although it is reported to be a huge boulder of Necomian sandstone, 12 feet × 5 feet × 5 feet (3·6 m × 1·5 m × 1·5 m), it lies in a marl pit with only its tip showing.

Michael Burgess, in his paper on *The Standing Stones of Norfolk and Suffolk*, presumes that it lies somewhere in the region of 144:895993; and if that is so it could form part of a moat alignment from 144:877030 (at Low Common) to the north, through Mickle Mere and St Chad's Well (144:934832) to the south. While he was looking for the elusive stone, Burgess met a grandchild of the fifth Lord Walsingham, who had a reputation for being an 'enquiring sort of man'. His curiosity led him to get all the villagers together to try and move the stone. They were not successful, but such an orgy followed the attempt that a number of the villagers owed their existence to 'the time of the old stone'. The old Elizabethan hall of Merton was once 'the home of the wicked uncle' in the story of *The Babes in the Wood*, and it was in nearby Wayland (or Wailing) Wood nearby, that he was supposed to have tried to lure the children to their deaths. This is now an oak-ash woodland in the hands of the Norfolk Naturalists' Trust, and can be visited by prior arrangement with the Trust (Norwich 25540).

The full title of the sad story according to the ballad, which is the source for the modern version, is *The Babes in the Wood, or the Norfolk Gentleman's Last Will and Testament*, for the father of the unfortunate children was a Norfolk man, who when he was dying bequeathed his children to his cruel brother. According to W.A.Dutt, who retold the story in *Highways and Byways of East Anglia* (1901), fate punished the uncle severely for his evil deed. 'His barns were fired, his lands made barren, his cattle died, his two sons drowned while on a voyage to Portugal, and in the end he came to beggary and misery, and died in jail. As for the babes, they still wander in Wayland Wood, and on dark and stormy nights you may hear their wailing, which has earned for the wood its local name.'

The track you are now on goes east into the village of Merton, past the round-towered church in Merton Park, to the forest road that goes over Sparrow Hill and joins the Peddars' Way. Now you have entered the land taken over by the Army, and it is a special concession that you are able to walk this part of the ancient track. Army territory lies on either side of you, and it is likely to contain unexploded weapons. For

your own safety, obey any military notices on either side of the Way here. This restraint is sadly frustrating for the Way runs through one of the most historically important areas of all Breckland. To the west of the Way lie meres that were once the lakeland homes of Stone Age men; and barrows and tumuli, some of outstanding age and interest, lie hidden on either side of the track, refuting W.G. Clarke's supposition that no road was here until the Romans came.

Yet he is still the best guide along the Way, for the sheer enjoyment he had in the surrounding countryside, although

Peddars' Way

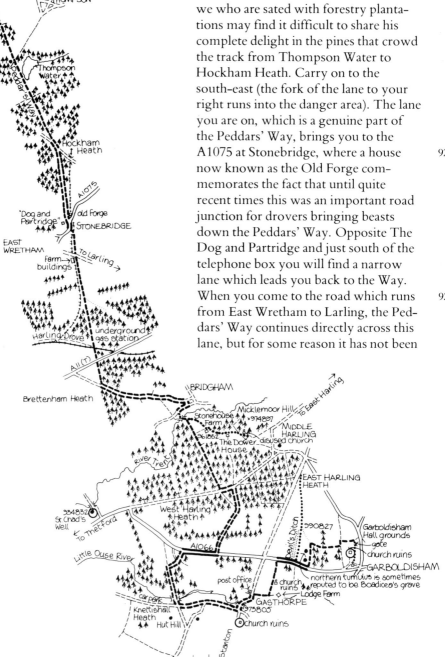

we who are sated with forestry plantations may find it difficult to share his complete delight in the pines that crowd the track from Thompson Water to Hockham Heath. Carry on to the south-east (the fork of the lane to your right runs into the danger area). The lane you are on, which is a genuine part of the Peddars' Way, brings you to the A1075 at Stonebridge, where a house now known as the Old Forge commemorates the fact that until quite recent times this was an important road junction for drovers bringing beasts down the Peddars' Way. Opposite The Dog and Partridge and just south of the telephone box you will find a narrow lane which leads you back to the Way. When you come to the road which runs from East Wretham to Larling, the Peddars' Way continues directly across this lane, but for some reason it has not been

92790

92889

marked here with either the Ancient Monument sign or the footpath blue arrows. But it is quite a clear track with trees and high hedges on both sides and, at first, old Army buildings to the west. Just before you reach the railway line, you will see a track on your right. This is the westerly edge of the Harling Drove, which some claim to be the oldest road in the country.

After you cross the A11 the Peddars' Way is once more clearly marked, running over Brettenham Heath. Throughout the summer the sandy heathland is a mass of wild flowers, the most delicate being the purple stars of basil thyme.

Although the Way continues across the next lane you come to, quite soon it peters out into private land. So you must go towards Bridgham. Do not go right into that village, but take the lane which runs south from the pub, and then follow the forestry road to a bridge over the River Thet. The track that you are now on, running directly to the south-east, is not the Peddars' Way but part of a line of footpaths that I shall describe later in this section.

From here you can go on to East Harling, or continue to trace out the remaining fragments of the Peddars' Way across Knettishall Heath. If you choose

Peddars Way
Knettishall Heath

Knettishall Church,
Garboldisham

the first alternative, take the track to the Dower House, and then on to a disused St Andrew's church, which now stands on the edge of a field and can only be approached through it. The church is locked, but the keys are available from Mr Barker who lives at the farm at Middle Harling. Covered by trees, north-east of the church is Micklemoor Hill, where an Iron Age farmstead once stood on the bank of the River Thet; some of the inhabitants lived in what appears to have been one of the first rectangular houses in East Anglia.

94852

If you are going to continue along the Peddars' Way, go south-east across West Harling Heath to the A1066. You must walk along the main road until you find the lane which takes you down to Knettishall Heath, a patch of heathland managed by Suffolk County Council for public use. You reach it by an arched structure of mellowed bricks which bridges the Little Ouse. Just by the bridge on your right, you will find a notice board showing you how the Peddars' Way runs across the heath. At the southern edge of the common land you come to an abrupt end in a patch of woodland. W.G.Clarke noted that on the survey map of 1837 the route of the Peddars' Way from here lay across the Sapiston to Barningham road, and in that case it would seem to make sense to assume that it would have continued south-east to the Roman villa which stood at Stanton Chare, which was excavated in 1936.

57820

50795

There is nothing much to be seen at that site now, which can only be reached

by lanes, and I think that your best course would be, when you reach the edge of Knettishall Heath, to walk around its perimeter before retracing your steps across the Little Ouse to the A1066. That way you will have made the most of Knettishall Heath by walking over Hut Hill with its attendant tumulus.

If you have decided to go to Garboldisham rather than Thetford, and that village is certainly worth a visit, then turn right when you get to the cross-roads at the eastern edge of the heath. This will take you past the old brick works, and on to a second crossroads. In the south-east corner of the crossroads you will find the ruins of Knettishall church, an important alignment in the track described later .

973802

Continue north-west to the tiny village of Gasthorpe (a post office, a telephone box and three thatched cottages), and head up to the A1066.

Walking towards Garboldisham you will see traces of yet another Devil's Ditch, one of the many defensive earth-works which protected the main routes of East Anglia from successive waves of invaders up to the time of the Danes. This particular ditch is just that, with low, tree-covered banks on either side of it. A public right of way runs through the ditch, but in summer this is so over-grown that you must walk along the headland of the fields on either side. A footpath from 144:990827 is meant to connect the dyke with the woodland to the east of Garboldisham Heath, but when I was there it had been ploughed

988817

107

over. You can insist on your rights and make your way across, doing as little damage as possible, or you can continue along the dyke until you reach the road for East Harling. If you do this, you will still be able to see the great tumuli which stand on Garboldisham Heath, one of which, 'Soldier's Hill', according to A.J. Forrest's *Under Three Crowns* could be the final burial place of Boadicea, the last queen of the Iceni.

If you take the path across the heath you will find a gate on your right, which leads through an avenue of trees to the ruined tower, which is all that remains of Garboldisham All Saints. The present church, which stands by the main road, is reached by another narrow footpath.

near Garboldisham

Thetford and Breckland

Part C.
The Harling Drove

O.S. map 144

Because of its great antiquity it's worth walking part of the Harling Drove, although much of it runs through forestry land, which can sometimes be rather monotonous. Although the eastern part of the Drove has got lost in railway tracks, it is worth visiting its starting point at East Harling, which can almost claim to be the capital of 'alternative' East Anglia. If you want to look further into that, call at the 'Nuts and Raisins' shop by the market square, where you can pick up some relevant literature and have some interesting talks along with the soya beans. Or walk along School Lane to Laurel Cottage, where Gangadar, an Australian Buddhist, makes and sells clay whistles or Ocarina, based on the ritual instruments of Pre-Columbian Central and South America. If your mood is more traditional, you can visit the fifteenth-century church on the outskirts of the village. It still retains much of its original stained glass.

986

The actual walk starts further to the west, where the Drove joins the Peddars' Way. You begin with a long stretch of forest walking, to the small area of East Wretham Nature Reserve. The entrance to the main part of this heathland reserve is approached through a parking space. It is worth while calling at the Warden's house for a copy of the

12883

two-mile (3·2 km) nature trail round the reserve, and for information on the birds and plants you can expect to find there. Over this section of the heath, dogs must be kept on a lead.

There are two spring-fed meres on East Wretham Heath, and apart from the one at Stow Bedon, they are the only Breckland meres to remain outside Army territory. Ring Mere, which lies to the south of the Drove, is believed to be the 'Hringmere' of the sagas, and it shares with Rymer – 3 miles (4·8 km) south of Thetford – the distinction of being the possible site of the great battle on Easter Day, 1010, when the Danes and Saxons died together in their hundreds. In 1978, the mere was a slightly spongy marsh, but it has been known to be absolutely bone dry. Its fluctuations are extreme; Olive Cook reports that, in 1950, it was so high that it overflowed the Drove.

Lang Mere, to the north of the Drove, is now a wired-off nature reserve. You can see its reedy beds just past the small monument that lies to the left of the path commemorating Sydney Herbert Long, who founded the Norfolk Naturalists' Trust in 1926. It all seems gentle enough, but Olive Cook relates that in the past: 'The waters were shunned as the haunt of the Devil. Fish and water fowl bred there unharmed when the waters were high, and when the basins were dry neither sheep nor cow might graze upon the juicy vegetation.' Any farmer foolish enough to drive his cattle out to pasture on the long peninsula that runs into the mere always suffered some disaster. Tradition had it that the evil was caused by the witches of Wretham, and it was in the waters of this mere that any person suspected of witchcraft was ducked. If the waters drowned her like any other mortal, then she died innocent; if she survived the ordeal, she was clearly receiving supernatural help and must die, guilty.

When the Drove enters the forest of Croxton Heath, the path is a wide walk with a belt of deciduous trees, mostly silver birches, to the north. The forest way joins a lane – which passes Fowl Mere. All the northern side of this lane, which is still a part of the Harling Drove, is in Army territory, but it is possible to take a footpath to the south, just to take a look at the pit known as the Devil's Punchbowl; although the tumulus which lies to the south of it is now obscured by the forest. The stories about Fowl Mere are mostly concerned with the great fluctuations in its water level, which it shares with Ring Mere. In an 1887 issue of the magazine *Leisure Hour*, the sad story was told of how a boy from Croxton employed as a bird scarer nearly drowned in the mud here. In 1906, the mere was so dry that it was ploughed and harrowed; swedes and cabbages were grown on its bed. The best story about the mere is again told by Olive Cook, and concerns an airman

883891

877892

110

who, looking down from his plane, saw 'the sorrowful face of the most beautiful woman covering the surface of the mere'. He saw this vision twice, and it so haunted him that he took a friend to walk along the banks of the mere. Of course, there was nothing to be seen on its surface, but just as the two men were leaving they looked up at the sky. There the airman saw the clouds taking the shape of the face he had seen on the mere.

The Drove crosses the A134 and continues through the forest, without interruption, until it meets the by-road leading to Weeting. From there it goes to Hockwold and the fens (see p.203). If you have had enough of forest walking, you could leave the Drove when it meets the A134 and walk to Two Mile Bottom picnic park. From here you can take the forest road going west.

According to a 1695 map of Norfolk, this forest track was once the main road between Thetford and Brandon. Now it follows the course of the railway line towards the headquarters of Thetford Forest at Santon Downham. The railway is mostly well-shielded from view, and there is a pleasant open path to walk on. To the north a tumulus, known as Blood Hill, is hidden in the trees. Various bridle paths run by it, going uphill opposite the steep bank, which stands over the railway at 144:840874. This bank marks the site of the Saxon chapel of St Helen, which stood here at least until 1574. Nearby is St Helen's Well, reputed to have holy powers. In the eighteenth century the name was corrupted to Tenant's Well, and it is now

BRANT

83980

8487

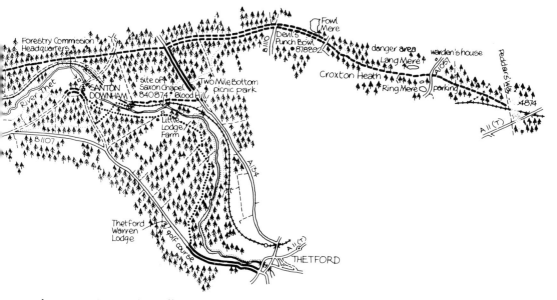

known as Tanner's Well. However, the Forestry Commission have preserved Helen's name for the car park by the river. To reach St Helen's Park (much less formal than the name suggests) you will pass the tiny church of Santon, with its octagonal tower and painted wooden ceiling.

29872

It is worth following the track west to visit Santon Downham, where the Forestry Commission has its Thetford headquarters, to get information about nature trails and the colonies of red squirrels who live in these woods; and to look at Santon Downham church, which has a small priest's doorway, probably of Saxon origin. In the late seventeenth century, the whole doorway was buried in one of the heavy sandstorms to which the Breckland was prone before the trees were planted, which almost blocked the river. From Santon Downham, you

16877

must make your way by road, either going to Brandon or to Thetford.

If you cross the river by the footbridge from St Helen's Park, and go straight along the path which runs across a field, you come to a choice of three ways. You can turn west to go to Santon Downham church, climb the hill ahead of you to the Thetford road, or go east along the bank of the river. If you choose the third alternative you will come out on a forestry road leading to Little Lodge Farm, and will see a tumulus in a small field immediately opposite you. You can head straight for the Thetford road or, if you feel like more forest walking, you can take the bridle path (marked by horse shoes), choosing either to go south to the Thetford road or to go along the river by Thetford golf course. There is no bridge across the river until you reach the town.

825873

837870

Part D:
Thetford and Breckland

O.S. map 144

There is a shadowy path that runs through this area, slightly to the east of the Peddars' Way. I first suspected it when I took the footpath which runs north-west from the ruined church by Roudham Hall, which lies to the west of Harling Road. This church is dedicated to St Andrew, and is on a slight elevation with a marked ditch to the north. Although the building is a complete ruin, the graveyard has been used up to recent times. The latest burial that I noticed there was in 1970. In 1931, there was a village here with a population of 151; now only a few cottages remain inhabited around the church, and even in his day R. Rainbird Clarke could find no one who could recall the sites of the two inns that flourished here in the nineteenth century: The Dolphin and The Three Hoops.

From the church, seven ways used to run out of Roudham; now there are only four left. Two are sizeable lanes. The one we want goes north, and starts off as a narrow metalled lane, which runs past an unattended level crossing over a fairly busy two-track line. After the A11, it

955872

953874

112

becomes a real footpath leading to the village of Illington. Illington church is worth visiting.

Take the lane which directs you to the village, and then turn right to the farm buildings belonging to the Hall. When I went, I had great difficulty in finding the church, and eventually asked some children where it was. They told me to take 'the grass road', and directed me to a rough path running east along the headland of a barley field, to the north of which was a line of old Army huts. After a while the path becomes more tended and leads to the ruined gates of a little flint church. The door is locked and, if you wish to look inside, you must time your visit so that you arrive at 4 p.m. on the third Sunday of the month, when a service is held there. I have not yet managed to do so, but am told that it is well worth the effort.

This church aligns with the church at Thompson to the north, and the alignment then goes to the Norfolk coast, crossing the Nar by the pilgrims' rest house to the south of Litcham, which we discovered in Section 1 to be a meeting place of several lines; through Syderstone church to Brancaster Staithe, a little to the west of the Roman port of Branodunum. To the south it aligns with the ruined church of St Andrew at Roudham, from where we started, another ruined church to the east of Knettishall Heath, and the churches of Hepworth and Walsham le Willows.

From Illington church you must go back to the lane and join the Peddars' Way just south of Stonebridge.

9479

9309

9289

Section 3

Important alignment points

Balsham Church	154:588508
Burwell Castle	154:586660
Ditton Green: Water Tower	154:656583
Fleam Dyke Tumulus	154:548543
Icklingham:	
All Saints Church	155:777725
Marmansgrave	144:840797
Noon's Folly Farm	154:394413
Royston Cross	154:356407
Swales Tumulus	154:708721
Thriplow Church	154:443470
Tuddenham Corner	155:743679
Whittlesford Church	154:474486

Section 3: The Icknield Way

The great dykes

In the summer of 1912, O.G.S. Crawford, for twenty-five years the archaeology officer of the Ordnance Survey, walked the white, dusty roads between King's Lynn and Dunstable, tracing what he believed to be the most likely path of the Icknield Way. He marked the course he took on the Ordnance Survey Sheet of *Britain in the Dark Ages*.

It was a *herepath* (a war path), he claimed, the only route along which great armies of men could be moved, and so interspersed with the sites of great battles. Those we know about took place mainly between the Saxons and the Danes, and before that between the East Anglians and the Mercians. But there were, no doubt, earlier struggles when the Celts bitterly defended their territory against the Romans, and before that when they stood out against the expansions of the people of Essex. It has been suggested that the name of this famous route is derived from Icen-Hilde-Weg, 'the war road of the Iceni'. Certainly the Way dates from pre-Roman times, and it was probably in use for at least four or five millennia before the legions took stretches of it for their own military communications, for it follows the natural line of the chalk across the eastern and southern parts of England, stretching as far as Wiltshire.

Yet despite Crawford's careful plotting, the actual route of the supposed Icknield Way has remained conjectural. The researches into the documents relating to its course, which he undertook in the Bodleian while he was still a student, were used indirectly by Edward Thomas in *The Icknield Way* (1913), the last book that he wrote on the English countryside before he took to poetry. Thomas carefully traced the history of the speculations about the Way. From the seventeenth and eighteenth centuries he quoted Michael Drayton, who in his *Polyalbion* (1616) traced the Way to Yarmouth, 'by the Iceni then being generally possest'. A second source was an essay, supposedly by Roger Gale, in Hearne's *Leyland* (1710) which traces the road from Barley in Hertfordshire through Ickleton (see Section 6) to Burgh Castle near Yarmouth, via the Gog Magog Hills and over Newmarket Heath. He also used William Stukeley's *Itenararium Curiosum*, which takes the road by the Roman camp at Great Chesterford 'towards Ickleworth [present day Ixworth] in Suffolk'.

Among the more recent sources from which Edward Thomas quoted are Dr Mason, rector of Orford in Suffolk, (*Archaeologia* XXIII, 1829) who takes the Way as running on from Ixworth to

Buckenham and from there to Caistor and Burgh Castle; Arthur Taylor (*Archaeological Institute: Memoirs*, 1847) who connects the Way with Norwich Castle Hill, arriving there from New-market, Kentford, Cavenham, Lackford and Thetford; and W.G. Clarke (*Norwich Mercury*, October 8th, 1904) who traced the route east from Norwich Castle Hill by Sprowston, Wroxham and Stalham to Happisburgh. This last was a route which Thomas felt could not be jus-tified, but which, as we have seen, has links with the great alignment running east across the country from Avebury. However, he allowed for a westerly extension of the Way towards Land's End.

Along all these suggested routes we shall find alignments marked by churches on pre-Christian sites, by vari-ous tumuli, and by the rare long barrows originally made in this stoneless land out of turf and timber covered by earth. One such barrow stands to the south-west of Royston on Therfield Heath. Yet there is no single way defined by these way marks, and indeed we will find the name of Icknield Way given to a whole net-work of roads and footpaths. Edward Thomas gave the usual and fairly obvi-ous answer as to why this might be: 'Until the enclosures and the metalling of roads the ruts and hoof-marks of the Icknield Way were probably spread over a width of from a hundred yards to a mile, according to convenience or neces-sity: from century to century its course might vary even more.' This idea of var-ious tracks for various weather condi-

tions has been widely accepted. But lat-terly a new idea is gaining favour. It is that the tracks spread over a far greater width than Thomas envisaged, and that in some areas the parallel west-east tracks could stretch up to 10 miles (16 km) at least from north to south. This theory has the advantage of accounting for the great dykes, which were certainly long enough to protect such a territory.

No one has been able to give a definite date to these dykes, one of which (Devil's Dyke by Newmarket) exists almost in its entirety. They were prob-ably used as defensive earthworks by the Normans, and probably even in later barons' wars; but when they were origi-nally constructed is not yet known. For a long time, scholars took it for granted that the Saxons threw them up against the Danes, and they certainly made use of them; but it seems that the earth-works may well have been constructed to mark the divisions between the late Celtic kingdoms, possibly were even built during Bronze Age times.

The case for such an early construction is strengthened by recent archaeological surveys of Britain carried out by Jim Pickering. He has already plotted the course of a dyke running for 110 miles (176 km) along the Jurassic Way through Lincolnshire and Northamp-tonshire. He calculated that this earth-work once stood 13 feet (3·9 m) high, and was extended across three ditches and two banks to a total width of 55 feet (16·8 m). He dates the dyke around 1400 BC, and believes that it was a tribal boundary. He thinks that there is likely to be a similar system in East Anglia, and if he is right the dykes we shall walk along could simply be the vestiges of a much longer and more elaborate network of earthworks than has previously been thought.

Edward Thomas was uninterested in the dykes. It didn't seem to occur to him to walk along them; he was too engaged in pursuing what he considered to be the main track of the Icknield Way back to his beloved Wiltshire. He was more impressed with a railway cutting than with the earthwork of Devil's Dyke. He tramped past Fleam Dyke on what is now the A11, taking some pleasure in the stretch of cornlands to the north and in the belt of trees on either side of the road, but little in the dyke itself. And such pleasures as he had on the way did not compensate him for 'the paper wrappers of sausages, etc, thrown out by motorists from Cambridge'. He would have found the road much less endurable now; it is partly for that reason that I have walked the extent of both dykes to the west of Newmarket, and partly because such an arrangement makes it possible to cover the whole width of the Icknield Way. Unlike Thomas, I have travelled in an easterly direction, and I have enjoyed it.

For what I have done in this section is to follow the northern and southern edges of the territory through which the tracks of the Way ran, from Royston to Newmarket, and then trace the routes as they converge at Lackford, before spreading out again towards Thetford.

116

Undoubtedly the trading route went on to the Wash, and was probably identical with the Puddingstone Track, which I have followed from the north to the south in the first two sections of this book.

Once more the paths of animals coincide with those of men. For the high ground of the Icknield Way was a drove road for centuries, extending naturally from the busy route of the Berkshire and Oxfordshire Ridgeway. It was used as such almost within living memory. At least, I know an Oxfordshire farmer whose grandfather's shepherd as a lad regularly drove sheep along the high chalk from Warminster to Thetford market. It took three weeks.

Paul Dyke

Part A
Ashwell Street and the ways to Thetford

O.S. maps 144, 154, 155

384411

The maps will show you how the conventional course of the Icknield Way runs along the A505 from Baldock to Royston, and continues east along the main road to Newmarket, leaving it by the farm track to Noon's Folly Farm. That name probably has nothing to do with a sun alignment; Nigel Pennick of the Institute of Geomantic Research believes that the name comes from a corruption of Celtic words indicating an enclosed piece of ground. He has found similar names in Cornwall.

The route from Noon's Folly Farm, and the way along the first dyke that runs across it, is described in Section 6 of this book. So are some of the parallel roads that lie to the south, notably the one that runs between Barley, Great Chishill and Elmdon, which has also been labelled as the Icknield Way.

The route I'm going to describe now runs north of the A505. It is generally known as the Roman road to the north of Royston. You can pick it up where, as a footpath, it crosses the A14 (which covers the Roman road of Ermine Street). The track is known as Ashwell Street, from its starting place in Ashwell, a village to the north-west of Royston. We will be able to find traces of it as far east as Mildenhall in Suffolk.

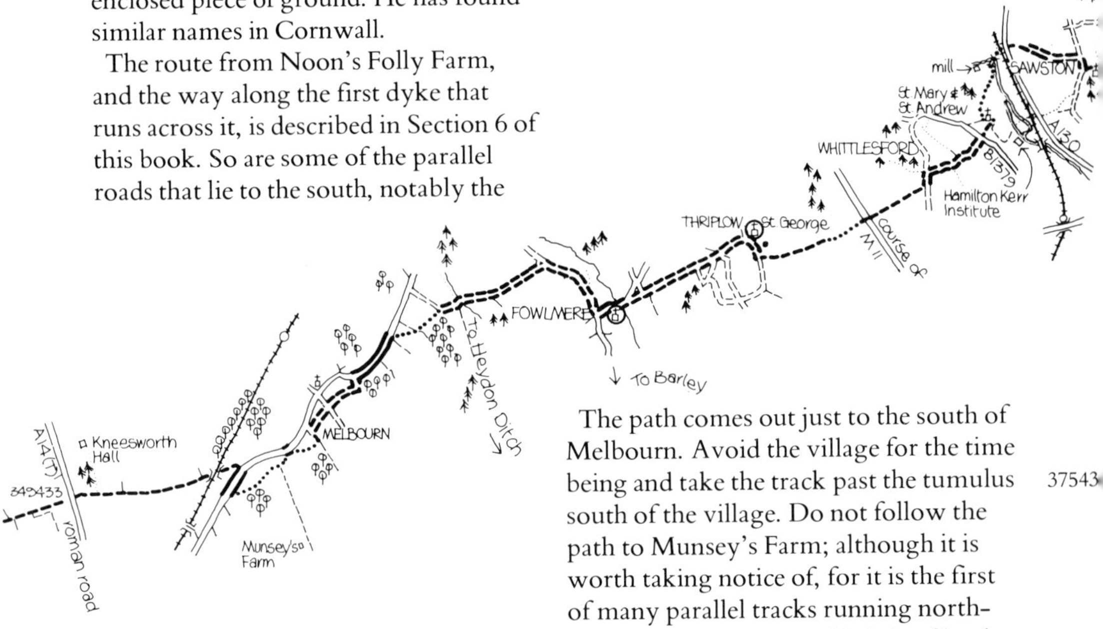

34843

mill
SAWSTON
St Mary &
St Andrew
WHITTLESFORD
Hamilton Kerr
Institute
THRIPLOW St George
Course of
FOWLMERE
To Barley
To Heydon Ditch
MELBOURN
Kneesworth
Hall
A14
349433
roman road
Munsey's
Farm

The path comes out just to the south of Melbourn. Avoid the village for the time being and take the track past the tumulus south of the village. Do not follow the path to Munsey's Farm; although it is worth taking notice of, for it is the first of many parallel tracks running north-west/south-east across this belt of land, which includes several dykes and earth-

37543

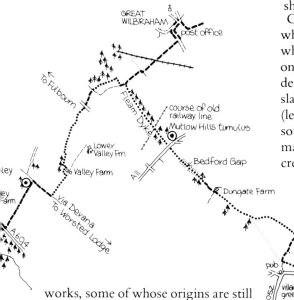

GREAT WILBRAHAM
post office
To Fulbourn
Fleam Dyke
course of old railway line
Mutlow Hills tumulus
Lower Valley Fm
Bedford Gap
Valley Farm
...ley
...ey ...arm
Via Devana
To Worsted Lodge
A604
Dungate Farm
Green Road Farm
BALSHAM playing fields
pub
village green
B1052

shows must once have taken place there.

Continue along the lanes to Thriplow – which has a lot to offer: a village smithy which has been preserved as a museum on the village green; a Norman church dedicated to St George the dragon-slayer; and the remains of a tumulus (levelled in 1800) which stands to the south-east of the church and once marked the site of eleven Bronze Age cremation burials.

444468

works, some of whose origins are still unknown.

You can avoid the A10 through most of Melbourn by taking the parallel side streets but they will eventually bring you to the main road, which you will have to walk along until you join the footpath at 154:393455. This path joins the lane to Fowl Mere. You will pass a farm track going to the south-east. This probably covers the northern part of the first ditch (counting from the west) across the territory of the Icknield Way in East Anglia. It is known as Bran Ditch, or Heydon's Ditch in its southern part, which runs to a village of that name (see p.219). Bran is the Celtic god of death and also the word for crow or raven, and it could be that the earthwork got its name from the birds attracted by the slaughter resulting from the fierce battles which archaeological evidence

403460

Ashwell Street continues along a field road, straight towards Whittlesford church, though its direct course is interrupted by the building of the M11 (the latest earthwork across the Icknield Way). Presumably it will eventually cross the motorway by footbridge, and from that height you will be able to see how this path, which is a little to the south of Ashwell Street, runs parallel to the alignment between the churches of Thriplow and Whittlesford, and even perhaps how that alignment stretches to Fowl Mere in the west and Sawston church in the east.

474486

423459
487493

T.C.Lethbridge, the Cambridge archaeologist and dowser who unearthed the Gog Magog figures at Wandlebury to the south of Cambridge, considered Whittlesford to be a place of great significance in the configurations of the landscape in this area. In his book entitled *Witches*, he pays particular attention to its church, which stands near the River Cam. This building, with its central tower, dates from the eleventh century. Below the clock on the tower there is a curiously carved stone which particularly delighted Lethbridge for it shows the pagan fertility image of a Sheila-na-Gigg. The church is dedicated to St Mary and St Andrew, an unusual combination. Lethbridge links St Andrew with Apollo, and there is the obvious connection between St Mary and the mother goddess. Apollo seems to have had a particular significance for the Iceni, whose coins, modelled on Gallo-Belgic designs, carry that god's head on one side.

You can cross the Cam, which is not very wide at this point, just north of the old mill (now the Hamilton Kerr Institute of the University of Cambridge). It is a neat cycle track, which runs eastwards to meet the A130. From Sawston church a footpath takes you north of Babraham to the A604.

503520

Ashwell Street continues on the other side of that road, a little to the south. Here it starts as a farm track which climbs over the high ground that lies to the south of the old Roman road from Cambridge to Haverhill (described in Section 5 of this book). You will pass a small wooded hill which encloses a

509531

tumulus. It is, unfortunately, on private ground and inaccessible, but its presence is the expected sign of an important crossroads, although Ashwell Street and

120

the old Via Devana do not form an exact cross here, and you have to walk to the south for a little way before you see the path to Valley Farm.

51652

Follow the footpath which runs downhill to join the lane south-east of Fulbourn – a farm track continues the route on the other side. Now on towards Fleam Dyke, the third of the great earthworks across the Icknield Way.

52655

53755

The second dyke, Brent Ditch, cannot be walked along. It runs on either side of the A11 from the moats to the north of Pampisford to Abington Park in the south-east. It crosses that road at 154:516474. It is a large, deep ditch without high banks, and it is now completely filled with trees and scrub. In June 1850, when the A11 was a narrow, dusty road much like the one that Edward Thomas walked along half a century later and generally known as the Icknield Way, Mr S. Tymms read a paper to the Bury and West Suffolk Archaeological Institute, in which he described the first five dykes across the Icknield Way. Of Brent Dyke, he said: 'Towards the middle it has been filled up for the Icknield Way to pass over it, which shows it to be older than the road' – an observation that confirms the theory that the Icknield Ways, which are certainly a good deal older than the earthworks set up to protect them, never consisted of a single track.

To return to Fleam (or Flight) Dyke. At this point on Ashwell Street you have to make the decision as to whether you will carry on with that route, or whether you will now take the opportunity to walk the 5-mile (8 km) length of the dyke, and so join the southern track of the Icknield Way, which is described in Part B of this section.

I shall take that second alternative first. Fleam Dyke, which was once a regular pack-horse route, is quite high at its northern end, and you will be glad of the steps that help you climb up to it. You walk along the top of the high bank for just under 2 miles (3·2 km), the route being broken once for the course of the old railway, which Edward Thomas, who was thoroughly bad-tempered at this stage in his walk, found much more pleasurable than a prehistoric dyke.

Devil's Dyke
Reach

548542

After the A11 the walking becomes much more difficult, for the path goes through the tangled undergrowth. In a sad mood, a contemporary poet, Michael Vince, wrote of the dyke: 'It twists the miles with nettles towering over' ('Enforced Absence' [Fleam Dyke]); and so it does. The trick is not to try and walk this stretch of the dyke in high summer.

There is one gap in the dyke before you come to Dungate Farm, but otherwise the path runs along the top of the earthwork until you reach the end of the belt of trees. From that point, a farm track takes you through to a wide, green road. This is a stretch of the Icknield Way which runs along the high ground to the south of Ashwell Street, and which I will describe later in this section.

From this point, you can follow the track and path indicated by the public footpath sign across the fields to Balsham church. In the church you will find 588508 an Anglo-Saxon coffin lid, which was unearthed in the graveyard, that must date from a very early period in the history of the village. For in Danish times the whole population of Balsham was massacred as punishment for the stand that the Saxons who lived here took against the invader. Only one man is reported to have escaped; he did so by taking refuge in the doorway of the tower of the church, and defending himself so savagely that the Danes left him alone. According to Nigel Pennick, there is a place near Balsham which used to be known as the middle of the world, but I have not been able to find it.

121

To return to Ashwell Street and the north-western end of Fleam Dyke: if instead of walking along the dyke you decide to continue along the original route, you will take the track that runs to the north-east into Great Wilbraham.

553574 Take the farm road after the post office which leads you to a green lane, whose hedges have sadly been lopped. The green lane, for a little while, makes a very pleasant walk indeed, going between high hedges set about three yards (2·7 m) apart. But this pleasant path (known as 'The Street') is soon disrupted by the new road being built to the north-west of Newmarket, which follows Ashwell Street through Exning.

So the walker's best course is to desert Ashwell Street where it is crossed by another track at 154:574587 and head north-west towards Bottisham. Follow the lanes through Swaffham Bulbeck to

Swaffham Prior, which boasts two churches side by side in one Saxon churchyard. These villages, like Reach and Burwell to the north-east, which we shall also visit, stand on the edge of the fens, and each has its 'lode', an artificial water-course running into the River Cam to the north-west. The villages themselves are now mainly dormitories for Cambridge; there is a regular bus service from here to the city.

From Swaffham Prior you can see the most impressive of all the dykes which cross the Icknield Way, looking exactly like a high railway embankment stretching across the flat lands to the south-east. This is one of several East Anglian earthworks known as Devil's Ditch; it is natural to attribute anything whose origin is unknown, or which has been created by another race, to Satan. This dyke extends for some 9·5 miles (15·2 km) from Reach in the north-west to Ditton Green in the south-east. You can join it where the B1102 goes through the dyke. On the south side a Roman house, described in Cyril Fox's *Archaeology of the Cambridge Region* (1923), was excavated in 1893.

I find it more satisfactory to take the lane through to Reach, and to walk the dyke from its furthest corner, if only for the sake of the brilliant sainfoin, a large flame-coloured vetch (which Edward Thomas also noted) that grows in great profusion here. The dyke begins within the village and is quite unmistakeable. You will want to walk along it for a little way, at least as far as the field path to Burwell, where you must decide again whether you want to continue along the area of Ashwell Street, which will mean a lot of road walking, or whether you prefer to follow the course of the dyke and look at the stretch of the Icknield Way which lies to the south and west of Newmarket.

Once again, I will take the second alternative first. Apart from the early stretch from Reach, you will find that the walk along Devil's Dyke is much simpler than that through the tangled undergrowth of Fleam. Indeed, in many parts this dyke is a smooth, treeless, chalk mound. It is crossed by several roads and tracks running parallel to Ashwell Street. The first, which I have already mentioned, is the Swaffham Prior-Burwell road; then there are two parallel farm roads running to the south-west; and then Ashwell Street itself, with the new road running beside it. Once you are across that you will be on the edge of Newmarket race course, and if a race is in progress you have a fine, free, grandstand view. The dyke runs towards the A11, and once across that road it goes to the south of the steeplechase course. I find it a happy coincidence that Newmarket and Newbury (in Berkshire) are now the chief centres for British race horses. For the horse was the totem animal of the Iceni, and it seems that they may well have taken the cult with them as they journeyed east and west along the Icknield Way.

To continue our own journey along Devil's Dyke. This section is still bare of trees and the chalk path is easy and

123

pleasant to follow, until a stile takes you on to the railway line, which you cross at your own discretion. When you rejoin the dyke on the other side you very soon find yourself walking through a thicket, and then scrambling down the edge of the earthwork, which is now cut by a fairly busy B road. Immediately across that road you pick up the dyke again. The path climbs to the top of the earthwork through a dense stretch of woodland, interspersed with sizeable box bushes, which have almost grown into trees. It is from here that you can most easily appreciate the great extent of the ditch to the west side of the dyke, but unfortunately it is impossible to explore

632604

Devil's Dyke

it. The dyke runs through the Stetchworth estate, and only the narrow path on the top is open to the public.

There are several breaks in the dyke along its course to Ditton Green, and this means quite a lot of scrambling up and down. At its southern end you will find yourself in a field. Walk around the headland towards the road, which you reach by a footpath running alongside a cottage garden.

65758

You can now get back to Newmarket by another route. Follow the lane round by the water tower to the farm buildings, and then climb the bank to the south-west of the valley. This path leads to a couple of farm cottages. Beside them you will notice a well, and just past them, in the field on your right, you will see a large boulder. I have not been able to find any reference to this stone, but its presence so close to the well, and indeed to the water tower, is interesting.

6565

From here the path goes through an avenue of lime trees, and then runs along a wide farm track known as Dane Bottom. All the land on either side of this track belongs to the Stetchworth estate, which is very jealous of its rights, so it is important that you should keep to the path, which heads for the B1061, about half a mile (804 m) south-west of Newmarket. Do not be put off by the lack of public footpath notices on this route, or by the warning signs on each side of the path telling you that the land is private. The path itself is a right of way.

63360

If you now want to rejoin the walks along Ashwell Street, walk to the clock tower in Newmarket and take the road to Exning. This village was the birth-place of Etheldreda, queen and saint (see Section 5). It was here that her father Anna, King of East Anglia, had his palace, and from here he conducted his defensive campaigns against the maraud-ing armies from Mercia, led by King Penda. Etheldreda was baptized in St Mildred's Well, a spring which was once an important object of pilgrimage and which still bubbles in a piece of land belonging to the Jockey Club.

Etheldreda's baptism was performed by Felix the Burgundian, Bishop of Dunwich. In her early youth she made a vow of perpetual virginity, which was accepted by her first husband, Tonbert, an East Anglian chieftain, and initially by her second, Egfrid, whom she mar-ried five years after Tonbert's death. But in 670, when he inherited his father's throne of Northumbria, presumably desiring an heir of his own he tried to persuade his wife to break her vow. Stormy disputes culminating in divorce occurred when she would not agree to do so. Nor was that the end of the mat-ter, for although Etheldreda entered a nunnery, Egfrid soon regretted his deci-sion and tried, with the help of a band of soldiers, to force his wife to come back to him. Etheldreda fled south until she came to the island in the fens which we call Ely, where she set about building a retreat house for both men and women recluses. She lived there as abbess for six years, and then fell victim to the plague. It killed her in three days. Sixteen years later her body was exhumed and found to be still free from corruption.

From Exning, the natural continuation of Ashwell Street goes north-east through Snailwell to Chippenham, but before you take that road it makes sense to visit Burwell Castle. This is the point 586660 at which you will arrive if you decided earlier that you did not want to walk along the Devil's Ditch, but preferred to leave it just before coming to the old railway cutting to the south-east of Reach. The footpath that leaves the dyke goes straight along the old field division, and leads on to a lane. You can choose 582661 between following the public footpath sign across a field to Burwell and mak-ing a slight detour to visit the earth-works of the castle. The land to the south of the castle earthworks can be very swampy. If you take the first path, you will find that once you have crossed the little bridge over the stream that originally fed the moat your best course will be to walk round the outer wall of the castle, going anti-clockwise. Some-where near here, Geoffrey de Man-deville, an outlaw taking refuge in the fens during the nineteen years' war bet-ween Stephen and Matilda, was shot by an arrow. From the north of the castle you will find a lane that takes you to Burwell church. It is dedicated to St Mary and has a St Christopher wall painting. A disused St Andrew's church is to the north-east of the village.

From Burwell you have to go by road to Snailwell, where you can take the path south-east past the new road build-ing and by a belt of trees to the A11. 659652 These trees, according to an article by John Harris in the 1969 autumn issue of

125

Devil's Dyke
near Swaffham

Drive, are haunted by one of the ghostly black dogs which are a particular psychic phenomenon of East Anglia, and which are generally met with in north-east Norfolk and along the Suffolk coast.

The lane that goes on from Snailwell to Chippenham closely follows the course of Ashwell Street, but leaves it to go round the edge of the park. When the lane crosses the B road, you will find a terrace of startlingly elegant cottages, once tied for workers on the estate of Chippenham Hall. A barrow to the north of the village, at 154:659711, contained a bronze dagger of Wessex craftsmanship, one of the few instances of this culture (about 1600-1400 BC) to be found in East Anglia; they are nearly all clustered round the Icknield Way. Follow the lane past Badlingham Manor

and on to Rectory Farm. This last stretch of the lane marks the end of the present public way along Ashwell Street, though the route continues along the farm track to Worlington.

6837

This is the point at which we must now turn towards the remaining paths that run through the central section of the Icknield Way, for the scattered tracks running east across Cambridgeshire gradually converge to cross the River Lark. The best way is to go through Herringswell to Tuddenham. Head for the A11 from Rectory Farm. On that road lies Swales Tumulus, one of the four long barrows of East Anglia. According to Helen Clarke in *East Anglia: Regional Archaeologies*: 'Swales Tumulus consists of a small Neolithic mound covered by a later Bronze Age

7087

barrow. A body appears to have been cremated on a funeral pyre and subsequently covered by a simple earth mound.' She believes that this site dates, as do other long barrows, from the early Neolithic period.

Continue the route along the lanes to the south of the A11, take the lane towards Kentford, and then follow the forestry path which comes out just to the west of Herringswell. Make for Hall Farm and then follow the (unmarked) public footpath to Tuddenham (a stile by the entrance to the farm road would seem to confirm a right of way). At the top of the hill the way divides and you have a choice of walks. If you turn left, you go through a gate into a narrow field bounded by a river. At the other end of it is an old brick bridge across the river. Follow the lane round and you will find that you come out on to the road opposite the telephone box in Tuddenham village.

From here you can take the lane going north to Tuddenham Heath and the nature reserve, but this has no immediate connection with the Icknield Way. The way to the crossing of the Lark at Lackford lies to the south and now it is the lane between Cavenham and Lackford that is known as the Icknield Way, which you can join at Tuddenham Corner. Tuddenham church is dedicated to St Mary the Virgin, and dates in part from the thirteenth century, although it has suffered heavy Victorian restoration.

If you did not go into Tuddenham village, you can take the field path via Charity Farm to Tuddenham Corner.

Head north-east through Cavenham. When Edward Thomas passed that way, he noticed that beside the modern bridge over a tributary of the River Lark, which runs to the east of this village, there was 'an old single arch about seven feet broad of narrow bricks, still firm but all grass-grown over its high-curved crown which passengers used to mount like a barrel'. You will pass the faint remains of dykes known as 'The Black Ditches' – generally believed to be the remains of a Roman sewage system. These run for just under 2 miles (3·2 km) to the south, first on the east and then on the west side of the stream. To the north, some more fragments of the ditches can be traced over Cavenham Heath.

The lane that is known as the Icknield Way joins the A1011 at Lackford. Turn left here and go across an ordinary road bridge towards Icklingham. The way that is generally known as the Icknield Way runs through the forest by a strip of firs known as the Icklingham Belt, which well pre-dates the present forestry plantation. If you make your way along it, it will bring you out south of Elveden. Olive Cook reports that the southern part of this stretch of the Way, which lies near the river, is supposed to be haunted by a headless rider. This could be the Archbishop of Sudbury, who was beheaded and left lying in the Lark by the followers of Wat Tyler.

Before going on towards Elveden and Thetford, it is worth investigating some of the other possible routes and taking a look at the ancient village of Icklingham itself. A Roman house was discovered

127

here in 1877, and it is a place where there is plenty of evidence of much earlier occupation. In particular you will want to see the disused, thatched Saxon church of All Saints. Beside it a footpath runs north-east and parallel to the Icklingham Belt. This was a pilgrims' path to Walsingham. Do not be put off by the fact that it runs through a very muddy patch, virtually a deep slurry pit, just after it passes the church. With a bit of a struggle you can negotiate that by climbing along the fence, but don't try to do it if you have young children or dogs with you. The subsequent walk is well worth the effort.

The path goes across Telegraph Plantation, so called because it marks the site of the Admiralty signalling station in use at the time of the Napoleonic Wars.

790746

The route passes a tumulus, goes over Berner's Heath, and then you can head

818767

east to join the Icknield Way just before it reaches the B road.

Another way to reach Elveden is to take the lane that goes east to West Stow from Icklingham. It goes past the gate leading to the West Stow reconstruction of the Anglo-Saxon village, mentioned on p.99. As I noted earlier, the banks of the Lark were heavily populated in Saxon times; Edward Thomas, who came this way before the extensive excavations, remarked that this was a place where Anglo-Saxon coins and weapons were found.

Continuing east from there, you will find the Forestry Commission's 23-mile (36·8 km) King's Walk on your left; but there is a more interesting route to the

128

north-east, although you have to be prepared for a long stretch along the main road into Thetford at the end of it. If you can face that, or can arrange to have a car parked at the other end, then go further on to the east, and take the wide path

8377

running along the eastern edge of the King's Forest. This path passes two tumuli. The first is known as the Hill of

8377

Health, presumably a corruption of Helith, the Celtic sun god. The second, hidden in the forestry plantation to the west of the path, is called Traveller's

8427

Hill. Near the second tumulus you can make a choice: you can either turn towards the main road or go through the forest to its northern edge and follow a path over Culford Heath to a point a few yards further to the north on the A134 to

8647

Thetford.

There is no doubt that the river crossing in Thetford marks a focal point of the Icknield Way. This town and the paths and roads that lie between it and Grime's Graves are described in Section 2, pp.90-95.

If you have already visited Thetford on that route, you may now like to take an alternative route to the north-west, walking over Thetford Heath from Barnham. A tumulus lies to the south of the road. The western end of Thetford Heath is flanked by Marmansgrave Wood, an old plantation, which joins the

8407

New Barnham Slip; the tracks going through the belts of woodland go south-west, and join the Icknield Way across the B1106. According to Olive Cook, Marman, whose grave lies where the track crosses the lane, was either a

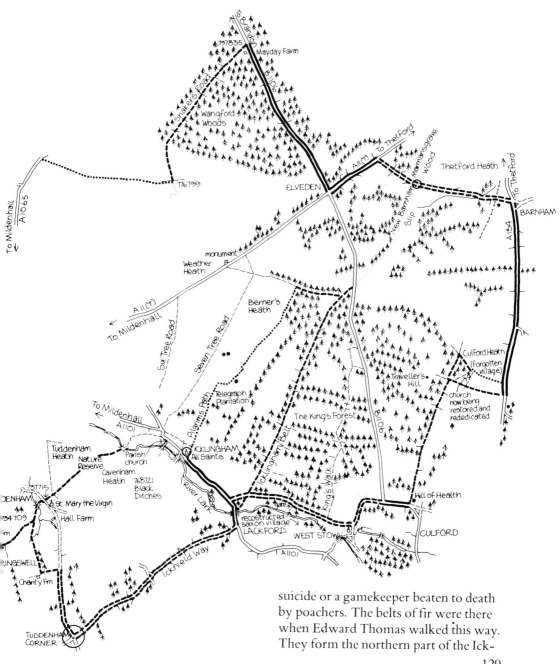

To Brandon

797835

Mayday Farm

Shaker's Road

Wangford Woods

To Mildenhall A1065

716799

Wangford Drove

A11(T)

To Thetford

ELVEDEN

New Barnham Slip

Warmans grove Wood

Thetford Heath ↑

To Thetford

BARNHAM

A134

monument

Weather Heath

Berner's Heath

A11(T)

To Mildenhall

Six Tree Road

Seven Tree Road

Culford Heath (forgotten village)

Traveller's Hill

church now being restored and rededicated

Telegraph Plantation

Pilgrims Path

The King's Forest

B1106

To Mildenhall

A1101

Tuddenham Heath

Nature Reserve

Parish church

ICKLINGHAM All Saints

Icklingham Belt

King's Walk

Cavenham Heath

768721 Black Ditches

River Lark

Hill of Health

Hall Farm

737715

DENHAM

St Mary the Virgin

734709

reconstructed saxon village

LACKFORD

WEST STOW

CULFORD

RINGSWELL

Charity Fm

Icknield Way

A1101

TUDDENHAM CORNER

suicide or a gamekeeper beaten to death by poachers. The belts of fir were there when Edward Thomas walked this way. They form the northern part of the Ick-

129

lingham Belt. Continue through Elveden and head towards Brandon.

795835 About half-way between the two you will find a forestry road, beside the entrance to Mayday Farm. If you have already been to Brandon, Weeting and Grime's Graves when you were following the Puddingstone Track, you might like to turn south-west here. This very ordinary forest path is known as Shakers' Road and Olive Cook believed it to be one of the ancient tracks of the Breckland. The name of the track indicates that it was once a 'sheep run'. 'Shakland' is a term (as far as I know peculiar to East Anglia) denoting the pasture where sheep graze. The other ancient tracks that she lists all run from the neighbourhood of Icklingham. They are the Pilgrims' Path, which we have already looked at, and Seven Tree Road and Six Tree Bend which go north from the west of the village, unfortunately through private lands. The latter is the southern continuation of the Shakers' Road through Wangford Woods.

774798 The Shakers' Road from Mayday Farm is crossed by a broad track. If you continue to the south, you will come out on 774768 the A11, to the west of the high way memorial which dominates Weather Heath, which was set up to the memory of the men of the Elveden estate who died in World War I.

The path to the west at 144:776799 goes across heathland, and comes out on the 737806 road to the south of Lakenfield airfield. Turn left along the main road towards 7174 Mildenhall, which lies some 3 miles (4·8 km) to the south. Just by that little town, the road covers what was once known as Hurst Fen, where grain storage pits belonging to the middle Neolithic period have been excavated. Two other important artefacts have been found here which give us some insight into the daily lives of the people who settled at the point where the territory of the Icknield Way was crossed by the River Lark.

There is a polished greenstone axe from the Lake District, a treasured possession and even more effective than the local flints for clearing the forest. Its presence indicates that even at that early date there was some traffic across Britain. The other objects, of more local interest, are the decorated pots made of clay inter-mixed with flint and sand. Pottery of this distinctive type was obviously carried along the Icknield Way, for it has been found in the Chilterns, together with other pots known to belong to the western edge of the chalk ridge.

Today, Mildenhall is a pleasant little town, with an excellent private museum run by members of the local history society, which is open most afternoons. From Mildenhall it is possible to follow some of the walks in the fens, which you will find in Section 5, or to continue south to Barton Mills (see p.132).

As for the Icknield Way, there are many theories as to how it could have run north from Grime's Graves to the Wash; but, as I noted in the introduction to this section, most of the suggested ways coincide, at least in part, with the Puddingstone Track, which I have traced in the two previous sections.

Part B
The southern way to Herringswell

O.S. map 154

The paths and lanes that make up the southern part of the Icknield Way are much less coherent than the westerly part of Ashwell Street. For our area I take the southern route as being partly covered by the Roman road of Beard's Lane to the west of Saffron Walden. This is described in Section 6, p.216.

However, due to the building of the M11, it is now almost impossible to walk far to the north-east of Beard's Lane, so it would be better to start this route across the Granta at Great Chesterford, where the Romans set up a temporary fortress at the borders of the Iceni territory. From there, take the farm track towards Dell's Farm and past 525463 Abington Park Farm to Linton. This track is obviously part of a much longer way, probably a continuation of Beard's Lane, and certainly once linked to the green lane to the north of Balsham.

To continue north-east from Linton, you must abandon the natural continuation of the path across the A604 and head into the village. Take the path north of the hospital and climb Rivey Hill to the 568479 water tower. Here you will meet a substantial track, which takes you downhill to the B road between Balsham and Linton. Take the footpath that runs to the 576491 east of it as far as the Via Devana (see Section 5, p.185).

Follow the footpaths, passing briefly along a farm road, to Balsham village.

From the playing field behind the church there is a stile leading to the path described on p.120, which outlined the walk to the south-west from Fleam Dyke.

On this walk, when you come out on the wide lane, do not cross over towards 579512 the dyke, but continue to Green Road Farm – a very pleasant, slightly hilly 595531 walk. This path continues across the lane, but after it reaches a second lane at 598538, it peters out into private land.

Between this point and Herringswell (see p.127), only a very few short scraps of the Way remain along footpaths. Your choice is between taking a zig-zag road walk between the villages to the south of Newmarket, or going to the north and picking up the route along Ashwell Street. If you do the first, you will turn right to Weston Colville from where you start the journey to the north-west, going through Dullingham, Woodditton, Cheveley, Moulton and Kentford to Herringswell. But it is probably more satisfactory to take the lane on your left before you get to the village of Weston Colville, and head for Little Wilbraham – crossing the A11. At the point where the overhead cables cross the lane, you will find that the 562580 green road of Ashwell Street does too. So you can turn right here and pick up the brief walk described on p.122.

On the other hand, if you could arrange

131

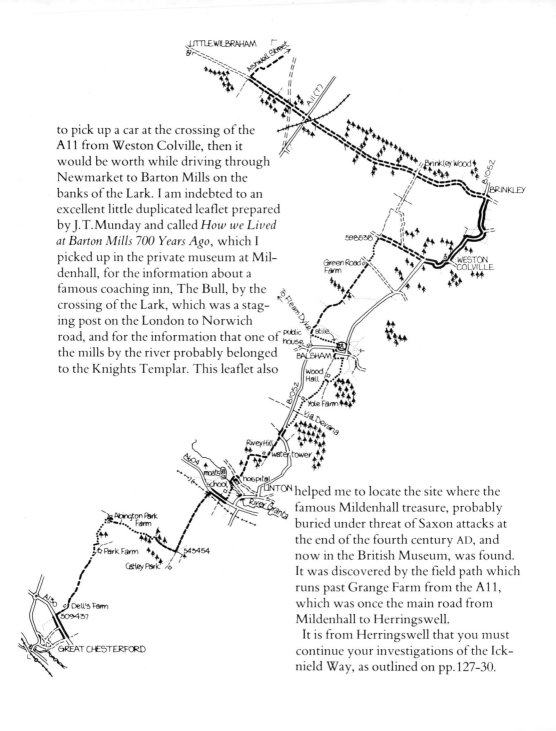

to pick up a car at the crossing of the A11 from Weston Colville, then it would be worth while driving through Newmarket to Barton Mills on the banks of the Lark. I am indebted to an excellent little duplicated leaflet prepared by J. T. Munday and called *How we Lived at Barton Mills 700 Years Ago*, which I picked up in the private museum at Mildenhall, for the information about a famous coaching inn, The Bull, by the crossing of the Lark, which was a staging post on the London to Norwich road, and for the information that one of the mills by the river probably belonged to the Knights Templar. This leaflet also helped me to locate the site where the famous Mildenhall treasure, probably buried under threat of Saxon attacks at the end of the fourth century AD, and now in the British Museum, was found. It was discovered by the field path which runs past Grange Farm from the A11, which was once the main road from Mildenhall to Herringswell.

It is from Herringswell that you must continue your investigations of the Icknield Way, as outlined on pp. 127-30.

Section 4

Important alignment points

Blythburgh Priory	156:450756
Blythburgh, Toby's Walks	156:440743
Bradfield Combust	155:893575
Bradfield St George	155:917600
Bungay, St Mary's Church	156:336897
Creeting St Mary	155:094567
Crowland Moat	155:009702
Dunwich	156:475706
Garboldisham (old church)	144:008819
Glemsford Church	155:835484
Haughley Castle	155:024626
Hesset Church	155:936618
Ilketshall St Andrew	156:379872
Kersey Church	155:002439
Kersey Priory	155:997446
Kettlebaston Church	155:966503
St Chad's Well	144:934832
Sizewell Power Station	156:462632
Thurston Church	155:929652
Walsham le Willows	155:999711
Westhall Church	156:423803
Weybread Church	156:241801
Woolpit Church	155:974625

Section 4: Suffolk

Witches, moats and ghosts

O.S. maps 144, 155, 156

One of the nastiest men in the records of English history is Matthew Hopkins, a seventeenth-century Essex busybody, commissioned by Parliament to tour the eastern counties putting down witches. He did this to such effect that, within sixteen years, he brought several hundred men and women to trial for witchcraft, and in Suffolk alone hung over sixty of them. For these services he was paid twenty shillings for every town he visited; but when he came to Stowmarket, in the very heart of Suffolk, he was rewarded with £28 for ridding the town of the ungodly – or more properly of the eccentric and nonconforming. It is a sad reflection on the age that Hopkins' activities must have been sponsored by Milton's tutor, Thomas Young, who was then the vicar of the town.

Yet we cannot be smug. The tales of Hopkins' investigations read too much like the accounts of modern political witch hunts, in which the victims of interrogations are kept awake for days on end. In the seventeenth century, people accused of consorting with the devil were not allowed to sleep during the time of their interrogations, and these could last for several days on end. So the wretched prisoners were kept walking up and down because, as Hopkins explained, 'if they be suffered to couch, immediately came their familiars into
134

the room, and scareth the watchers, and hearteneth on the witch.' When the poor creatures were proved guilty and executed, anyone brave enough to have remained their friend was refused the right to give them a Christian burial and, like any other felon, the witches were interred at crossroads or along the highways. That, as we shall discover, is one of the links between witchcraft and ley lines.

Perhaps it is partly because of Hopkins' activities that so many stories of witches still abound in Suffolk; people tend to find what they look for. But there is another reason, linked with the Horsemen's Society that flourished in East Anglia, and particularly in Suffolk, until the turn of the century.

This secret society was always much more than a trade guild for carters and men in charge of farm horses, although it was that too; for in the old days its members were thought to have access to the white magic of the witches.

The distinctive, chestnut Suffolk Punch is a remarkable animal, squat, sturdy and practical; not being as heavy as the Shire, he is more suitable for working the heavy clays of the central area of the county. To think of this beast in any magical context, or to link him with the Iceni's Epona, may seem ludicrous, but it is the only explanation for the way the rituals of the Horsemen's Society of East Anglia (which has its only parallel in Britain in the similar Horsemen's Society of north-east Scotland) should have continued into the twentieth century. They are open secrets now, for with agricultural mechanization they are no longer pertinent; the folklorist and social historian George Ewart Evans has done no one an injury by revealing them in *The Pattern Under the Plough*.

The guiding principle of horse magic is simple. It depends on the fact that horses have a far keener sense of smell than most people appreciate; and that men can be shown how to exploit this so as to give themselves complete control over the animals without any resort to cruelty or force. It is less easy to account in plain, straightforward, practical terms for the energy that was needed, and the expedients that were resorted to, in order to preserve this secret through the centuries. That power could only come from the force of the old religion, and as such, like all relics of pagan times, it was associated with witchcraft.

Everything connected with the rites of the Horsemen's Society, from the fetishes used to control the horses to the initiation ceremonies which new members had to undergo, has direct links with pre-Christian ritual. George Ewart Evans is fairly certain that the horsemen were often identified with witches, and that this forced them into even greater secrecy. So, for centuries, talk of witchcraft has been in the air in Suffolk; and both men and women may be accused of it. Stories of witches, now almost completely divorced from any human context, abound and are often tied up with significant points along the ley alignments.

In this flat land, the alignments often run through moats; for where there are no natural rocks for way marks, as Alfred Watkins proved, water must be used in its place. In *The View Over Atlantis*, John Michell has worked out the alignments in the much-moated area around Ixworth, between Bury St Edmunds and Stowmarket. These moats, which often seem to be no more than scrappy, muddy, duck ponds, are often found near an earthwork or castle mound; presumably they once provided both a measure of defence and a source of water. But there seems to be much more to the connection than that.

Many of the moats are very deep, and legend often makes them even deeper. The one at Haughley Castle, just outside Stowmarket, is reported to be so deep that in the last century a miller's horse and cart were both swallowed up by it. This is one of many similar stories I have come across throughout England, telling of horses being drowned in moats and ponds. I cannot help connecting them with the ducking of witches.

At Haughley the Norman castle was built on an existing artificial mound, which has now become completely overgrown. So flat is the surrounding countryside that, I am told, if you climb one of the trees growing on top of the mound, you can see Ely Cathedral 30 miles (48 km) to the north. Like most castle mounds in this area, it is reputed

135

to be connected by underground passages to other castles, earthworks and halls. This tradition is probably occasioned by the forgotten knowledge of the underground streams associated with the ley lines running between the moats.

Some of these alignments are still public rights of way, but many of them have been enclosed and ploughed over, and only a few are actually indicated by public footpath signs. Yet, although it is only rarely possible to follow the alignments from moat to moat, there are several old green lanes traceable between them; and often where these lanes cross

136

there are reported to be graves of gypsies, suicides and felons, buried with a stake through their hearts to anchor the evil, in a way which is reminiscent of dragon killing.

We shall also find many ghost stories along the Suffolk alignments. One of the most curious was reported in the area of Bradfield St George, to the south-east of Bury St Edmunds. The ghosts were not of people but of two houses, seen on at least three recorded occasions, the last being in June 1926. The story of the appearance was retold in the *Bury Free Press* in September 1978. The 1926 manifestation came to the daughter of the

Ely Cathedral

rounded by a most beautiful garden. It was seen in 1860 by Robert Palfrey, while hay-making on the other side of the road. The second sighting of that same house took place one June around the turn of the century, and was related by a man who, in his youth, spent his Saturdays accompanying a local butcher on his rounds. The appearance of the house was heralded by a sudden dramatic drop in temperature, which caused the butcher's horse to bolt and the butcher to be thrown from the cart. When the horse could at last be checked, the narrator of the story returned to the site to pick up the frightened butcher. He reckoned that was about ten minutes after the start of the incident, and recorded that he was just in time to see the house disappearing in a shimmering mist.

It is difficult to make an exact location of these two houses, for researchers have found no buildings of any sort recorded on old maps or mentioned in documents. But if we join them on an alignment that runs through the church, from whose tower I am told that it is possible to see sixteen other churches, the line runs south-west through Bradfield Combust, where it crosses the Roman road covered by the A134, to the church at Glemsford. Bradfield Combust, as its name suggests, must be associated with the inexplicable fires that from time to time are reported to break out along ley alignments. It is also the birthplace of the eighteenth-century Arthur Young, who became the first secretary of the newly formed Board of Agriculture, and

newly-appointed rector of nearby Rougham Green and her walking companion. They saw the wall and gates of a great mansion, just where the lane from Little Welnetham turns sharply to the right by the church of Bradfield St George. Being strangers to the neighbourhood, they were simply impressed by the grandeur of the building; it caused them no undue surprise until they found that nobody had ever heard of it. So later they returned to the place to look for it again. It was not there.

The second house was seen to the north of the first. It was a much more homely Georgian red-brick dwelling, sur-

whose reports on the conditions of farming throughout the British Isles speeded up agricultural reforms in his own time and form the basis of our present-day records of agricultural history. In looking for the supernatural along ley alignments, it is important not to forget the human side. I have not done the research but it would seem to me likely that sources of energy would infuse the people who were born at important points along the lines.

Glemsford, a wealthy wool town in mediaeval times, is linked to the other dragon-killing power, St Michael. A fifteenth-century wood carving of the angel with the flaming sword stands as a pub sign for The Angel Inn. In the Bury St Edmunds' zodiac, which we shall be looking at in this section, it stands on the neck of Leo.

To the north-east, the alignments from Bradfield St George run to the church and moat of Stowlangtoft, on the site of an old encampment.

The next ghost story takes us to the east of the county, and on to one of the alignments radiating from the drowned cathedral city of Dunwich, going through the priory lands of Blythburgh. The story is a sad one, its central character being an early victim of racial hatred. On Friday, September 14th, 1750, Tobias Gill, a negro drummer attached to a regiment of dragoons at Blythburgh, was executed by being hung in chains on Blythburgh Heath, for the supposed rape and murder of Anne Blakemore of Walberswick, whose body was subsequently found to be uninjured. Up to the

138

moment of his execution, Gill protested his innocence; and even as he stood beneath the gallows he made one more frantic bid for his life. Seeing the London mail coach approaching, he asked if a halter could be put round his neck and the other end of the rope attached to the coach, so that he might try to run with the horses for his life. His request was refused, and now he is said to haunt the area, driving a black hearse pulled by black horses.

Although I have not been able to find any records of sightings in recent years, Tobias Gill is remembered in the naming of Tóby's Walks, the lanes to the south-west of Blythburgh Priory, which run along the alignment between Westhall Church to the north-west and Sizewell Power Station to the southeast. Both places, for quite different reasons, are important to our story. Excavations at Westhall have unearthed remains of an Iron Age chariot, and a first century AD disc brooch inscribed with a pony; while Sizewell was noted as a portentous place long before the discovery of atomic power.

In this section, I have worked across Suffolk from west to east, starting with the recently discovered zodiac to the south-west of Bury St Edmunds. In the centre of the county I have traced some of the walks connected with the alignments between the moats; and I have followed Dr Rudge's Puddingstone Track as far south as the village of Kersey. Finally, I have gone east to the coast, and then turned westwards again along the Waveney Valley.

Part A
The Bury St Edmunds Zodiac

O.S. map 155

Before you trace the walks round the Bury St Edmunds zodiac, discovered by Michael Burgess in February 1976, and fully described by him in a paper put out by the East Suffolk and Norfolk Anti-quarians in 1979, you might like to look at the discussion on terrestrial zodiacs in the general introduction to this book; and to compare the Suffolk effigies with the corresponding figures in the oval Nuthampstead zodiac, described in Sec-tion 6.

The zodiac to the south-west of Bury St Edmunds is considerably more com-plex than the Hertfordshire one. The Suffolk symbols are drawn on two intersecting circles, centred on Hawk's Leys, an L-shaped patch of woodland (which was once triangular) with Hawk's Farm (now used most discreetly as a garage for Cuttings' coaches) at its northern end. Unlike Cross Leys (the central point of the Nuthampstead zodiac), which lies on private ground, Hawk's Leys can fortunately be approached by footpaths, while the coach company uses the unmade road which runs from the farm to Brockley Hall. In its main aspect this zodiac is like the one at Nuthampstead in having Leo to the south and Capricorn to the north; like both the Nuthampstead and the Glastonbury zodiacs, it also has a westward-facing guardian hound,

whose back legs stand on the castle ruins at Clare on the banks of the River Stow.

At Nuthampstead, I have chosen to walk round the whole zodiac, and then to trace the outline of one figure in detail. In this case, I want to make a tour along the paths which link the figures; as it is most convenient going clockwise round the circles, this means taking zodiacal figures in a reverse order. We will start from the ruined abbey of Bury St Edmunds, which was once a holy place only rivalled in importance by Glastonbury.

The ruins of the great abbey stand on the east side of the city by the bank of the Lark, between the church of St James (which became a cathedral in 1913 when the diocese of St Edmundsbury and Ipswich was created) and St Mary's church, the burial place of Mary Tudor, sister of Henry VIII. You reach the abbey grounds through the gate to the north of the cathedral.

On this site in 633AD, when the town was known as Beodricsworth, King Sigebert, the first Christian King of East Anglia, founded a religious community. Nearly three hundred years later, the body of Edmund, the king who had been martyred by the Danes in 870, was brought to Sigebert's church. The relic brought good fortune, for in time the Benedictine Abbey of Bury St Edmunds

857643

139

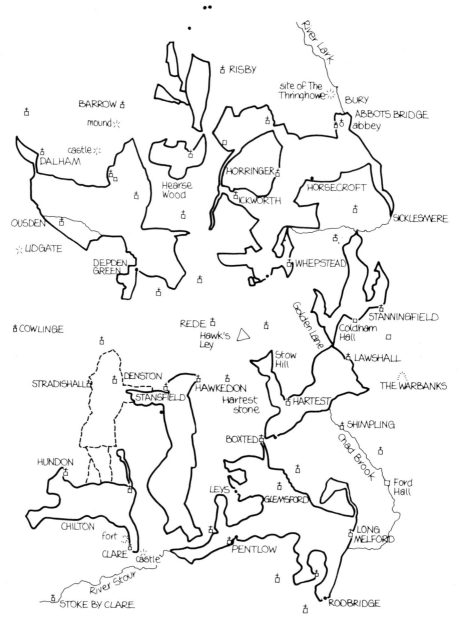

BURY ST. EDMUNDS ZODIAC based on Michael Burgess's Map

became one of the richest monastries in England. Its abbots knew what they wanted. When Herfast, the first Norman Bishop of East Anglia, wanted to remove the bishopric from North Elmham (see p.58) to Bury St Edmunds, the abbot made a pilgrimage to Rome and successfully implored the Pope not to make any changes in the status of his abbey. The bishopric went to Thetford instead.

St Edmund's Abbey continued to flourish until its dissolution on November 4th, 1539, when the abbot, the prior and forty-two monks signed the surrender document to the crown. W.A.Dutts lists some of the relics which the commissioners found and presumably destroyed. They included: the parings of St Edmund's nails; his banner and sword; one of his shirts and one of his sinews; and a 'pardon bowl' whose property was to grant pardon for five hundred days' sins to anyone who drank from it in 'the worship of God and St Edmund'.

Dutt mentions another more obviously pagan miracle connected with the shrine. It was a fertility rite – known as 'The Oblation of the White Bull' – performed for barren women, probably at the price of a high fee to the abbey. This is how Dutt describes it: 'The white bull, decked with ribbons and floral garlands, was brought to the south gate of the monastery, and led through the streets until the west gate was reached, the interested dame walking by its side with the monks and townspeople forming an attendant procession. From the west gate the bull was driven back to its pas-

ture, while the dame went on and prayed at the shrine.'

Perhaps St Edmund was felt to be so potent because his story fits in so well with the folklore connected with the severed head. This was one of the pagan symbols adopted by the Church, and it concerned the practice of placing skulls or even whole heads around (or in) the walls of sacred places to ward off evil. Stone heads which represent them bear a sign upon the neck to indicate where it was severed from the body; and it was the faint red ring round St Edmund's neck, which remained when his head was miraculously rejoined to his body, that was particularly remarked upon.

Tradition has it that he was killed by Danish arrows and decapitated at Hoxne, where a stone cross is said to mark the spot of his death, but the event probably took place at Hellesdon near Norwich. Dutt tells the old story: 'After the battle at Hoxne the Danes departed, leaving Edmund's headless body fastened by cords and arrows to a tree. There it was discovered by some of the dead king's followers, who, when the country was clear of their victorious enemies, crept back to the battle-field to bury the bodies of the slain. Edmund's body they buried in a small chapel near by. Then they went in search of the severed head, and after forty days' searching, were guided by a voice crying. "Here, here, here!" to a thicket, where it was found between the paws of a wolf. The beast offered no resistance to their taking it, and when they had done so disappeared into a wood. This "uncouth thing and strange ageyn nature" caused the Saxons to marvel greatly; but a greater wonder followed. When the head was carried to the chapel and interred, it became joined again to the body, leaving only a faint red line to mark where it had been cut off.'

In 903, the restored body was taken to a

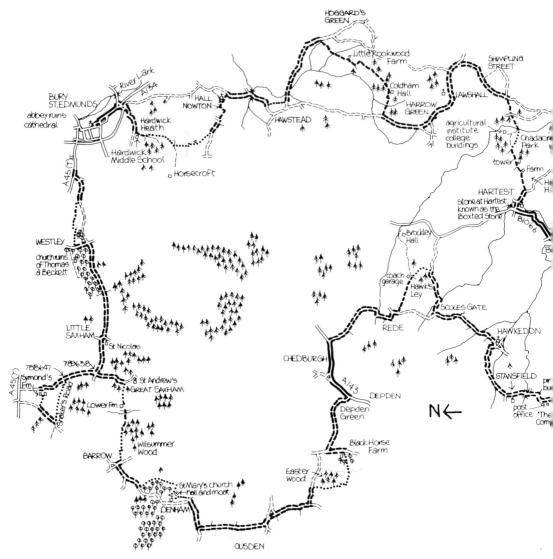

prepared shrine at Beodricsworth and the name of that place was changed to St Edmundsbury, from where we will now take up the pattern of the zodiac. Your best course is to leave Bury St Edmunds by the Sudbury road, A134, and then take the minor road running south-west at the second roundabout, when you come to the edge of the town. This will bring you to Hardwick Heath. A footpath by Hardwick Middle School goes south through this park, taking you through the belly of Sagittarius to a lane

defined by the River Lark flowing south from Bury to Sicklesmere. Do not go as far as the farm, but to continue your journey south leave Sagittarius ·ius when you come to this lane, by taking the first footpath on your left.

Go through Hall Nowton and take the road south to Hawstead. As soon as this road takes you across the Lark, you enter Scorpio, by the very tip of his sting. The tributary, which flows into the river a little to the east of the road bridge, outlines the eastern side of the animal.

864596

Before you reach Hawstead, take the public footpath going south just after the lane turns to the west. When that footpath reaches another lane, turn east. This lane will take you across the brook at Scorpio's back. Follow the lanes and then the footpath, which will bring you through the body of Scorpio to Little Rookwood Farm.

862592

874569

Continue past the farm and make for the sixteenth-century Coldham Hall, which is held in Scorpio's jaws. That creature's spiteful, November sign might well have influenced the seventeenth-century Ambrose Rookwood (whose home it was) when he took part in Guy Fawkes' November Gunpowder Plot.

From the Hall, follow the track now running north-west to a lane; you are now on the road that defines the animal's left claw. As you follow this road past Harrow Green to Lawshall, you leave Scorpio and enter the figure of Virgo. She is leaning to the south-west with the tip of her hood at Boxted. Like the Virgo figures at Glastonbury and

1632

which defines the creature's back and runs towards the appropriately named Horsecroft Farm. This Sagittarius is a traditional centaur/archer holding his bow to the west. His rump and tail are

143

Bury St. Edmunds

Nuthampstead, she holds a spica or a corn dolly. This one is represented by Stowe Hill. Her hem is at Lawshall church. After the church take the road towards Shimpling. You leave this road by a farm lane going west to Chadacre Park, the site of West Suffolk's agricultural institute. Continue west along the outskirts of the park, past the farm buildings of the college. Then follow the path over Hartest Hill. It goes along a lane by the Edwardian folly of Tower House Lodge, through Home Farm, where a noisy Alsatian may dispute your right of way. Finally, turn right down what must surely be the steepest road in Suffolk. It will bring you to what Michael

Burgess describes as 'the magical village of Hartest'. It stands at Virgo's heart.

I'm grateful to Mr Burgess for bringing the Hartest Stone to my attention before I had visited the village. It is a large granite boulder, 4 feet x 4 feet x 4 feet (1·2 m x 1·2 m x 1·2 m), standing at the northern end of the village green. It is said to have been hauled into its present position from Somerton Hill. This deed was done on July 7th, 1713, by twenty gentlemen and twenty farmers to celebrate Marlborough's victories in the War of the Spanish Succession.

I haven't been able to trace the site where it originally stood, and in any case Mr Burgess is sceptical about the story

8552

838522

of the shifting of the stone. But it is possible that its previous position could have been significant in the alignments radiating from the zodiac's centre at Hawk's Leys to the north.

From Hartest take the B road to Boxted, then follow the lane to Boxted church. That marks the point of Virgo's hood and the tip of Leo's ear. He is a rampant lion, similar to the one at Glastonbury, and like the Glastonbury lion a river (in this case the Stour) outlines his belly.

Leo's hind leg stretches from the village of Long Melford, where the poet Edmund Blunden spent his last years, and for whose beautiful, enormous church he wrote historical notes, surely the most literate (if not apparently the most accurate) of any in the country. If you want to visit that village, take the B road from Boxted. It runs just to the east of the River Glem, which defines the lion's mane.

If, however, you decide to carry on with the footpath walk, take the one from Boxted church to Fern Hill. It brings you out on a minor road north of the village of Glemsford, which stands on the lion's neck. From there, follow the B road south to the Stour and cross the A1092 (the Roman road running between Cavendish and Long Melford). If you have visited Long Melford, this is the point at which you can rejoin the walk. Follow a minor road across the river and then take the bridle path going west to Pentlow Street, where you join the road to Pentlow, whose church stands on the lion's foreleg. The rest of

that leg is defined by the river, until his paw is reached just to the east of Bower Hall; a footpath follows the course of the river going west.

When this path joins the road follow it through to Clare, but just before you get to the centre of the town take the first road on your right. You will then see a public footpath sign on your left. This goes along the banks of a stream, over part of the ground where Clare Priory once stood. The path will take you over the disused railway line, to the grassed mounds of Clare Castle. These earthworks and those of the Iron Age fort of Clare camp (sometimes known as Houndswell) mark the edges of the rear paw of the zodiac's westward facing watch dog, whose tail reaches north to Chipley Abbey.

It is well worth walking round Clare Castle and the fort to the north of the town, before continuing along the path that will take you to the next figure of the zodiac: the giant, hooded figure of Gemini, also pointing to the west. The rectangular fort is reached by a short by-road which runs just to the north of the public library.

Next follow the farm road that leads to Hermitage Farm; it is a public right of way although not marked as such. Go up the hill to the right of the farm house and buildings, along the path that leads to the poultry sheds, and then keep by the headland. At the top of the field, cross the dry ditch which runs by the trees standing on the skyline (as seen from the farm), then go straight across the field towards Houghton Hall. At the other side of this field you come to a clear track, which sadly comes to an abrupt end in ploughed land just south of New House Farm. From here you must find your own way, doing as little damage as you can, and keeping to the headlands of fields, for the old path has gone.

777481 You are making for the lane to the west of New House Farm. When you reach it, you will find, just opposite the farm buildings, that a green lane (cleared at the insistence of the local ramblers' association) runs to the north. When I walked there in November 1978, the clearance had reached almost to the

777490 point where the lane (following the bend of Gemini's knee) curves round to the north-east. At this point, the right of way has been ploughed over and you must make your way across two fields, between King's Wood to the east and Longwood to the west.

I was lucky when I went this way. Half-way across the second field, some deer running along the skyline showed us where the lane continued. It goes along high ground, hidden between neglected hedges grown into straggling lines of woodland. Yet, although it is so overgrown, it is a clear green lane with banks on either side of it; and I've since learnt that it was once the miller's lane between Stansfield and Cavendish.

This lane has again been broken off by ploughed land, and when you reach it you must follow the headland down to the stream, where you will see a small

783508 bridge. On the other side of the stream you will find a pink bungalow. The gate
146

on to the road for Upper Street is just to the south of it. Continue along the lane to Stansfield.

From Stansfield, Gemini points towards his phantom twin at Denston. This rather vague figure, which is looking towards the east, is considered by Michael Burgess to be somewhat spurious. He takes it that, in this zodiac, Gemini is chiefly represented by the sacred, limping god whose body we have walked along. Mr Burgess thinks the figure may be a representation of Mercury, Wayland, Vulcan, Hercules or Orion; but I suggest that he may also represent the wounded Fisher King of the Grail legends.

From Stansfield take the road to Hawkedon, which marks the top of Gemini's hood. Continue north to Scoles Gate, where you turn east until you see a public footpath sign pointing 8165 to a field path about half a mile (804 m) along the lane. This footpath takes you past the woods of Hawk's Leys. When the path reaches the old farm, go across the farm road, and possibly past two or 8155 three incongruously smart-looking coaches, and follow the field path west to the village of Rede, standing on the highest ground in Suffolk (for the significance of that name see Section 6, page 209).

From Rede, you will have to go by road to Depden to reach the next figure of the zodiac: the bull's head of Taurus. The bull's nose is marked by The Marquis of Cornwallis public house in Chedburgh. From the inn, the A road 7885 marks the bull's snout for a quarter of a mile (402 m), and then you may follow his profile by taking the lane through Depden Green to Gate Farm.

68576 Turn south at Gate Farm, along the road which outlines the bull's bent hoof,

58572 and leave the creature by taking the path through the orchards of Black Horse Farm. This path is going to take you up to Aries, the kneeling paschal lamb, which is in the same position as the one in the Nuthampstead zodiac. Appropriately enough, you reach it by the path that goes along the western edge of Easter Wood.

Follow the lanes past the village of

36597 Ousden, whose church, dedicated to St Peter, marks the lamb's hind legs. Your way does not lie there, but continues along the lane to Denham, about 2·5

57618 miles (4 km). Denham moat, by St Mary's church, marks the lamb's snout. From there you can take a footpath past the Hall, and round the eastern edge of a wide orchard. The path comes out on a

58627 lane just south of Barrow, whose crossroads marks the top of the lamb's head.

The next figure is the eagle, which as at Nuthampstead represents our more familiar water carrier, Aquarius. For a note on how that came about, see Section 6, p.219. The eagle is centred on the woods and estate of Great Saxham, with Wilsummer Wood (which you can reach by footpath) representing its western wing.

For the purposes of this walk, the best way is to keep to the northern edge of

87632 Wilsummer Wood and follow the track which will bring you out on a lane just to the north of Great Saxham's

fourteenth-century church, dedicated to St Andrew – whom Michael Burgess here equates with the Hindu Indra/Indara, the rain bringer and dragon-slayer. Now go north towards the next sign, Pisces, which as at Glastonbury and Nuthampstead is represented by three fishes. In this case, there are two small ones (one above the other) in the west, and a larger one standing on its own in the east, which Michael Burgess describes as a whale.

The underside of the most southerly of the two small fishes is marked by the ancient path, which in common with

Clare Castle

some other old ways in this area is an old sheep run indicated by the name of Shakers' Road (see p. 130).

To reach the Shakers' Road, continue north along the lane; you are now walking along the western outline of the large fish. When you come to a patch of woodland on the footpath you are walking along the part of the Shakers' Road that defines the small fish. You should leave the path when it reaches a lane and turn to cross the stream which outlines the other side of the same fish's body, and then take the footpath to Symond's Farm. The name is significant. Alfred Watkins found that Symond's occurred many times on his old straight tracks and associated the name with seamen; in this case it may relate to the line which Michael Burgess describes running from Great Saxham church to King's Lynn, which goes through the farm.

From there, unless you want to walk along the busy A45, you must retrace your steps and make for Little Saxham.

There is only one figure left in the zodiac, Capricorn, represented solely by a head and neck facing to the west, with St Nicholas' church of Little Saxham

785654

798637

marking its snout. It is an unsatisfactory creature for walkers, for much of its outline consists of parish boundaries that are not necessarily rights of way. The road from Little Saxham to Bury St Edmunds runs through the goat's head. It will take you to the village of Westley, with a ruined church dedicated to St Thomas à Becket (believed by some people to have been the sacrificial victim of a witch rite). From the parish church in Westley, you can take a footpath to Bury St Edmunds, and although that completes the walks in this part, it does not complete the story of the goat.

Michael Burgess believes that the amount of water to the east of Bury St Edmunds indicates that this Capricorn (unlike the one at Nuthampstead which is a more conventional animal) is a fish-tailed goat, and he thinks that the tail may spread out as far as Great Barton, which we shall visit in the next two parts of this section. As part of the evidence, Mr Burgess cites the stretches of water to the north-east of Bury St Edmunds, which on eighteenth- and nineteenth-century maps were known as Mermaid's Pits.

8246

Part B
Moats and Grundles

O.S. maps 144, 155

The most notable feature about the area of Suffolk that lies mainly to the north of a line drawn between Bury St Edmunds in the west and Needham Market in the east is the moats. Nowhere else in England is there such a concentration of them. Almost every village and farmhouse of any size has one, so it is not surprising that this is a region in which tales of underground passages and rivers abound. It also has a more peculiar phenomenon to offer: geological or man-made scars on the landscape known as grundles. This name, though apparently local and inexplicable, is sufficiently accepted to be used on the Ordnance Survey maps.

If the land were hilly, I would describe these grundles as hollow ways, like the ancient paths that are found along the Oxfordshire edge of the chalk, going from the ridgeway to the valley and sometimes following old water courses. But this is the flattest part of a flat county, so that explanation won't do. Anyway, the two grundles are much deeper and narrower than any hollow way I have ever come across.

David Dymond, the local historian and archaeologist, who lives in Grundle House, at the northern end of the Stanton Grundle, believes that they were natural formations used as trading routes. He derives the word from the

Old English 'grind' and believes that it relates to the gravelly nature of the soil on the grundle floor. To back this up he quotes a mediaeval document, in which the path by his home is referred to as 'le deep Grindle'.

He affirms that the Stanton Grundle was used as a drove way within living memory, but it takes a lot of imagination to envisage that today. For you have to walk along both grundles in single file; and the great, steep banks, rising to some 18 feet (5·5 m) or more in places, tower above you, overgrown with trees and scrub. Surprisingly, the gravelly soil beneath your feet is fairly dry.

I shall describe the grundles in some detail (see p.154), but before I go on now to outline the walks in the area as a whole, I should like to give my personal reaction to the name. I think of them as dragon paths, for grundle seems to me to be too like Grendel, the name of the monster Beowulf slew, to be completely coincidental.

In *The View over Atlantis*, John Michell drew some interesting alignments between the moats in this region, but unfortunately this does not mean that footpaths run between them. So what I have done is to work out a route in the area, using both lanes and footpaths, making it possible to follow the way by car, or preferably by bicycle, interspersed with

149

Entrance to grundle
Stanton

round walks along the paths.

I want to start the tour from the church in the village of Woolpit, south of the A45 (T) at 155:974625. In the church you will find a board, whose message, transcribed from a seventeenth-century manuscript in the British Museum (Harleian, 3873), refers you to a story related by the fourteenth-century chronicler Ralph of Coggeshall. Three hundred years previously, two green children were discovered in the pits that gave the village its name, and defended the inhabitants from the ravages of wolves up to the sixteenth century. These children were taken to the house of Sir Richard de Caine, while the villagers, in vain, tried to find out where they came from. Their skins were green, their speech was strange, and they could only survive on beans. When the children were able to communicate, they said that they came from a Christian country, where St Martin was worshipped, and that they were tending their parents' cattle by the river when the earth swallowed them up, and they eventually found themselves in the pits. The boy did not live long, but the girl grew to maturity, and is reported to have died a well-to-do matron of King's Lynn.

Their story has at least one parallel. In *Mysteries of the Earth*, Jacques Bergier relates that, in 1887, a green boy and a green girl appeared from a cave and were fostered by the peasants of Barijos in Spain. Again they would only eat beans, and again the boy soon died. The girl lived on for a further five years, during which time her skin lost its green

colour and she began to remember tales of her own country.

The similarities in the stories do not, however, get us any nearer to an explanation of this mystery. Some people look on the green children as visitors from another planet, and W.A. Dutt writes them off as 'fairies'. But remembering all the tales of underground passages and streams in Suffolk, I am inclined to a more terrestrial, but none the less dramatic, explanation of the children's appearance. I think that the boy and girl who turned up in Woolpit may perhaps have been tending their father's cattle at the edge of the River Lark, near to Fornham St Martin, when a Breckland sandstorm (such as the one that buried the Saxon settlement at West Stow, see p.83) blew up. Lost, blinded and bewildered, their settlement buried, the children may well have wandered into a passage that brought them up at Woolpit. Their unusual speech could be accounted for by the fact that they may well have belonged to some small Celtic community, eking out an existence among the Saxon serfs and Norman overlords. Or they may have belonged to even earlier stock. And their adventure would be enough to account for the colour of their skins.

A story dating from the early sixteenth century emphasizes how likely it was for people to get completely lost in that area. When John Perfoy died in 1509, he bequeathed a parcel of land to the church of St Mary in Bury St Edmunds. This land was to be used to raise the money to ensure that the church bell would be rung as many times as there are days in the month, for it was by the ringing of the bell that he had been saved when he was once completely lost in Fornham Marsh in thick mist.

It would be nice to come up with a direct alignment to some significant place on the banks of the Lark, either from the pits at Woolpit (which lie off a lane to the east of the church); or from its moat which lies to the north; or from the church itself; or from the Lady's Well (said to possess healing powers) which stands in the centre of the village. This I cannot do. John Michell's alignment from the Woolpit moat goes through Drinkstone and Hessett.

However, there is one interesting alignment to be traced from Woolpit moat. Its runs north-west to the stone in Thurston churchyard, and south-east to 928653 the village of Creeting St Mary on the Gipping (155:094567). From that village, a footpath to the south-east goes past Creeting College Farm to Malting Farm where it meets the Roman road, now 114557 covered by the A140. We know that in late Neolithic times there was a large settlement here, and that these people made the type of pottery, decorated with incisions, that the archaeologists classify as Rhinyo-Clacton ware. The only other settlement of such people in Suffolk, that we know of, was at Honington on the Black Bourn (see p.98). Although this is to the north of the alignment, I feel that we may have a hint here of a line of communications between the Neolithic Breckland settlement (Honington is on its eastern edge) and that in the Ipswich

152

area. These two regions were the most densely populated regions of East Anglia from Palaeolithic times to the Middle Ages, and the line of communication between them could possibly have some bearing on the story of the green children.

From Woolpit, I want to look at the moats in the north of the area, which means crossing the A45. There are some massive alterations going on at this intersection at the moment, and hopefully there will eventually be a more straightforward crossing than I found.

When you get over the highway, make for Elmswell, crossing the railway line by the mill. Now go north to Great Ashfield and Badwell Ash. Behind Great Ashfield church is the moat at Castle 99367 Hill. It falls on an alignment which runs through to the moat at Haughley Castle (see p.159).

Make your way through the lanes to West Street, where you turn north along the lane signposted to Stanton. Take the 9897 farm lane on your left. This is the beginning of the first of the round walks, and it will take you along the Stanton Grundle. Start off by following the lane past Pot-9847 ash Farm. Here there is a large sandstone, probably marking a stage in the old main highway from Walsham le Willows to Thetford via Bardwell, Little Fakenham to Euston, which runs to the south of the farm and forms part of this walk. It is not a very clearly defined right of way now, but you can just trace it running north-west across the wide expanse of hedgeless field and into a patch of woodland. I am told by John

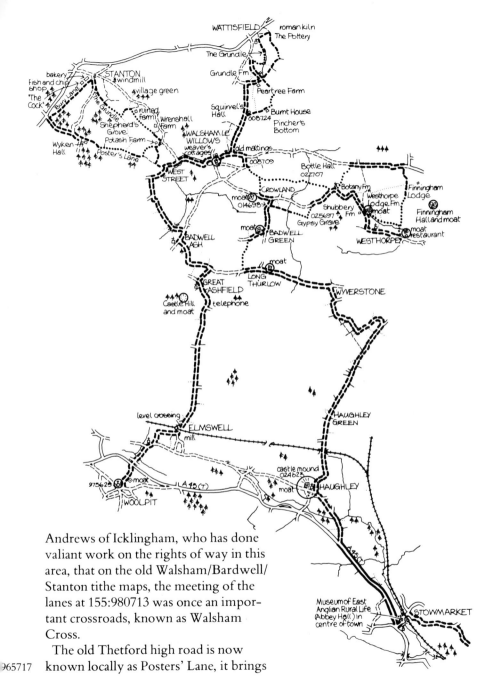

Andrews of Icklingham, who has done valiant work on the rights of way in this area, that on the old Walsham/Bardwell/Stanton tithe maps, the meeting of the lanes at 155:980713 was once an important crossroads, known as Walsham Cross.

The old Thetford high road is now known locally as Posters' Lane, it brings

965717

153

Grundle, Wattisfield

you to the lane by Wyken Hall. Just as you come in sight of the main road, you will see a lane going through the woods on your right. Known as Bury Lane, this was once a part of the main road from Bury St Edmunds to Stanton. It brings you to the crossroads and church in the centre of that village. By the church wall, there is a stone on which the village cross used to be mounted.

You don't have to go right up to the church, although it is worth visiting. The way to the grundle lies along the lane, past the bakery. On the outskirts of the village, follow a narrow gravel drive-way on your left. It leads to David

Dymond's house, and you will find the entrance to the grundle on your right, beside a seventeenth-century house known as The Lodge, which is thought to have once been a meeting place for people coming into Stanton from the grundle.

The entrance to the grundle is fairly wide and shallow, but quite soon the path gets narrower and the banks on either side steeper and more overgrown. From time to time you will find your way impeded by a fallen tree. The grundle extends for over half a mile (804 m), and when you scramble out at the other end of it you will find yourself in a wide, ploughed field. Most of the hedges have been removed, but some of the ditches marking the old field divisions have been left; across the one just ahead of you, you will see a small, nineteenth-century, brick bridge.

This area is known as Shepherd's Grove, and it was once very heavily wooded. David Dymond has traced 330 oaks used in the construction of his house and he is certain that they all came from the woods around Stanton. So we must imagine that the grundle existed almost as an underground passage through the trees.

At the end of the grundle turn across the fields to the east. The path becomes a considerable, but very overgrown, farm track. After passing the farm and its buildings, now deserted and decayed, you can choose whether to return to Stanton or carry on with the circular walk to Walsham.

If you decide on the former course, you continue along the green lane, known locally as Wash Lane (because it gets swamped in wet weather), to the road. The walk back to Stanton is just under a mile (1·6 km). You will pass the remains of the village green, a rather sorry little triangle of grazing land, and the village windmill. Almost opposite the windmill there is a cottage where the village carrier used to live. People can still remember his pony and trap taking rabbits into the Bury St Edmunds market.

Grundle, Wattisfield

If you decide to return to West Street from the old farmhouse, you will have to be prepared to assert your rights; for where the path has not been ploughed up, it has been allowed to get monstrously overgrown. Yet this was once an important thoroughfare, and is still an undisputed right of way, known locally as King's Lane. It runs south of Wrenshall Farm where it broadens out into a wide green lane. The imposing-looking earthwork on your left is simply a memory of World War II, connected with the old airfield of Stanton. Ignore the lane that runs immediately beside it to your left, and carry on to Potash Farm, and so back to West Street.

The next round walk takes you along the other grundle at Wattisfield. To get there, go straight through the village of Walsham le Willows, past the church on your right and a group of weavers' cottages on your left. On the outskirts of the village, turn left by the old maltings, where the beer for local farmers was once made and which have now been most neatly converted into private dwellings by an East Harling architect, who is noted for his work on the restoration and preservation of old buildings.

About half a mile (804 m) from the maltings, you will find a farmhouse known as Squirrels' Hall. It stands on your right, marking the starting point for the walk. The lane by the farmyard soon becomes a pleasant green road. The two houses that once stood near to it have been empty for many years. The first, which is quite a way from the lane, can be seen over the fields on your right. It is generally referred to as Pinchers' Bottom, an unfortunate corruption of Finches' Bottom; at one time the little house in its remote coppice must have been, at any rate in summer, a lyrical place to live. The name of the other house, a little further along the lane, is Burnt House, for obvious reasons. The lane ends soon after Burnt House, and you have to make your way across a field. There is a rough indication of a

Old Kiln, Wattisfield

00571

00872

footpath going to the south of Peartree Farm, and you have to follow it, for the original lane which comes out to the north of the farm is now completely overgrown and impassable in high summer.

Follow the lane between Peartree Farm and Grundle Farm to visit the Wattisfield Pottery. You will find a sign directing you to it, after you have passed the last of the cottages on your right.

)15745

Before you reach the pottery, you must first walk past the fearsome battery sheds belonging to the firm of Sappa Chickens. It is a nasty experience to know that all the birds are locked away in those grim barracks, and yet not to be able to see a sign of life (human or animal), and to hear only the persistent drone of the electrical installations. It is salutary though, for throughout East Anglia, Sappa Chickens offer farm-gate sales of 'fresh eggs'. Now at least you will know what that means. No one disputes that they have been recently laid.

The pottery is immediately past the battery farm. It is a busy commercial venture of quite a different character. The grounds are open to the public so that everyone can have a look at the old Roman kiln, which stands well to the right of the enquiry office and exhibition rooms. The kiln on show is one of more than a score of similar kilns to have been excavated within a radius of 1·5 miles (2·4 km) of the current pottery. But the Romans were not the first people to make pots at Wattisfield. There is evidence that Bronze Age and Iron Age potters were here long before them.

The path to Wattisfield church, and the grundle that starts from it, leaves the pottery beside a more recent, but still ancient, domed, brick kiln, which stands to the north of the workshops. The path goes downhill past the gate to the churchyard, and then you will see a field path which runs along the side of the grundle, so you can clamber down into it by one of several clearings in the heavy undergrowth. It is a scramble, for this grundle is even deeper and narrower than the one at Stanton. It is lined with hornbeam and, surprisingly for this part of Suffolk, its rim has a heavy growth of bracken. Occasionally, where the undergrowth is clear of the sandy banks, you can see a cross section of the field drainage systems that have been worked into it through the centuries.

012744

Although this grundle runs into a

Roman kiln, Wattisfield

stream feeding a large, gloomy farm pond in a great dip of trees, the ground beneath your feet is mostly unexpectedly dry. As you near the farm, you will find plank bridges crossing the grundle over your head. When you come to one that is made of concrete, not wood, climb out. You will find yourself in a field, with the wooded farm pond in a hollow on your right and a gate in the hedge opposite you. There is a right of way (but no path) across this field to the gate and the lane.

015736 You can get back to Squirrels' Hall either by the way you came, or by taking the lane going past Peartree Farm.

The last round walk in this area is also based on Walsham le Willows, and I have used it as a centre for looking at some of the moats and the legends associated with them. Leave the village by the path from 008709 and go due south to the moat at Crowland. This runs right round the house, and until quite recently was the only water supply for the dwelling, since the previous occupants refused to go on the mains, or do anything about the moat which frequently flooded their cellar. That attitude might be attributable to indifference or to a dislike of interference and change; or it may represent a genuine respect for the moats, which were perhaps something more than merely

Walsham le Willows

convenient sources of water and natural defences from men and animals. John Michell aligns the Crowland moat through the ones at Norton Hall and Hessett to the south-west, and south-east through Sudbourne Farm to the west of Wyverstone and Kerry's Farm, south of Bacton.

Follow the lanes to 014698, where you will find a wide green road. This lane runs almost parallel to an alignment from Crowland moat to the one at Westhorpe, which is included in this walk, and extends to the moat just north of Brockford Street on the A140.

The Crowland green lane goes uphill between hedges at the side of a field and then turns to the north along a parish boundary known as Hundred Lane. This 26696 turning marks the site of a crossroads, where a gypsy is said to be buried beneath an oak tree. There are two oak trees here, but I could find no trace of the grave. When you reach the lane, head 41698 past Botany Farm to the next moat at Shrubbery Farm. This is on a clear alignment with the moat at Finningham Hall to the south-east, and with those at Badwell Green and Stowlangtoft to the south-west.

From Shrubbery Farm, you can either continue along the lane past the church to Westhorpe village, or take the foot-path along the north side of the stream that links Shrubbery Farm moat with the one at Hall Farm, Westhorpe.

51690 On the green at the road junction at Westhorpe you will find lime trees, which when I saw them in February 1978 were festooned with great globes of mistletoe. It is there that you will find the entrance (also a public right of way) to Westhorpe Hall. The old Hall is now a fashionable country restaurant, but at one time it was the home of Mary Tudor, sister of Henry VIII, who married Charles Brandon of Suffolk and who is buried in Bury St Edmunds.

The footpath brings you to the north of the moat, behind the Hall; with the old wall behind, it is one of the most beauti-ful in the area. A wide causeway takes you north from the moat to a lane to the 051709 north of Finningham Lodge. This road 039698 leads to another green lane. It starts quite clearly, but soon degenerates into a head-land path going to Westhorpe Lodge 040702 Farm. Turn north here, and follow the farm road to the lane, where you turn left, and then take a narrow field path going south to Botany Farm. There you 032703 will find a footpath running west, which passes the site of a dwelling (long since disappeared) known as Bottle Hall, whose owner is supposed to have sold his wife for half a crown.

The footpath takes you back to the one between Walsham le Willows and Crowland, with which this walk started.

From Walsham, you can follow the lanes to some of the other moats by going south-east, past the moat at Bad- 012693 well Green, and continuing south to the one that stands to the east of the T junc- 014682 tion at Long Thurlow. Carry on going east through Wyverstone Street and then head south through Haughley Green to Haughley village. Here the moat, now 025624 not much more than a duck pond, par-tially surrounds a very overgrown castle

159

East Anglia originate. As Enid Porter describes them in *Folk Lore of East Anglia*, they are 'tiny sandy-haired and complexioned people' and they will 'work in exchange for hot cakes'. This seems to me to suggest that they were far more likely to have been members of a conquered race than elementals from another dimension; and even the remedy to stop them stealing horses, by hanging flint stones with holes in them over the stable doors, although seemingly far removed from any earthly warning system at least indicated that it was tinkers, horse-coopers and gypsies that the honest citizens were on their guard against. Stowmarket has long been a centre for showmen and travelling people of all sorts.

From this town, you can take the minor road to Creeting St Mary, which I linked with Woolpit on p.152. If you should take the walk from there via Malting Farm to Hungercut Hall, you will find yourself north of the Romano-British settlement of Combretovium. Near here an Iron Age well (now exhibited in the Ipswich Museum) was discovered in 1973, when the earth was being levelled to make the Claydon By-pass. It is thought to have been a holy well, sunk to meet a sacred spring.

This seems a good place to conclude our tour of the Suffolk moats.

mound, from which various stories of underground tunnels originate. On an immediately practical level, the porch of Haughley church, which stands near the old moat, is filled with ancient leather fire buckets.

From Haughley, you can only reach the town of Stowmarket by the A45(T). It is worth going there though to visit the Museum of East Anglian Rural Life, an open-air museum with a reconstructed water mill, which stands in the grounds of Abbey Hall. It is approached beside a magnificent mediaeval tithe barn, which stands off a lane, up a hill from the market square in the centre of the town.

It is from Stowmarket that most of the stories of confrontations with 'fairies' in

Part C
The Puddingstone Track (3)

O.S. map 155

This last stretch of the Puddingstone Track properly begins at Thurston churchyard, but before I describe it, I will take up the threads of the track as we left it at Great Livermere on p.99.

There are no significant puddingstones and not many useful footpaths between Great Livermere and Thurston, a matter of some 4·5 miles (7·2 km) as the crow flies and considerably longer by the twisting lanes which you will have to take. The most direct route is to follow the road to Great Barton. This part of the way lies along the route that must have formed part of the original track. Just over half-way along this lane, you will come to Red Castle Farm on your left. It has a fairly impressive stone outside it, whose history I have yet to discover, but I would like to think it may relate to our track. The farm buildings stand near the site of a Roman villa, which gives us a clue to the ancient importance of this lane.

If you went to West Stow from Great Livermere, you would have to make your way eastwards by slightly busier lanes to Great Barton.

Cross the main road at the village, and continue south until you reach the school, where you turn towards Thurston and Thurston church.

If you went by footpath from Great Livermere to Ixworth you have a more interesting walk to Thurston, for this takes you by the working mill at Pakenham, which regularly grinds animal feed, and which visitors are able to look over by arrangement. Continue along a stretch of Roman road to Thurston church. I have not yet been able yet to trace the stone in this churchyard, although for a time I fooled myself that it lay in the lumps of masonry from the old tower whose fall destroyed the original church in 1860. The church, dedicated to St Peter, is on a slight hill and the stone, which gave its name to the village, must have been one of the most significant on the route.

Nor have I had any better luck with the next series of stones. The first is reported to be somewhere in Hessett church. There is a small stone by the churchyard gate here, but I cannot believe that this was the one that Dr Rudge intended. Hessett can only be reached by lanes. Although I cannot tell you how to find the stone, Hessett church is worth visiting for its wall painting of the seven deadly sins and for the remains of the old cross in the churchyard.

If, at this point, you want to look at some of the moat alignments (see p.152), turn right to see the three moats which lie just to the west of Hessett; then return to take the overgrown footpath from Hessett churchyard to Drinkstone.

9457 The next stone is supposed to be somewhere in the village of Felsham, but I have no hint of a more definite location. The village has a notable well, and it would be good to think the stone was associated with this. Felsham lies about 2·5 miles (4 km) to the south of Hessett. The next stone is at Hitcham

977498 Chapel Farm to the east of Kettlebaston. You can make part of this journey along various footpaths running by clusters of moats. Start off by taking a path from Felsham church to the lane at Brooke

947562 Hall; the moat lies on your left.

The path goes south to Thorpe Wood, passing another moat to the east (155:948558). Continue south past Grove Farm, and follow the path till you meet the patch of woodland that stands

950544 between you and Moat Farm to the west. Now make for the village of Brettenham, and you will come to a moat just after the path joins the road. Head south through Devil's Hill Wood and, skirting Hitcham, take the lane towards the moat at Wetherden Hall, one of the few in Suffolk that doesn't look like an old duck pond. You are now on your way to the village of Kettlebaston. Take

966503 the footpath going south opposite the church.

Chapel Farm and the remains of the chapel, where Dr Rudge located the stone, lie to the east of this path. The ruins are on private ground and cannot be reached, so you must follow the path going through to the village of Chelsworth, which lies just over a mile (1·6 km) to the south-east, and which Norman Scarfe commends for its

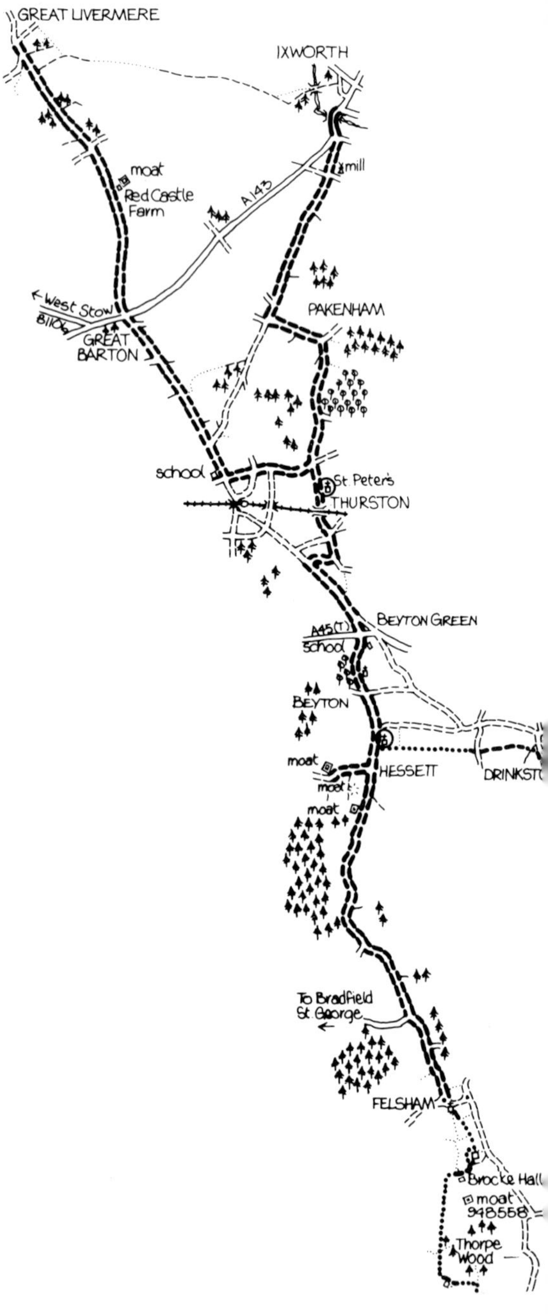

162

GREAT LIVERMERE

IXWORTH

mill

moat
Red Castle Farm

A143

West Stow
BitO
GREAT BARTON

PAKENHAM

school

St Peter's
THURSTON

BEYTON GREEN

A45(T)
school

BEYTON

moat
moat
HESSETT
DRINKST

moat

To Bradfield St George

FELSHAM

Brooke Hall
moat
948558

Thorpe Wood

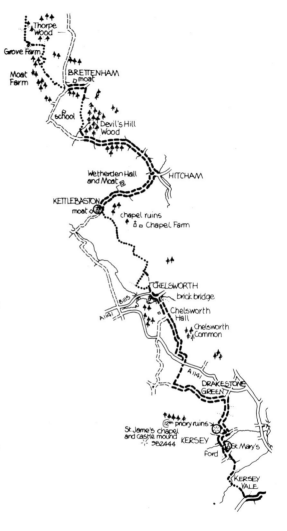

0478 'well-kept cats'. The church stands on the bank of the River Brett, just across the road from Kettlebaston Lane. The puddingstone is in the north wall of the church tower.

Dr Rudge found the next stone lying by the door of a farm on Chelsworth Common. I cannot tell you where the stone is, but the common is reached by taking the main road into the small village, and then crossing the river by a beautiful brick bridge. This lane runs past Chelsworth Hall and continues uphill to the common. The next stone – which again I have not been able to find – is reputed to lie in an orchard in Drakestone Green.

To get there, follow the lane going south from the common, cross the main road and carry on to Drakestone Green, which is a large farm and not a village.

7446 From there you take the lane that goes to Kersey. The remains of the twelfth-century priory, where a stone is alleged to lie among the ruins, is now inaccessible to the public, but the alignment from here is important. To the north-

6503 west, it goes through the church of Kettlebaston and then runs by the tumulus at Eastlow Hill. To the south-east, it

2439 goes immediately through Kersey

1385 church, to the church at Shelley, and so

2346 to Stratford St Mary, where traces of a henge, believed to be contemporary with the one at Arminghall (see p.65), have been found.

There are two puddingstones to be seen in Kersey itself. This village is most unusual for Suffolk in that it is built on two quite steep hills. The street runs

from the top of the one to the north where the priory stood, through a ford in the valley, to the top of the one to the south, which is crowned by the church of St Mary.

So the priory and the church are aligned by street and ford, and the

163

alignment runs north-west through Chelsworth and Kettlebaston. As if to emphasize this alignment, there are the two puddingstones. One bursts through the pavement at the north end of the village, across the road from the White Horse Inn and just outside a terrace of cottages that have mercifully escaped the over-restoration and prettifying that has overtaken so many of the other old weavers' cottages in this village. The other stone, sadly painted over, stands to the east of the ford, just outside the Suffolk craft shop.

Kersey and its neighbour, Lindsey, were once wealthy wool villages, and the church of St Mary, which was mentioned in the Domesday Book, bears

164

to have replaced an older chapel, which served the castle, now reduced to grassy mounds in the farmland to the south.

At Kersey we leave the Puddingstone Track; one way to do so is to take the footpath which runs from the lane to the south of the church, through Kersey Vale to Hadleigh. From there you can get a bus into Ipswich, or if you feel like a further walk take the Holton St Mary road through the town and leave it by the third road running east. This will take you to the old railway line, now a very pleasant walk; the sides of the old cutting are covered in wild flowers, including pyramid orchids. The line went through Raydon Great Wood, and at that point you can turn into the village of Raydon. The lane goes south to the A12, along which you will find buses running to Colchester and Ipswich.

003431

033422

060404

evidence to its prosperity in the Middle Ages. The present building dates from the early part of the fourteenth century, and the only trace of the earlier church is the eleventh-century font, which was restored to the church in 1927. For many years it stood upside down as a cottage doorstep. Like many other Suffolk churches, St Mary's of Kersey carries a reminder of St George the dragon-slayer. In this case, it is to be found in the faint remains of a wall painting.

There is one other building to look at before you leave Kersey – the thirteenth-century chapel of St James, which stands north of the village at 155:982444. The present building (which was used as a barn up to 1930) is thought

Puddingstone.
Kersey

Part D
The Coast and the Waveney Valley

O.S. maps 156, 144

Just over a mile (1·6 km) out to sea from the remains of the village of Dunwich, a Roman fort is supposed to lie. Divers have yet to find any trace of it, yet some historians believe that Dunwich must have been the site of the Roman settlement of Sitomagus. Their speculation is based on the fact that the Roman roads from the fort at Walton to the south, and from Burgh Castle and the signal station of Corton to the north, seem to converge at a mid-way point just beyond the present Dunwich coastline. A branch of the great Colchester-Caistor St Edmund road (Pye Street) also probably went to Dunwich. It left the main road north of Coddenham, going via East Soham to Peasenhall, and for that distance can still be traced. Another road from the north followed the line of Stone Street to Halesworth, then went east to Blyford (where a statue of Venus was found) and then to Dunwich.

That evidence, together with the Roman coins and domestic utensils that have been ploughed up round about or discovered on the beach, has been enough to start members of the North-East Essex Sub Aqua Club on a project to try to discover some tangible remains of the Roman occupation. Their task, started in the early 1970s, has not been an easy one. Underwater visibility in the North Sea rarely extends beyond 15 feet

(4·6 m) but six to twelve inches (15–30 cm) is the norm. Often everything is completely black and only very experienced divers, who can feel their way along the sea-bed, can attempt to make any investigations.

These divers, the handful of people living in the few remaining cottages, and the summer visitors drawn by the fascination of the place's history, its tiny museum (which contains a model of Dunwich in its prime) and its lovely cliff-top walks, are the heirs of a city which, until the fourteenth century, was in two vital respects the capital of East Anglia: the cathedral city and one of the busiest ports in the whole country.

We can only speculate about the settlements at Dunwich before the first half of the seventh century AD, but by that time it must already have become a very important place. For when Felix of Burgundy came to England at the request of Sigebert, the first Christian King of East Anglia, he made his way to Dunwich almost as soon as he landed, and it was there that the cathedral which carried his name was built.

Church-building was one of the great activities of Dunwich. There can never have been a city that boasted so many religious buildings. In 1573, two centuries after the main port of Dunwich had been swallowed by the sea, John

Day, a man famous in the history of typography for being the first English printer to use Saxon type, resolved to compile a history of his native town, where he still lived. According to his information, Dunwich once possessed six parish churches (including the Cathedral of St Felix), two of which, All Saints (which fell down the cliffs between 1904 and 1919) and St Peters (which fell on to the beach in 1688) were still standing; two friaries, the Grey Friars and the Black Friars with 'verie fayer churches and byldings'; two hospitals; three chapels; and an 'aunchent and verie old church called the Temple, the which church by report was in the Jews tyme'. This last was a church set up by the Knights Templar and one of the few round churches in England. There is one in Cambridge and another, now demolished, stood in north-east Hertfordshire, in the area covered by the zodiac described in Section 6.

Wherever I have gone in East Anglia, I have found that when I have encountered a place in which the old religion lives through local stories, buildings and place names, the area frequently proves to have been a stronghold of families connected with the Knights of this twelfth-century order (see p.206). Here the reference to the Jews, a community of whom helped to build up the wealth of Norwich in the twelfth century, would seem to indicate that the Templars, who were similarly renowned for attracting earthly riches, were also an eclectic order, evolving their own mystery out of the secret wisdom of varying groups of people.

On the completely practical level, it is no surprise at all to find that they were connected with a rich and busy seaport. The men of Dunwich had business with the sea both as ship-builders for the Navy, and as merchants and fishermen in their own vessels. Much of the history of the town, and our knowledge of the leading citizens in mediaeval times, is gleaned from documents concerning the building and furnishing of ships to meet the monarch's demands. But it is the trading adventures of her merchants, and the fishing expeditions to the Iceland seas, that I should like to learn more about.

Although there are many hair-raising tales of smuggling off the Dunwich coast in the eighteenth century; the holy men and worthy burghers of the mediaeval city seem to have left few ghosts behind them, although their earthly remains are still sometimes washed up on the shore. There are the bells of Dunwich, of course, which like the legendary bells of almost every drowned village are supposed to be heard at certain portentous times. These sounds must be ghostly, for clearly any bell that fell on to the sea-bed would soon get clogged with mud and sand and be incapable of ringing. However, if the church tower were still standing under the waves, the rise and fall of the tide lapping the belfry could ring the bell. Perhaps that was how, as late as 1855, another John Day (a master mariner this time), who was lost on a voyage to Bawdsey, was able to verify his position

167

Leper chapel, Dunwich

by hearing the sound of the submerged Dunwich bell.

The divers have found no trace of a standing tower or of bells in any condition. (Being very valuable, most bells were saved and taken inland when it was certain that a church was going to be lost.) Not surprisingly they do report strange experiences underwater. These are mostly connected with the strong sensation felt by a person alone in 'black' conditions that another presence is there. But this is an experience that is also shared by people like mountaineers who undertake hazardous adventures alone, and it could have more to do with human nature reacting to a certain sort of stress than with any actual place.

Yet the pull of Dunwich is very strong.

Ryder Haggard introduced the city into three of his novels. Edward Fitzgerald (the translator of *Omar Khyam*) was a frequent visitor, and in 1855 he drove Thomas Carlyle over to see the torn cliffs. The day he died, in Woodbridge, was one on which he had planned to visit Dunwich yet again. But it was left to Swinburne, a friend of Fitzgerald, who also loved the place and often came here, to write some lines for the ruined church of All Saints:

. . . one hollow tower and hoary
Naked in the sea wind stands and moans.
Filled and thrilled with its perpetual story;
Here where earth is dense with dead men's
bones.

So perhaps the ghostly strength of Dunwich consists in the hold it has over

168

people and that is why, although it was destroyed in the fourteenth century, people went on living for another four hundred years under the constant threat of the storms that tore at the coastline. In 1740 there was a particularly vicious one, an account of which was given by the local historian Thomas Gardner, whose *Historical Account of Dunwich*, published in 1754, is quoted in Rowland Parker's *Men of Dunwich*, an excellent reconstruction of life in the busy port in mediaeval times.

The section of Gardner's account of the 1740 storm that concerns us is his description of what was discovered when the ravages of the sea levelled the two hills of the town, and laid bare the foundations of the chapel of St Francis: 'where, besides the ruins of the Walls, were five round Stones near of a bigness; the Dimensions of one (I took) were four Feet the Diameter, and near two the thickness. There was likewise a circle of large Stumps of Piles, about twenty-four Feet Circumference.' Rowland Parker gives two possible explanations for those five stones and the circle of stumps. The first is that the stones might have been Roman millstones used for oil-extraction or stone-crushing, and that the circle represented the base of the mill; the second is that the circle of piles was the 'inner sanctum of a temple dating from long before Roman times, a miniature version of the one at Arminghall'. As Rowland Parker observes, 'nothing could be more normal than the Chapel of St Francis should be built on the site of pagan worship.' And he

makes us think about the hills, too. Known as Cock and Hen Hills, they are shown on a map of 1587 as standing to the north-west of Grey Friars, whose gates can still be seen at 156:476702. Were they natural or man-made hills, which according to Gardner 'stood upwards of forty Feet high'? 'Were they Roman burial mounds like those at Bartlow in Essex?' asks Rowland Parker. Or could they echo Silbury Hill? And could Cock and Hen even be a corruption of Gog and Magog, the deities of the old religion?

The frustration is that, as we can no longer give the circle or the hills any precise location, it is not possible to work out any convincing alignments from them. So what I am going to do in this part of the book is look at three groups of walks and investigate places on the way that could possibly fall into alignments from central places in Dunwich.

First, I shall go south-west to Snape. If you want to make a two-day expedition of this walk, you could base yourself for the night at the Youth Hostel at Blaxhall, 156:367571. Next I shall go north-west through Blythburgh to Ilketshall St Andrew, 156:379872. That route traces out an alignment which runs almost parallel to the Roman road of Stone Street, which is partially covered by the A144. From Ilketshall St Andrew, I have gone via the remains of the castle at Mettingham to Bungay. From there I have taken up the walks of the third group, which follow the course of the Waveney Valley to the west.

South-west from Dunwich

O.S. map 156

It could be a good idea to start this walk with a visit to the little museum' which stands in Dunwich's only remaining street. There you will be able to see what the coastline looked like in the heyday of Dunwich's prosperity as a Saxon cathedral city and as a flourishing mediaeval port, and guess yourself at the origin of the hills and the exact bit of North Sea that covers the possible site of a Bronze Age temple.

The walk starts to the south of the town, past the hill road that leads by the gates of Grey Friars and the lane which goes towards the coastguards' houses on the cliffs, where Edward Thomas came to complete his life of Richard Jefferies. 470690 If you follow the lane through to Cliff House, and turn south over the National Trust Land of Dunwich Common, you will have your first unlucky sighting of Sizewell Power Station. Your actual path, however, runs inland, and you turn west by the path that leaves the lane before it reaches Cliff House. Small sections of the path you are now on follow a possible alignment from the henge at Dunwich. It runs through the crossroads at Poplar, south of East Bridge, past Friston church (156:414605) and the tumulus that lies to the east of Snape (156:403594). At its northern end this bit of the path goes through pine woods and comes out by the R.S.P.B. reserve on the marshes of Minsmere.

170

Here it becomes a wide, sandy track, before joining a metalled lane, which bridges the marsh at East Bridge. 45466

Just as you get into East Bridge you will find a public footpath sign on your left. If you want to make a short walk back to Dunwich, you can take this path. It will lead you past a ruined chapel, 47565 which Thomas observed was 'half-fallen over', and in which a pill-box was set up in the last war. The field footpath goes on to the wide sluice gates, and then along the sea wall which runs north to Dunwich and south to Sizewell.

In the sixteenth century, Sizewell was an important port and a base for the Icelandic fishermen. It was also a great smuggling centre. But its real power probably dates from earlier and less explicable causes. In a letter to his friend Charles Keen, the poet, Edward Fitzgerald, who spent almost his whole life in Suffolk, said: 'I, like you, always have, and from a small child have had, a mysterious feeling about Sizewell Gap.' The present atomic power station, like the microwave tower at Haddenham (see p.193), may be another 'needle of power'.

If you continue along the lanes and footpaths going south from East Bridge to Leiston Common at 156:456633, you will meet the first of several paths between here and Aldringham, which run to the east and take you to Sizewell and along the coast walk back to Dunwich.

Continue your journey south, past Crown Farm, where the lane becomes a 45862 footpath again. When you come to a convergence of paths, just north of the 46361 tumulus, take the path to the south-west; it will lead you round Aldringham golf course to the B1353, which takes you directly to Aldringham. Another tumulus lies south of the road, and a third near the south-west intersection of the crossroads at the centre of Aldringham.

You should now take the lanes for Snape Street. To reach the Youth Hostel at Blaxhall from there, you can choose between following the lane to the west just after you have passed the maltings, or continuing along the main road and joining the bridleway across Blaxhall Heath. This passes another tumulus and brings you to the Youth Hostel in the centre of the village by the post office.

If you are not going to Blaxhall, you can return to Dunwich from Snape Street by taking the path that goes east through Black Heath Wood to the A1094. You can then go into Aldeburgh and then follow the coast to Thorpeness, past Sizewell to Dunwich. If you do not want to visit Aldeburgh, then before you reach the town you can take the path across the golf course, on your right, and then across the nature reserve which will take you into Thorpeness. From there you can pick up the coastal path.

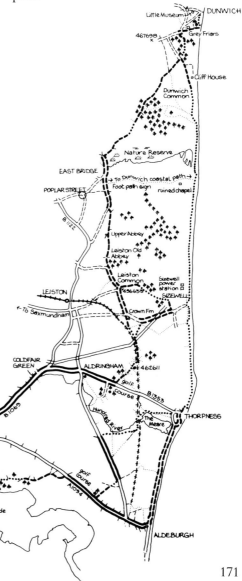

171

North-west from Dunwich

O.S. map 156

Two tumuli lie on either side of the alignment that runs north-west from Dunwich through Blythburgh church. A circuitous walk round Westwood marshes will enable you to visit them both. Start off by taking the path to the north just past Dunwich post office; and follow it between the woods and the sea. The path goes over the marshes to the 486737 old windmill, and across the marshes to the northern edge of the wood. Once clear of the wood, you will see the 453727 tumulus that lies to the west of the alignment.

Take the track which skirts the marshes to join the lane for Walberswick. You do not have to go into that village, for you 477742 will find a path running north on the eastern edge of a wood. After crossing The B1387, take the path along the southern edge of a wood. The tumulus lies at 156:474748. The path itself goes round the wide expanse of Blythburgh Mere and comes out just to the south of the church. It was to a church on this site that the body of King Anna was taken in 654 AD, after he had been killed in a battle against the Mercians. The battle itself took place on the site where Bulcamp now stands, a little to the west, on the road to Halesworth.

451753 Blythburgh church, standing on an island in the marshes, has an enormously spacious, uncluttered interior, in which I

172

have been told it is a delight to sing. The warm bricks of the floor have been left uncovered and across the ceiling spread the wide wings of wooden angels, looking all the better for being worn, and no doubt riddled with worm. Indeed, the whole church has aged in a marvellously mellow way. In mediaeval times it must have been like a fairground, if the one completely restored blue and crimson figure, hung around with tin foil (I am assured that that is no anachronism), was really repeated all over the church.

The significant places on the alignment between Blythburgh church and Ilketshall St Andrew are the remains of Blythburgh Priory; the moat at Mill Common (156:408819), to the west of Brampton; the castle mound to the west of Redisham; and the moat opposite 39883 Corner Farm, just to the south of Ilket- 38686 shall St Andrew itself.

The ruins of Blythburgh Priory lie just across the river from the church. Continue along the river bank until the second bridge, at which point you can head for the village of Blyford, once a centre 4276 for smugglers, who made their headquarters at the Queen's Head. Now proceed to Mill Common, passing Holton 41081 and following the path across an old airfield.

Before reaching Mill Common, you might well find it worth while to visit Westhall church. The inhabitants of this 42480 village according to Leonard P. Thompson in *Smugglers of The Suffolk Coast*, were deeply involved in smuggling enterprises; but, more important to our purposes, is the church itself – standing

church at Ilketshall St Andrew, which you can either reach by going directly along the lanes or by taking the field path from Back's Green.

386846

From Ilketshall St Andrew, you can either go east along the lanes to Beccles, where you can get a train to Norwich or Ipswich, or you can go west towards Bungay and the walks along the Waveney Valley. The third alternative is to start immediately to trace the alignment going south-west to Hoxne, which is outlined on p.176.

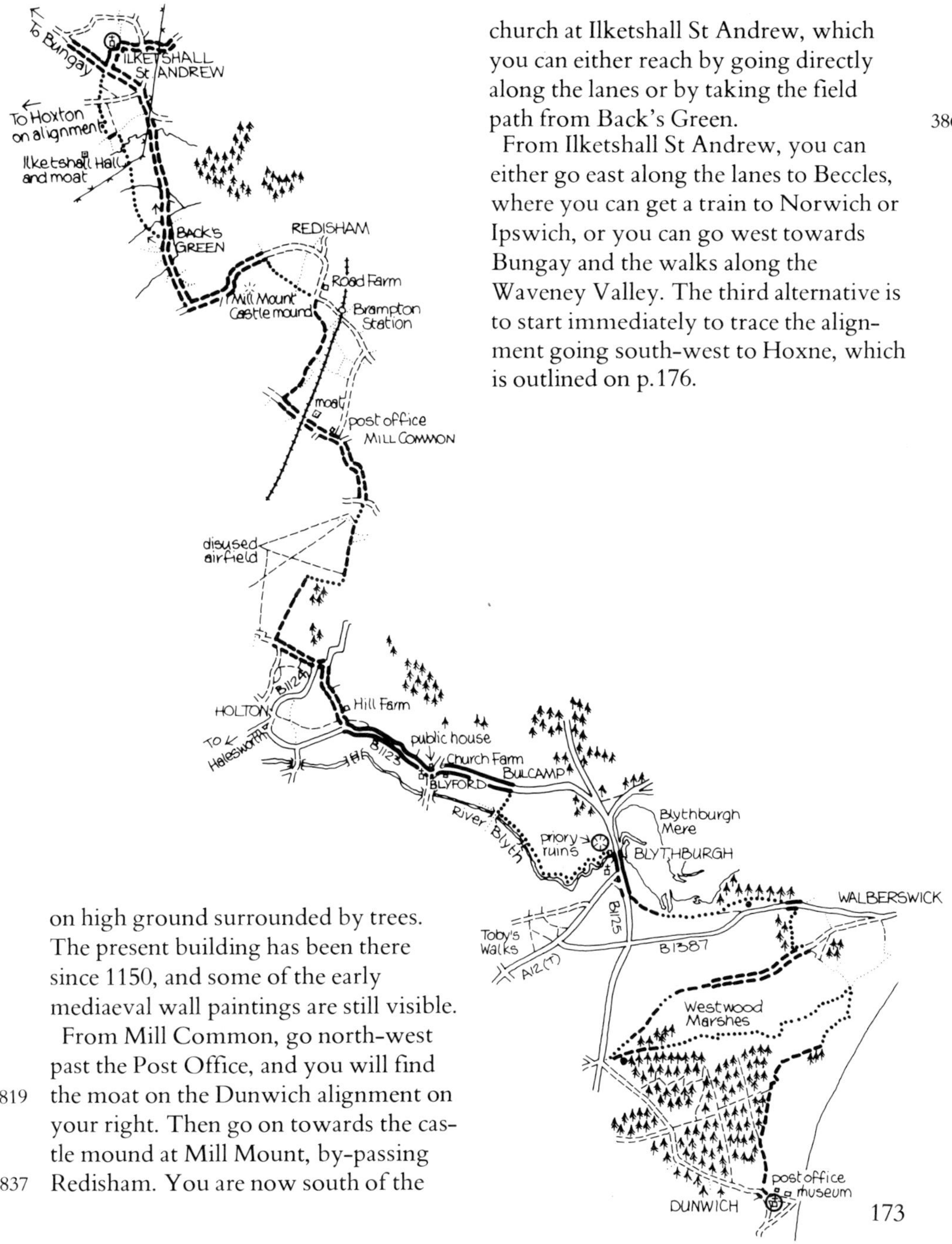

on high ground surrounded by trees. The present building has been there since 1150, and some of the early mediaeval wall paintings are still visible.

From Mill Common, go north-west past the Post Office, and you will find

408819   the moat on the Dunwich alignment on your right. Then go on towards the castle mound at Mill Mount, by-passing

398837   Redisham. You are now south of the

To Bungay
ILKETSHALL St ANDREW
To Hoxton on alignment
Ilketshall Hall and moat
BACK'S GREEN
REDISHAM
Road Farm
Mill Mount Castle mound
Brampton Station
moat
post office
MILL COMMON
disused airfield
HOLTON
B1124
Hill Farm
TO Halesworth
public house
B1123
Church Farm
BLYFORD
BULCAMP
River Blyth
priory ruins
BLYTHBURGH
Blythburgh Mere
WALBERSWICK
Toby's Walks
B1125
A12(T)
B1387
Westwood Marshes
post office museum
DUNWICH
173

The Waveney Valley

O.S. maps 156 and 144

From Bungay, the River Waveney runs south-west to Hoxne through a fairly steep valley and then flows over flat land almost due west into the Breckland. So the walks in this part are divided into two groups. In the first, I have followed the traces of three alignments running

239801 east of the river. They all converge on the moat by the round-towered St Andrew's church of Weybread, and run through an area (lying to the west of Stone Street, now the Halesworth to Bungay road) which is full of villages whose names all incorporate that of a saint. Tradition has it that the people of Ringsfield (a village between Bungay and Beccles) used to refer to the inhabitants of the 'Saint' villages as the Welsh – that is, strangers. It could be that for generations the Roman road was an actual divide between different races of people.

In the second group of walks, I have followed the walks along the course of the river from Hoxne, through Scole to Diss and the Waveney fens.

The alignments through Weybread
379873 start from Ilketshall St Andrew,
360887 Mettingham Castle ruins and Bungay
337897 parish church respectively. I shall take them in that order. Although there are occasional footpaths, you will find that long sections of these alignments have to be followed along lanes, for many of the paths have been ploughed over. The first point on the alignment from the hexagonal tower of the church at Ilketshall

31483? St Andrew is the moat at St Margaret, South Elmham, which you reach by crossing the Roman road of Stone Street (A144) and following the lane to Ilketshall St Margaret (another round-towered church). From there, go past St Peter's Hall (a farmhouse with chapel-shaped windows) to St Margaret, South Elmham. The moat stands just to the south of the church. Continue by footpath and lane in a south-westerly direc-

30783. tion past the ruined chapel and the mins-
271810 ter ruins and then on towards Withersdale Street. Now head for Mendham

262810 Priory, where you take the footpath to Weybread passing some farm buildings on the way. The footpath follows the alignment from the moat at St Margaret,

SYLEHAM

GREAT GREEN farmhouse castle remains &

Moat

HOXNE

WINGFIELD GREEN

post office

B1118

CHICKERING

EYE second hand bookshop open Friday and Sat

castle mound

B1117

South Elmham to the one at Weybread. The moat and church there lie at the end of the lane to the south-west of the village. From Weybread church, take the footpath going north and then you may follow the lanes to the church and moat of Hoxne.

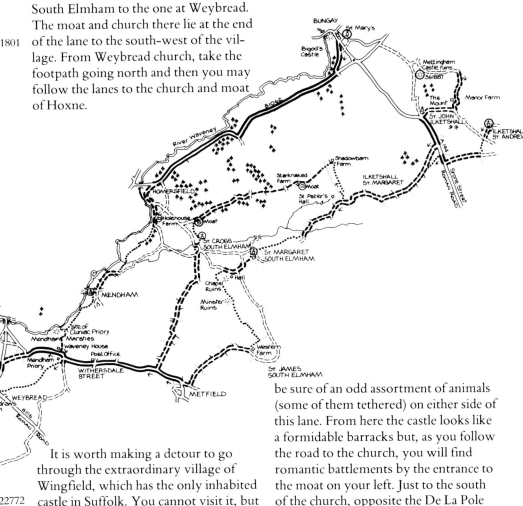

It is worth making a detour to go through the extraordinary village of Wingfield, which has the only inhabited castle in Suffolk. You cannot visit it, but to get the most imposing first view of it you should approach it from Wingfield Green, which you will reach by taking the lane from Weybread to Great Green.

Wingfield Green is a large expanse of common land, whose grazing rights are fully utilized by the surrounding families. This means that you can always be sure of an odd assortment of animals (some of them tethered) on either side of this lane. From here the castle looks like a formidable barracks but, as you follow the road to the church, you will find romantic battlements by the entrance to the moat on your left. Just to the south of the church, opposite the De La Pole Arms, is an eighteenth-century farmhouse built on the site of a chantry college, which was founded in the fourteenth century.

From Wingfield, the road to Hoxne (pronounced Hoxen) is the B1118. In the fourteenth century, when abbeys and priories were vying with each other to be chosen as places of pilgrimage, the tradition started that Edmund, king and martyr, was killed by the Danes at Hoxne. A marble cross stands on the site of the tree where he is supposed to have died.

Alternatively, you can go past Instead Manor House and follow the river path to the bridge at Syleham. From there, follow the lanes to Hoxne.

The next alignment starts from Mettingham Castle (156:360887) and goes 299842 through St Cross, South Elmham, by 147738 Weybread moat to the castle at Eye. Mettingham Castle ruins lie beside a moat, which can be reached by lanes from either Bungay or Ilketshall St Andrew, which are virtually equidistant.

From the castle ruins, go south by The 369880 Mount and moat by Manor Farm and 336854 then head for St Peter's Hall. A footpath and farm track will take you from here 326857 to the moat of Starknaked Farm, which is on the alignment that runs between the ruins of Mettingham Castle and St Cross, South Elmham.

I've yet to find the local explanation of its name, but it is probable that, like various farms with 'Hungry' names throughout the country, there must have been a time when it did very badly. Perhaps ill-luck dogged it because the farm buildings were actually set across the ley line, which has long been considered a siting that will bring dire misfortune to the inhabitants of any building. In Ireland, it is considered foolish to build a house over an old road, for the ghosts of bygone travellers will constantly pass through it, and this Celtic

176

belief may well be part of a general folk memory. However, a more practical explanation could be that it stood on a stretch of very poor land. The farm track continues through some woods and just after you pass a moat there is a footpath 2978 leading to the church of St Cross, South Elmham.

From this village, follow the lanes to the B1123 and Withersdale Street, then take the footpath to Weybread church and moat. The paths from Weybread to Hoxne are described above.

From Hoxne you can only reach Eye by road and so I advise taking the lane which runs west from the post office. Turn right when the lane is crossed by the B1117 and follow the road towards Eye. Just before you reach the town you will see the castle mound on your right, to the west of the church. Unfortunately, the mound is overgrown and almost inaccessible. In Eye there is an extremely good bookshop which specializes in books about East Anglia. Since it is only open on Fridays and Saturdays do take this into account when planning your visit.

The third alignment begins at Bungay, but before you leave the town there are two important places to visit. The first is the ruin of Baron Hugh Bigod's fortified castle in which, 'while Christ and all his angels slept', his people lived out the turbulent years of Stephen's reign. So strong was the castle that Holinshed had him boast:

Were I in my castle of Bungaye
Upon the water of Waveney,
I would ne set a button by the King of Cocknaye.

The entrance to the castle is kept locked, but you will find the keys at the nearby Swan Inn. The earthworks around it, which you can walk along at any time, are much earlier than Bigod's stout walls.

The second visit is to the unused priory church of St Mary to the north of the town. Here the black shuck – the ghostly calf-sized dog, who haunts the coasts of Norfolk and Suffolk – terrorized the congregation on August 4th, 1577; killed three people, and the body of one 'shrunk up as it were a piece of leather scorched in a hot fire'. This description comes from a pamphlet written at the time of the visitation, which also records that it took place during a violent thunderstorm 'the like whereof hath been seldom seene'. From Bungay the fearful hell-hound went to Blythburgh, where it killed a further three people and 'burnt the hand of a fourth'.

In St Mary's churchyard, you will find a glacial erratic standing about three feet high. It is known as the Druid's Stone, and legend has it that it has the power, if the right rituals are performed around it, to grant wishes or summon the devil.

To continue the walk from Bungay, you must take the B road that runs alongside the river to Homersfield. From there, follow the lanes to Holehouse Farm, which stands on the alignment and perhaps gets its name from the fact that a space was left in the building to allow the ley to pass through as sometimes happens with the so-called Lepers' Windows in churches which stand on a ley line. Now follow the footpath which runs by a stream and go into the village of Mendham, whose church of All Saints stands by the bridge across the Waveney, which here divides Suffolk from Norfolk. From the bridge, a footpath takes you over Mendham marshes and by the ruins of a twelfth-century Cluniac priory, where it becomes a right of way going south to Waveney House. It is 1·5 miles (2·4 km) to Weybread from here.

The next walk takes you just out of Suffolk into Norfolk. Using O.S. sheet 144, I have started the last walk along the Waveney from Scole, across the river from Hoxne, where the Roman road crossed the river. This Roman road was probably the most important highway in East Anglia, running from Colchester to Caistor St Edmund (see p.67). At Scole there was a posting station where travellers could change horses, and a Roman farm, which appears to have been abandoned in the second century AD. Opposite the post office in Scole, you will find a bridleway which leads to Frenze Hall and then past the woods and across the railway line to Diss.

It is well worth going into the town. The church stands high on a hill to the north of the river. It was here that the sixteenth-century poet John Skelton, during his time as vicar, held his illegitimate, naked baby out to the congregation and asked who could find blame in such innocence. Today Diss's most famous citizen is the novelist Doreen Wallace, now in her eighties, who still has a regular column in the *East Anglian Daily Press*. To farming people

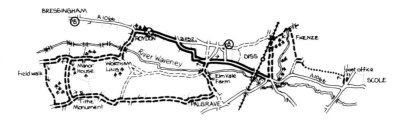

she is best known as the widow of R.H. Rash; and is renowned for her part in trying, by a most determined act of passive resistance, to put an end to the iniquitous tithe levy. She was not altogether successful, for tithing went on until the autumn of 1977, but the fact that it ended at all must be partly due to the stand the Rashes took in the 1930s. There is evidence of it at their old farm; and the story is told by Doreen Wallace herself in *The Tithe War*.

From Diss, I want to make one short walk, which is really an excuse to look at the Waveney fenlands. It starts off along the alignment that runs from the church at Diss, through the churches of Roydon and Bressingham, the ruins of the old church at Garboldisham (see p.108), across the Devil's Dyke to the west of Garboldisham Heath, to the crossing of the River Thet at St Chad's Well.

The first part of the alignment is partly covered by the A1066. Follow that road out of Diss, through Roydon, and then turn off for Wortham Ling. From here you can take the road through the fens, and past Manor House where the Rashes lived. Now you can either take the road going south or, if you want a field walk, carry on past that turning and take the farm track at 144:068797. Both routes bring you on to a lane which will take you to Palgrave. At 144:078787, you will see what looks like a very ordinary war memorial at the side of the road. In fact the war that is being remembered there is the Tithe War, and the homage is to 134 pigs and 15 bullocks which were impounded from the farm by the tithe bailiffs on February 22nd, 1934.

From Palgrave, you can go north across the Waveney and return to Diss.

0887•

0767•

Section 5

Important alignment points

Aldreth Causeway	154:438729
Balsham Church	154:588508
Barrington Church	154:397500
Belsar's Hill	154:423703
Boxworth Church	154:349645
Cambridge Castle	154:445592
Copley Hill	154:509531
Coton Church	154:409590
Cracknow Hill	154:383508
Denny Abbey	154:495688
Ely Cathedral	143:542803
Great Eversden Church	154:366533
Haddenham Water Tower	143:467753
Hockwold Church	143:725880
Littleport	143:565869
Little Eversden Church	154:374533
Little Thetford Church	143:532764
Mark's Grave	154:595483
Money Hill Tumulus	154:407515
Reach (end of Devil's Dyke)	154:568661
Rampton (Giant's Hill)	154:431681
Sawston Church	154:488493
Shippea Hill	143:664846
Soham Causeway	154:697729
Southery ruined church	143:624948
Strethall Church	154:485398
Swaffham Prior	154:568639
Wandlebury Hill Fort	154:495534
Waterbeach Church	154:498651
Whittlesford Church	154:474486
Worsted Lodge	154:528519

Section 5: Cambridge and the Fens

Gods, saints and engineers

O.S. maps 143, 154

On a hillside in an undulating wooded area some 3·7 miles (6 km) south-east of Cambridge, the figures that made up the trinity of the Old Religion are engraved in the chalk. The shapes of Gog, Magog, and Wandil (the East Anglian devil who swallows the springtime) were rediscovered by T.C. Lethbridge during the course of an excavation in the 1950s; but, as with so many other chalk hillside figures, nobody knows exactly how or when they came to be there. Yet, during the last millennium, there have been records of their existence and of the rituals attached to them, many degraded into the form of merry- making.

It would be interesting to know if they were there when, some time in the fourth century BC, the Iceni built their fort on Wandlebury Hill, creating a defensive earthwork enclosing some fifteen acres, which was largely destroyed in the eighteenth century when Lord Godolphin built his mansion there and laid out his parklands.

At least up to Roman times, and probably long after, Wandlebury was both a religious site and a strategic military installation. Scholars believe that the Iceni set up their fort here as an urgent defence against the expansion of the Belgic Celts from the south. There is much archaeological evidence that fierce fighting took place in this area. Later,

there was a new enemy for Boadicea's people, and the earthworks known as war ditches at Cherry Hinton probably date from one of the stands which the Iceni made against the Roman invaders.

It seems natural that the trinity on the hillside should preside over conflict, for although they are nature deities, connected with the rituals of the seasons and the fertility of the land, the vestige of a chariot discovered in the carving suggests a link with energy that can be channelled to both good and evil purposes. It points to a link with either the chariot of the sun, or the horse goddess Epona.

This is borne out by a mediaeval legend of Wandlebury, which tells that long ago the fort was ruled by a mysterious horseman, who rode round the hill at night on a great black stallion. Anyone ho wanted to challenge him had to ride to the hill when the moon was full, and call out: 'Knight to knight, come forth.' No one dared to make this challenge, until Sir Osbert, a Norman knight jealous of his own reputation, decided to brave the encounter. So he called out the Knight of Wandlebury, and to his surprise and great satisfaction managed to unseat him. But as Sir Osbert was triumphantly leading the black horse back to Cambridge, the fallen knight threw his lance and pierced his thigh.

And although he managed to get the stallion back to the city and stabled there, by the morning it had disappeared. Every year thereafter the wound on his thigh opened and bled afresh.

This story must be an echo of the initiation rites that took place on the hill. There is also a rather amusing coda to it. In the eighteenth-century landscaped grounds in the area of the hill fort, is the grave of a famous racehorse of the period, whose remote descendants may even now be training on nearby Newmarket Heath.

If you look north from the top of Wandlebury Hill on a fine day, it is possible to see the spire of Ely Cathedral, the Christian centre of this region. East Anglia has two powerful saints, to whom through the centuries the people have turned in times of trouble. For centuries Edmund, king and martyr, was the one who was most reverenced. But some three hundred years before he was killed by the Danes, the twice-married virgin princess, Etheldreda, daughter of the Christian King Anna of the Saxons, founded her abbey on the fenland island of Ely. Here she and Anna's other holy daughters lie buried and the Normans started to build the cathedral we see today.

Ely stands on one of the highest points of the fenland and for centuries it was virtually an island, approachable only by narrow causeways across the marshes – whose whereabouts, as you will remember from the story of Hereward the Wake, were kept a closely guarded military secret.

Yet even in Hereward's time the fens around Ely were made to be somehow productive. There is documentary evidence that in the eleventh century AD the Isle of Ely boasted nineteen plough teams, and for centuries the black, stagnant waters of the marshes yielded great quantities of eels from which the city probably got its name. And the discovery of salt pans in the fens suggests that monastic landowners were able to preserve and store this food.

In this section, I have dealt mainly with the stretch of fenland which runs south from Ely to Cambridge and east to the western edge of the Breckland. This area, formed after the last Ice Age, is composed of the peat which condensed in the shallow marshes. In the Ely region five buried forests have been traced – made up of oak, fir, birch, yew, alder, willow and pine. And among the animal skeletons preserved in the peat are the bones of aurochs (the original wild cattle), wolves, beavers, brown bears, otters, weasels, pelicans and swans. I owe these lists to C.P. Chatwin's H.M.S.O. booklet of the area, published in 1937.

Peat has one important characteristic for anyone wanting to construct the history of a landscape in his imagination. In most places, you have to remember that the ground you are walking on is considerably higher than the land which bore the imprint of our ancestors' boots, even in comparatively recent times. With peat, the story is reversed. The intervention of human intelligence and skill in draining the fens to make fertile fields has obviously caused the peat to shrink. This progress has been much accelerated in recent years.

In 1932 the depth of the fenland peat was calculated to be about 11·3 feet (3·4 m), but even by the time Chatwin came to make his study, improved cultivation had brought it down to 6 feet (1·8 m) and in many areas it levelled off at 3 feet (0·9 m).

It is important to keep this shrinkage in mind when you visit Wicken Fen, for this area, which has been preserved in the state of the early fenlands, has to have water artificially pumped up to it now to keep the peat at a viable level.

The story of the farming of the fens really starts from the Bronze Age, although there is plenty of evidence that nomadic hunters and fishermen were making a living here long before that. But it is to the men of the late Bronze Age, living in what are now the Cambridgeshire fens, that we owe the first traces in this country of any sort of road-building. Their achievement is enshrined in the bushwood and timber causeways that have been found in narrow stretches of fen between islands of higher ground. To me these feats of engineering, and the human ingenuity that went into them, are just as important as the numinous powers of the trinity on the Gog Magog Hills, or the miracles performed by holy Etheldreda. For the natural and the mystical cannot be separated, and one interest in walking in the fens is to see how the causeways and the ley alignments so often coincide.

The first large-scale draining of the fenlands took place in Roman times, no doubt with the aid of Iceni slave labour. Aerial photographs show that some two thousand years ago most of the region was cultivated in small fields; and to prove the success of this arable farming the remains of bread wheat have been found in the fen near Littleport, to the east of Ely.

The greatest feat of Roman engineering was the construction of the Car Dyke, some time in the middle of the first century AD. It was used both for navigation and as a way of carrying food north to the garrisons at Lincoln and York. A short stretch of the Car Dyke can be seen near Cottenham and we shall take a look at it on one of the walks, but it is sadly neglected and silted up now. Its state is a symbol of what happened right through the fenland, when the Romans withdrew the legions and the conquering Saxons, superstitiously avoiding whatever the Romans had left, allowed the natural fen to re-establish itself. So for a thousand years the fens were a virtual wasteland, and looked much as the region of Wicken Fen looks today. Small island areas like Ely were cultivated, and the population existed on what could be farmed there and on the eels, fish and fowl they caught in the marshes. It was subsistence living, but it bred a tough race, the 'fen tigers', who protested violently when in the seventeenth century Dutch engineers, directed by Cornelius Vermuyden, were invited by Charles I to set about reclaiming the land. This meant destroying the wild life of the swamps on which the people of the fens lived.

The Dutch project was undertaken with the financial backing of the Duke of Bedford and his Gentlemen Adventurers, and was completed in 1653. It is that feat of engineering which is largely responsible for the landscape we shall see on these walks, and for the naming of Adventurers' Fen.

In the first part of this section, I have looked at the ancient roads and the alignments running south from Cambridge on the relatively high ground; in the second part, I have followed the alignment between Cambridge and Ely, and traced parts of the pilgrims' paths running across the eastern fens towards the Breckland.

When Alfred Watkins' son Allen lived in Cambridge, the older man worked out many alignments in this area, and most of the alignments I have used have been based on these. Although we shall not walk in the western fens, I like to remember what Watkins said of John Bunyan, that Bedfordshire exponent of the narrow way. The geography of *The Pilgrims' Progress* is not entirely based on the Bible, he averred, for 'the stone causeways through the morass he did not find there but in his own watery and native land, with just such straight causeways as he pictures.'

Ely Cathedral

Part A
Cambridgeshire (south)

Wandlebury and the Via Devana   O.S. map 154

495534 The Iron Age hill fort of Wandlebury stands to the east of the A604 Haverhill – Colchester road, to the south of the city of Cambridge and just past the golf course. This area, which was the scene of fierce battles for several centuries, has been the focus of much academic wrangling in recent years. The current squabble was occasioned by an article which appeared in the *Sunday Telegraph* of March 19th, 1978, describing the researches undertaken by Tim O'Brien of Thaxted. His work led him to agree with the conclusion put forward by Alfred Watkins that the earthworks of Wandlebury outline a solar and lunar observatory which was in existence long before the hill fort.

O'Brien also discovered a series of stones tracing a line from the fort to Hatfield Forest. His views are strongly contested by William Clark, the resident warden at Wandlebury, and by Sylvia Beamon, of the Cambridgeshire Preservation Society, which owns and administers the area. Whatever the truth of O'Brien's contentions, there can be no doubt at all that people lived on this hill long before the Iron Age. Many Neolithic finds have been made in the area. But the great mystery of the chalk figures, who must have given the Gog Magog Hills their name, has yet to be fully resolved.

T.C. Lethbridge gives his own account of the excavation and the discovery of the figures in *Gog Magog: the Buried Gods* and in *Witches*; he claims that the area within an hour's walk of Wandlebury Camp 'contains more traces of the old gods than any area I have yet examined'. One of these traces is at Whittlesford Church, described in the section on the Icknield Way (p.119).

The outlines which Lethbridge uncovered in the chalk represent images of a male and a female deity, together with an indication of a third creature, which he took to represent Wandil. In recent years these figures have become overgrown again, and until a few months ago the hillside on which they stand was used as a children's slide. Happily, they are now at least preserved by a net of ropes, but they are still barely decipherable among the scrub and grasses.

If you go to Wandlebury by the A road, you will find the site of the chalk figures, now rather patronizingly known as 'the Lethbridge diggings', on the hillside to your right. As you leave the car park and walk round the earthworks to the main entrance of the fort's enclosure, where the eighteenth-century mansion stands, you will see the orange nylon net protecting Lethbridge's figures on the slope beside you.

There is another way of reaching

Wandlebury. It is to approach it from Fulbourn, which lies to the south-east of Cambridge beyond Cherry Hinton. From Fulbourn, take the road running to the low hills in the west, and you will come to a wide, sandy track running to your left at 494547. This is the start of the Via Devana to the south of Cambridge. It follows the course of the Roman road which is supposed to have linked Colchester and Chester, and which to the north-west of Cambridge lies under the A604 (Huntingdon Road).

Although this is an obvious Roman road, which was given its present name by Dr Mason (Professor of Geology at Cambridge, 1734-62), who first put forward the hypothesis that the road stretched to Chester, it has a history that extends on either side of the Roman era.

Watkins believed it was a prehistoric route aligned through Cambridge castle mound. Its later history is summed up by its popular name of Wool Street, and it has been suggested that this refers to wolves, or to a Saxon thane named Wulfa, but it must obviously reflect the connection with the wool trade throughout the Middle Ages. This traffic is further remembered in the

Wandlebury

528519 name of Worsted Lodge, which stands at the place where the track crosses the site of an even older road – the part of the Icknield Way that now lies under the A11.

When you start to walk on this track from the Fulbourn road, you will soon find that you are heading straight to the south-east. You will come to a lesser 505535 path going off to your right. Take the

signposted way through the woods (which are carpeted with white violets in the spring) and you will come to the earthworks surrounding the fort.

The Roman road itself, in this part about ten yards wide, makes a very pleasant walk to the south, with several opportunities for making a circular tour using the Icknield Way and Fleam Dyke. These routes are described in Section 3 (p.120).

Just before the lane at 595484, you will find a round tumulus standing in the

186

field to your right. It has a low, brick wall to one side of it. This is presumably Mark's Grave, which seems to be incorrectly marked on the O.S. map as lying on the other side of the road. I have not been able to trace any particular history to this tumulus, which would account for how it acquired its name, but I would guess that 'Mark' denotes a landmark rather than signifying a named individual, although Watkins thought it was the traditional burial place of a suicide with a stake through the heart. However, he gives no alignments going through this point, although he usually pays considerable attention to crossroads in working out ley lines, and this particular crossroads seems to have been an important one, for there is a trace of an earthwork and ditch across the Roman road before it climbs the hill going south-east towards Streetly End.

There are three alignments that I can suggest from here. They are:
a) Going north-west through Mark's Grave to the Gog Magog figures at Wandlebury, to the megalith which

99590
49645
stands on the access path to Coton church, through to Boxworth church, from where there is a footpath running parallel to the Roman road beneath the A604.

488493
b) If you take the line west from Mark's Grave through Sawston church, when it would cross Ashwell Street, you can follow it over Rowley's Hill to Barrington 397500 church, which is the point from which Watkins drew an alignment going to the earthworks to the south of Ely. This alignment runs partly along the course of the Roman Akeman Street, and it is one we shall touch on again in the next part of this section.

c) Going north from the tumulus 588508 through Balsham church, the alignment from Mark's Grave runs through the 578569 crossroads at Six Mile Bottom (which is on the central section of the Icknield Way), through to the twin churches of 568639 Swaffham Prior, and on to the northerly 568662 end of the Devil's Dyke at Reach.

When you continue from Mark's Grave south-east along the Via Devana, you find that the Roman road which started out so grandly from Wandlebury, with a width of some 30 feet (9·1 m) has shrunk to a narrow path; when it comes out into a field, some of the sections of the path are so muddy as to be virtually impassable, but it is worth persisting. It leads on to the road that runs between Streetly End and Horseheath. At this 615477 point, there is not so much as a public footpath sign to indicate the Roman road. Ideally the right of way along the Via Devana continues across the road towards Haverhill, but you must be warned that parts of this stretch of the way have now been ploughed up. If you do succeed in making your way through, you will come out on the lane that leads to Withersfield. The Roman 637472 road again seems to become the A604, for south-east of Haverhill there is a tumulus beside the main road, which 688444 suggests that this section of the A604 was a continuation of a main thoroughfare – most probably the Via Devana going towards Halstead and Colchester.

187

The Mare Way

O.S. map 154

The Mare Way (the name simply means boundary) is a ridgeway track going along the top of the low hills to the south of Great Eversden. It probably once stretched over Orwell Hill in the south, a site once famous for its maypole ceremonies, and then went east by Cracknow Hill to the tumulus at Money Hill south of Haslingfield; but unfortunately there is no longer any trace of the track on that part of the ridge which lies between the stretch of Roman road covered by the A603 and the A10 to the south of it.

A good way to start this walk is by taking the train from Cambridge to Foxton, and then going along the lane towards Barrington church, which as

4094

3975

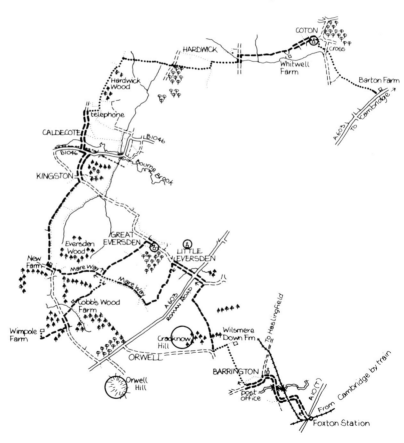

188

Alfred Watkins points out in *Archaic Tracks Round Cambridge* aligns with the earthworks to the south of Ely. That ley line runs along part of Akeman Street and through Leckhampton House to the south of Cambridge.

8507

Take the footpath from Barrington post office to Wilsmere Down Farm and continue northwards over Cracknow Hill and across the A603 to Little Eversden. The name of Eversden indicates a boar's wood, or boar's hill, and T.C. Lethbridge believed it could refer to a boar effigy carved in the chalk of the hill. The path before Little Eversden climbs fairly steeply past a disused quarry, to the only bit of the ancient Mare Way which still exists. The path runs along the hill-top. As you follow it, you will find a ditch and a bank on your left. Across it are traces of a hedge, one lone oak tree and several intermittent large stones.

53

2528

There is a slight valley between Great and Little Eversden, which runs to the north-east, and as you stand above it on the ridge you can see both churches which, as Watkins noted, align with each other on a ley line that stretches to the tumulus at Copley Hill in the wood to the west of the Via Devana and extends as far east as Carlton church. At the meeting of the paths, you have a choice to make. The one on your left goes to

53525

Cobb's Wood Farm, and eventually brings you to the parkland around Wimpole Hall. The one on your right takes you down towards Great Eversden village. It is a wide farm track which becomes a lane passing a pig farm; then it joins the lane that links the two villages. You might like to visit Great Eversden's tiny Jacobean church, before picking up the bus for Cambridge.

365533

There remains one other path on the ridgeway. It goes straight ahead and is a continuation of the Mare Way. Go along it for a very little way and then take the farm road past New Farm to Kingston. You may then continue north and follow the path around Hardwick Wood, then due east to Coton. From here you can take the river path to Barton Farm, just outside Cambridge. I have yet to find the significance of this path. It seems to be a deliberate siting, on account of the distribution of the puddingstones in Coton village; the main one stands by the entrance to Rectory Farm just west of the church. There is an ancient cross on the lane going south. Whitewell, the name of a farm to the west of Coton, suggests both a spring and possibly the route of a salt track. Watkins gives much weight to place names which include the word 'white'. I suspect that the history of this path would be worth investigating.

337527

3557

4058

427576

Part B.
The Fens

Aldreth Causeway

O.S. maps 154, 143

The route to Ely from Cambridge across Aldreth Causeway follows part of the alignment which Watkins noted as running from Strethall church (which is mentioned in the next section on p.218). to the Great Ouse. We cannot be sure that this was the way that William the Conqueror's army came when he tried to storm Ely, but popular tradition has it that it was so. We can be certain, however, that this was a trading route, and one frequently used by pilgrims.

Begin by taking the road from Cambridge to Histon. There is quite a frequent bus service. The original track, which runs slightly to the west of the alignment, starts in a very unpromising way at the edge of the town just north of Histon church and it is not easy to find. The road you want to reach is called Clay Street. To get to it, take the road going west from Histon village green, past the King William IV pub, until you reach a modern housing estate. The path you want starts close to Barrow Road, which comes on to Clay Street, just to the south of the one old house in the area. It is by that house that the path starts. There is no public footpath sign to indicate the start of this ancient track, which runs across country to Rampton, only a civic notice carrying a prohibition about the disposal of rubbish.

The track, although very muddy, is an easy one to follow. It goes straight to the north-west, and comes out opposite the castle ruins known as Giant's Hill. These are most shapely earthworks, but unfortunately they lie almost entirely in private grounds. If the path by the dyke is very overgrown, you may have to reach Rampton village by following the farm tracks to the north.

Turn into the village of Rampton and you will see the thatched roof of the eleventh-century church of All Saints, which stands back from the road. It is worth walking up the lane to see it. Inside you will find Saxon coffin lids, which prove that it stands on the site of an even earlier church. Even more relevant to a main route to a causeway, there are remnants of a wall painting of St Christopher. This figure is also found in Willingham church, and I like to think that both were painted as a protection for pilgrims from Cambridge to Ely.

And not only for pilgrims; it is always tempting to wonder how much these old ways were used by tramps right up to modern times. At Rampton the thought is particularly pertinent, for a board, now in the Cambridge Folk Museum (opposite the castle mound) once warned wanderers in Rampton: that 'All vagrants who are seen begging in this town will be apprehended and punished as the law directs.'

436643

4326

4286

190

From Rampton, the way to Belsar's Hill Fort lies north of the village green, which still has the base of its old stone cross. You will follow a lane taking you across heavily cultivated land, which soon becomes a field path – leading to the road which runs past Belsar's Hill. It is supposed to take its name from the Norman commander who led the campaign against Hereward. The hill fort stands just to the east of Willingham. This was the Wyvelyngham of Saxon times, owned by Uva (a good man who lived in the tenth century and is still properly remembered in the church), who gave the village lands 'to God and his dear virgin Etheldreda . . . to be held of right on perpetuity'.

From Belsar's Hill, the path leads to the causeway. It runs right through the centre of the fort (once again there is no footpath sign to guide you). Although no conclusive evidence of Norman use has been found at this earthwork, the very fact that the track runs through the centre of it (a most unusual arrangement) suggests that it must have been set up in connection with a river crossing. The land on either side of the path is now in private hands. It belongs to Chivers Jellies, who have a factory in Histon, and who use the field to graze great, white, Percheron horses, and these beautiful French beasts are the nearest you are likely to get to any relics of William's army.

The path is extremely muddy. Near the road it has unfortunately been used as a tip, and the part that goes through the ditch surrounding the inner earthwork gets so flooded that, in some seasons, it can be quite impassable without waders. The track heads across peaty land towards the river. If you choose to walk this way in dry, windy weather, you may encounter the opposite hazard of mud. I have happily never experienced a 'fen blow', but I am told it can be like a desert sandstorm.

In *Hereward the Wake*, Charles Kingsley imagines the Norman army going along this path to the river, where they had planned to build the bridge that would take them to Ely. He saw them carrying 'timber and faggots cut from all the hills that they might bridge the black half mile'. As they walked, they made 'a narrow firm path through the reeds and down to the brink of the Ouse, if brink it could be called, where the water, rising and falling a foot or two each tide, covered the floating peat for many yards, before it sank into a brown depth of bottomless slime. They would make a bottom for themselves by driving piles'.

The archaeologist T.C.Lethbridge went to look for those piles. He did some excavations at the causeway, in an attempt to find out the truth of the story of William's crossing, and describes his dig in *Merlin's Island* (1948): 'I dug trenches all round the old bridge site at Aldreth Causeway over West River. It was very hot and the peat stank abominably. Men came and looked at us and remarked that we would soon get quinzies and all our silver would turn yellow in our pockets. Neither of these misfortunes overtook us. We found no trace of the Normans, but we found a

thirteenth-century hythe with pottery
and bones of animals including a bear.
That was all.'

438722   The causeway over the dyke is now an

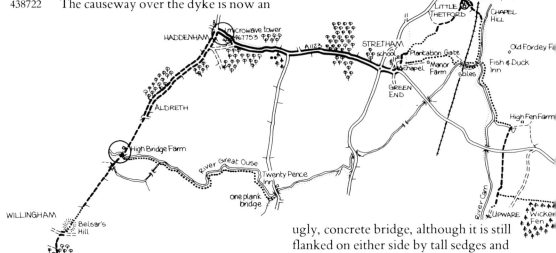

ugly, concrete bridge, although it is still
flanked on either side by tall sedges and
reeds. The bridge is raised high enough
over the water to allow the pleasure
boats to go along the river. The towpath
here runs along the south bank of the
river and, at this point, should you
decide not to make for Ely, but to join
one of the routes nearer to Cambridge,
which are described in the next group of
walks, you can turn towards the east.
This will give you a riverside walk of
just over 2 miles (3·2 km). But you need
to be warned that to reach the road at the
end of the walk, you will have to cross a
shaky, single-plank bridge over Cot-   47870
tenham Lode – safe enough if you are
not too heavy. If you risk that – or swim
– you come out opposite the Twenty
Pence Inn.

   However, if you decide to take the path
over to Aldreth, once across the bridge
there is a pleasant green lane. Just after

the derelict buildings of High Bridge Farm, you will find, in late summer, a thick bank of the deep pink spears of persicaria, grown to twice their usual size, nurtured on the rich fenland soil. On the horizon in front of you, slightly to your right, is our modern equivalent of the standing stone and the holy spring (see Tom Graves' *Needles of Stone*). On the high ground beside the A1123, a microwave tower and a water tower stand close together.

A dyke runs close to the west of the lane from the causeway, but the high bank screens it from view, and it becomes even more hidden by trees as you approach Aldreth itself. Kingsley thought the name was simply a contraction of Audrey's Hythe (or quay), for Audrey is quite a usual corruption of Etheldreda, founder of Ely. He also relates that St Audrey's Well once stood on the slope above the village, and it could be this spring that gave rise to the siting of the water tower.

The road through the village brings you past some modern housing, in an estate courteously and aptly named Hereward the Wake Close, just off the road to the village of Haddenham. Here there is a much restored, thirteenth-century church, standing on the site where Etheldreda's Celtic steward, Ovin, built his cross in 673, the year of the founding of the monastery at Ely. This modest village cross now stands in the cathedral nave.

To get to Ely along the old roads from Haddenham, you follow the main road to Stretham. A Roman road is said to have once gone that way, but being neglected and unused throughout the Dark Ages it sank beneath the peat. Make for Stretham chapel – the turning is off a heavily cultivated piece of fenland, known as Green End, which lies to the south. There is a small lane to the north of the chapel, which takes you to the old, steep-roofed houses at Plantation Gate. They stand at the entrance to the private road leading to Manor Farm. This road, although prohibited to cars, is a public footpath. It takes you alongside the edges of the fields which lie to the north.

As you continue east you will see the spire of Little Thetford church. When the path turns towards the north, you will find that it is flanked by a narrow dyke which you will be able to cross by a farm causeway. The path then runs through fields to the point where the railway, the Great Ouse and the Cam converge. There is not much to mark this meeting place. The Great Ouse is crossed by a high, derelict, wooden bridge, which brings you to the railway line. To get over that, which you do at your own risk – it is a busy track, but you can see for a long distance in both directions – you will find a pair of stiles.

For the purposes of following the old road to Ely, and considering how the Normans might have tried to make the crossing on to the island, you don't need to go over water or rail. What you should do is go under the railway arch on your left, and climb the bank of the river cutting to your right. This will bring you on to the tow path that follows the western bank of the Great Ouse

WICKEN

4675

521746

5374

535746

into Ely, passing Little Thetford (once known as Thetford-in-the-Isle) on the way.

There are, however, three reasons for crossing the bridge. The first is to visit the Fish and Duck Inn, a very up-stage hostelry, designed for the use of racehorse owners from Newmarket and American airmen from Lakenheath. Unless your pocket comes into those categories, you'd better miss it out – a pity, because it's on a beautiful site, and in the old days when it was a real fen pub a ferry took you back across the river.

The second reason for crossing the bridge is to take the lane that runs along the western bank of the Cam, towards Wicken Fen. At the A1123 you leave the river and follow the paths to the edge of the National Trust fen. From there, you can either go north into Wicken village, or south-east to the official entrance to the fen. You are asked to sign the visitors' book before you go into the enclosure. The fen is a marvellous piece of historical and natural conservation, for the sluggish black dykes and thick banks of rushes you see here must be much like the fenland that William had to get his army across. For me, one of its most fascinating present-day aspects is its colonies of pink and white orchids.

The third reason for going on to the bridge and walking round towards the inn, where the two rivers meet, is to look at the alternative route which William might have attempted in getting his men to Ely. T.C. Lethbridge, disheartened by his work at Aldreth, looked at the alternative causeways and based his

194

researches on the chronicle *De Gestis Herwardi Saxonis*, in which the monastic writer affirms that the distance King William had to cover over marshy ground was half a mile (804 m). At Aldreth the distance is much more. But at this point it is considerably less, and not only the old tradition of the ferry at the Fish and Duck Inn, but also the name of Old Fordey Farm, slightly to the north-east, indicates that this must once have been a regular crossing point. The other sign we shall come to as we follow the tow path north towards Little Thetford. T.C. Lethbridge wrote an account of his researches in this area and his speculations about William's manoeuvres in *Merlin's Island* (1948).

The tow path that runs along the western side of the Great Ouse will give you one of the most beautiful views of Ely Cathedral, which seems at this distance to emerge straight from the fen.

You will also notice that the inaccessible path on top of the opposite bank, to the east, is much clearer than the one you are walking along. If the high clumps of stinging nettles get too much for you, as they may if you walk this way in high summer, you will be glad to know that there is a wide green field path at the foot of the bank, following its course towards Little Thetford. The price you pay for taking it is the loss of the view of Ely. Whatever you do though, climb the bank once more when the field track comes to the bit of dead road from the railway level crossing outside Little Thetford. The little bit of land across the river at this point is known as Chapel

537723

564704

5357

Hill, and it is probably here that the hermit lived, whose worldly task would be to keep the causeway in repair and to help travellers on their way. There is no crossing now, nor unfortunately is there a way into Ely from Little Thetford.

Your choice is either to follow the river-bank path to the city, to go across through Little Thetford to the A10 for Ely or Cambridge, or to walk back to Stretham through the fields. If you choose either of the two latter courses, it is just worth taking a look at the lost footpath to Ely. Just past the village church, you will find a path on your right by house number 33. It takes you to the playing fields of the little village, and there stops. At the north end of the playing fields there is a ditch spanned by a now well-overgrown, beautiful, arched brick bridge. Beside the dyke is a high, impenetrable hedge, and the field the other side has been ploughed right to the limit.

The field path to Stretham starts immediately opposite the lane by number 33. It is a pleasant, wide, green lane running through the fields, whose hedges gradually reassert themselves as you get further to the south. When it nears the village it becomes a wide cinder track.

Wicken Fen

The abbeys to the south and east

O.S. map 154

At Exning, just outside Newmarket, where tradition has it that St Etheldreda was born, a man dreamt that the martyr King Edmund, killed by the pagan Danes, told him of a road that once ran from Fordham Abbey over Soham Causeway and which should be renewed as far as Ely Cathedral. Alfred Watkins, who told this story, did not add that most of that alignment is covered by a main road, now the A142. It is useless for walking.

I have found that the best thing is to follow the road (by bus if necessary) from Ely to Soham, where Felix of Burgundy founded an abbey. From there you can take a footpath to Wicken village. (See p.194 for a description of the National Trust's enclosure of Wicken Fen.) To continue the walk, you take the footpath that runs along the northern edge of the fen, reached by the lane running south-west of the village, and follow it to the Cam, where you go along the tow path to Clayhythe, crossing by the bridge which leads past a small, not too flamboyant, motel.

From the church in Waterbeach village Watkins drew an alignment to the moat that lies south of Landbeach, through Oakington church to Noon Folly Farm (384647). One of the most interesting things in Waterbeach church is the sculpture of two cherubs, one of whom is

196

blowing a trumpet. It comes from Denny Abbey about 2 miles (3·2 km) to the north. The abbey was used as a farmhouse for many years, but it has now been stripped back to its original structure and is in the care of the Department of the Environment.

Because of the barracks and the airfield to the north-west of Waterbeach, there are unfortunately no footpaths from the village to the abbey, although there is reported to be an underground tunnel. Tales of underground passages are quite common in East Anglia, despite the fact that, except in the solid chalk belt, it seems very unlikely that anything other than a carefully constructed drainage system could exist for very long inside the marsh. However, the tales are always worth listening to. I believe them to be the folk memories of the aquastats (the term used by Guy Underwood in *Patterns of the Past* to refer to the watercourses, which run beside the ley lines, which I discussed in the general introduction) that were known to have run beside the ley lines. The other tunnel from Denny Abbey is supposed to run as far as Bulmer Bridge on the Newmarket Road out of Cambridge, where a leper chapel stood. The gentlemen who told me about that one said that a canary which had been put down into the tunnel 'came up dead', so no excavations were undertaken.

So, from Waterbeach, if you cannot face the long road walk to Denny Abbey, you can return to Cambridge by following Watkins' alignment to Landbeach. To do this, go first into Landbeach. You will find the moat alignment on your left just after the crossroads. Follow the road as it bends sharply to the south-west covering a stretch of the Roman Akeman Street, which in the north lies under the A10. Going to the south it soon becomes a farm road, leading to King's Hedges on the outskirts of Cambridge. Just before you reach the railway, you must turn left and make your way through side streets to the city.

If you want to visit Denny Abbey from Waterbeach, head for the A10 north of the village. Look for the Roman canal, the southern section of Car Dyke, which connected Cambridge with Lincoln. This channel, which was probably dug with great labour by Iceni slaves, was the first effective drainage of the fens that we know of, is now choked by weeds and litter as it comes up to the road. To walk beside it for a little way, you must take the public footpath.

Denny Abbey's appearance, like that of a great stone barn, is unlike any other abbey ruins I have encountered. It is a reminder of how the abbey could have been used as a farmhouse for so many years. The main altar of the church, however, and many of the cloisters connecting the dormitories and refectories are outlined by fragments of wall between carefully mown grass, in the way

to which we are accustomed with public ruins.

In the mid-twelfth century, Denny was a cell of the Abbey of Ely, inhabited by the Benedictine monks. This could only have been for a few years, for in 1170 the building and its adjacent grounds were taken over by the Knights Templar who (as we shall see in Section 6) seem to have had a great interest in shaping the landscape around them, for occult religious purposes as well as for the practical ends of increasing their great wealth. The abbey was held by the Knights Templar and used by them mainly as a hospital for members of their own order, until they were suppressed at the beginning of the fourteenth century. The suppression was partly occasioned by the Church's jealousy of the Templars' wealth, but the instrument that was used to get them disbanded was the accusation of heresy. The particular heretical behaviour that seems to have frightened the people of Cambridgeshire was their habit of exhuming their dead after three years, and dividing the bones into several pits.

For thirty years after the Templars left, the abbey seems to have been empty; then, in 1338, it was taken over by the extraordinary Countess of Pembroke who, although not a professed religious, lived in the position of abbess to the Franciscan Minoresses (Poor Clares) whom she caused to be removed from their abbey at Waterbeach.

There is no charge for going into the abbey, although you are not allowed to do so without a guide. It is worth it, for

197

the remains of the walls and staircases which lay hidden for so long by the farm rooms have now been completely uncovered, and no traces of modern domestic use remain, apart from a rather heavy, early Victorian, iron fireplace in one of the upper rooms. But on the whole, it is much easier to imagine how Mary, Countess of Pembroke, lived and prayed among the nuns than to reconstruct the life of the Cambridgeshire farmers who worked here.

Although the interior is bare of any sort of furnishings – apart from the fireplace – it has two sculptures, which were found in the grounds. One is of a most decorative animal head; the other is a stone human head. This is reported to be either an image of St Leonard, who shared the dedication of the original monastery church with St James, or of Christ. The latter seems more likely to me, for the head bears a very close resemblance to the image of the Turin shroud, which was once in the Templars' possession.

The long years of practical use as a farmhouse do not seem to have taken the numinous quality away from this building. Animals appear to feel it, and the present curator's wife told me that when she and her husband first came to their house, which stands to the east of the abbey, in the summer of 1978, they noticed that every evening their dog's hackles rose, and the placid animal became restless and suspicious. This in itself was odd, but they became even

Map labels: River Great Ouse · Twenty Pence Inn · Cottenham Lode · B1049 · moat · COTTENHAM · Car Dyke · Denny Abbey ruins · airfield · Roman Road · DENNY END · LANDBEACH · moat · WATERBEACH · Oldfield Farm · HISTON · A10(T) · MILTON · To Cambridge · KING'S HEDGES · To Cambridge · Lock · CLAYHYTHE · Inn · Telephone · UPWARE · Lock · Wicken Fen · New River · WICKEN · A1123 · Lock · Coll·

more curious when they noticed that this always happened at exactly twenty past eight.

The students who helped to excavate the abbey ruins also had a strange experience. They kept hearing somebody drawing water from a well. Although there was obviously a spring near the building, no well had at that time been found. Two of them have now been discovered. They are quite close together, just by the west door. A little to the east of them is the one remaining grave. A Knight Templar lies there.

From here, you can either go south along the A10 to Cambridge or take a longer walk along the tow path of the Great Ouse. This is a clear, easy path, which brings you to the bridge opposite the Twenty Pence Inn (see p.192). From there you can either take the walk into Ely, which you will find described in the previous section, or go down Twenty Pence Road (B1049) to Samuel Pepys' home village of Cottenham. The village is worth seeing. Its church tower is crowned by four decorative minarets, and, although it doesn't feature in any of Watkins' alignments, it is delightful in its own right. From here you can get a bus into Cambridge.

Pilgrims' paths

O.S. map 143

The Pilgrims' Way between Ely and Walsingham led across the wide expanse of fenland, which stretches between the Great Ouse flowing north past Littleport to the western edge of the Breckland and from Methwold in the north to Mildenhall in the south. There was also a pilgrims' route to Walsingham from Thorney Abbey to the west of Wisbech, which went through Littleport and approached it by Friars' Way through Wood Fen. Although that is outside the scope of this book, and has in any case almost completely disappeared as a result of the seventeenth-century fenland drainage, it would still be a good idea to start these walks from Littleport.

The station is out of the town beside the river, and although it lies to the west, in the direction the walk will take you, it is worth visiting the town before you start. Here, on the evening of Wednesday, May 22nd, 1816, a group of men met at the Globe Inn. They were fired by the discontent of the fen workers, who had started to complain actively about their conditions in Southery and Downham Market which lie to the north. The Littleport discussions led to one of the most turbulent chapters in our farming history; for the men were in a black mood and their meeting took place at a time when farm wages never rose above nine shillings a week, although the

Napoleonic Wars had pushed up the price of food to the extent that wheat cost 52s 6d a quarter.

An account of the Littleport Riots, that sprang out of that Globe Inn meeting and stirred hundreds of fen workers into active protest, was written up in 1893 by C. Johnson, a lay clerk of Ely Cathedral. His story makes sad reading. By the end of June the rebellion was over, five of the leaders were executed, and the rest were imprisoned or transported.

Yet those men's lives were not wasted. Work on the fens is always hard. Although the land is flat and fertile, it is too wet to be easily manageable and much of the work still has to be done by hand. Long before 'prairie farming' became fashionable in other parts of the country, wide areas of the fens were held under single ownership, requiring a labour force that could be employed as cheaply as possible. The people working in the fen fields today can thank those early pioneers, whose protests led to the gradual improvements in their conditions.

All this is a long way from our main topic of ancient paths. Yet the rich land round Littleport, where tracks are renewed with each fresh drainage scheme, has been inhabited since Mesolithic times. The Littleport Riots were just one step in the history of the people of the fens, whose earliest records lie in the earth below Peacock's Farm, Shippea Hill (628848). The significance of the excavation there is lucidly described by Helen Clarke in her contribution on East Anglia in the regional

archaeology series published by Heinemann in 1971. According to her account, the microliths in the lower levels of the soil have a radio-carbon dating for the sixth millennium BC, and those of the higher levels about a thousand years later. This suggests that men in Palaeolithic times hunted around this area for many generations. Analyses of pollen grain show that this was then a wooded area, which possibly once formed part of the Breckland.

There is no trace in the pollen found at that level to suggest that the people who lived there at that time made any attempt at cultivating crops. That took place around the fourth millennium BC, with the arrival in Britain of people from the main continent, who had a tradition of crop cultivation and made pottery to store their produce. Shippea Hill is the earliest site in East Anglia to show any record of this revolution in human progress. Excavations of the upper layers of the land here have revealed sheep's bones (which shows that the people were herdsmen as well as arable farmers) and pottery shards.

Unfortunately there is nothing much to remind you of all this today. If you go past Peacock's Farm you have to use your imagination fairly strenuously. The site is on the north side of the A1101 between Littleport and Mildenhall. The fen is heavily cultivated right up to the side of the road, and Peacock's Farm consists of modern farm buildings, flanked to the west by a site for agricultural machinery. The only building of any historical interest at all is a deserted

Brandon Creek

brick farmhouse standing a little way back from the road.

So the best way to start walking from Littleport Station is not to take the road to the south-east, but to follow the course of the Great Ouse as far as Brandon Creek. The last part of the way can be done along the tow path. This will bring you to the Ship Inn. Surprisingly to those who find that too much fen scenery induces melancholy, Mark Twain chose this inn to stay at while he was recovering from a nervous breakdown.

North of Brandon Creek is the straggling township of Southery. In 1861, all that land was submerged in 'The Great Drown', one of the worst recorded fenland disasters. The tales of that time are included in W.H.Barrett's *Tales from the Fens*. You can make the walk to the east direct from Brandon Creek, but if you want to visit Southery first, you must continue north along the road.

Be careful if you go there on May 29th, for that is the day of the old Southery Fair. If you hear a dog howl on that day, you may be dead within the year. The story has it that the Saxon fenmen who built the old church, whose ruins still stand to the east of the town, kept a wolfhound, who hunted for them and brought them meat. Disastrously, this hound was killed by one of the soldiers in the employ of the Bishop of North Elmham. The restless spirit of the poor creature continues to haunt the buildings with awful cries of doom, and on the charnel house at the north end of the church you can see how the hard stone

201

blocks look as though the rats have been at them. That is not so, they will tell you; those are the tooth marks of the wolfhound who comes each fair day to try to get at the bones inside the tomb.

If you are interested in a fen walk in this area, take the lane to the west of the present church in Southery. After a short distance take the path going south, and when you join the next track turn left and follow it through to the fen road going past Sedge Fen Farm. Follow this track east and then north, till you come out on the road to the west of Feltwell. Turn right here and then take the first footpath on your right, running on top of the drain that marks the west of Feltwell Common. This brings you to the crossing place at 657902.

If you do not visit Southery, you can walk by the Little Ouse from Brandon Creek and then cross Feltwell Anchor Fen to 657902.

W.H. Barrett, in his *Tales From the Fens*, tells a rather horrific story about this fen. It has a curious connection with ley alignments, for the name of the character who is reported to haunt these parts is Dowser. In his life he was a

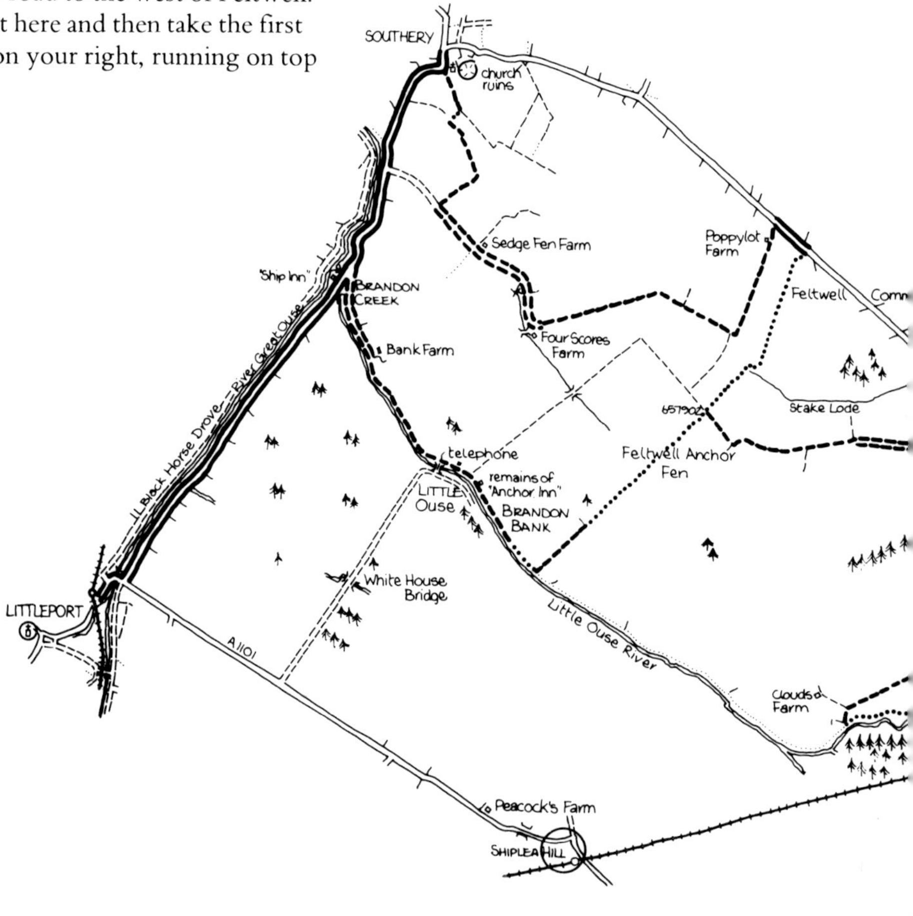

622945
623940

672922

SOUTHERY
church ruins
Sedge Fen Farm
Poppylot Farm
'Ship Inn'
BRANDON CREEK
Feltwell
Com
Bank Farm
Four Scores Farm
657902
Stake Lode
River Great Ouse
Black Horse Drove
telephone
Feltwell Anchor Fen
remains of "Anchor Inn"
LITTLE Ouse
BRANDON BANK
LITTLEPORT
White House Bridge
Little Ouse River
A 1101
Clouds Farm
Peacock's Farm
SHIPLEA HILL

remarkably unpleasant man, who lived in about 1865, and who used the isolation of his farm to indulge in various domestic cruelties, such as harnessing his wife to the plough. Eventually his own destructive nature grew too much for him. He went mad and killed himself.

Another ghost story of these parts reflects the hard-working fen men's dislike of the friars, who seemed to have an easy life of it, bullying and begging their way between Ely and Walsingham. All sorts of despicable activities were attributed to these holy men, rape included. The story is that on a bank leading to one of the lonely farms, a dog came to the rescue of a young girl, who was innocently engaged in cutting mint when the friar attacked her. But the dog died of the injuries he sustained in the encounter and was buried by White House Bridge (610878) to the southwest of the Little Ouse. So it is the ghostly dog and not the friar who prowls these dykes today.

Head east to the bridge over Cut-Off Channel, which marks the eastern edge of the fens. Unless you are interested in following the Pilgrims' Path through to Weeting (see section 2), the main attraction of Feltwell is a small, private, local industry museum. The village is now almost completely dominated by the Air Force, and has little of interest for the visitor, apart from the outstanding size of the church porch, and the ancient almshouses at its western end. If you want to go through to Weeting, follow the B1386 and take the lane beside the Foss Ditch. You are now at the start of the walk that is described on p.88.

The other possibility from Cut-Off Channel is to visit Hockwold cum Wilton – a most attractive village – and you can stay overnight at the New Inn by the river. This would give you a chance for another fen walk, 3·5 miles (5·6 km) or so around Hockwold Fen. The path, indicated by the public footpath sign, is called Cowle's Drove (an extension of the Harling Drove, see Section 2). These fen droves are tracks leading from distant farms to the nearest road or village, and from higher lands to river banks. In a summer wind they can be almost impassable on account of the black dust, and in winter they are likely to be deep in mud.

On this walk, you don't go to Clouds Farm, but follow the Little Ouse back to Hockwold.

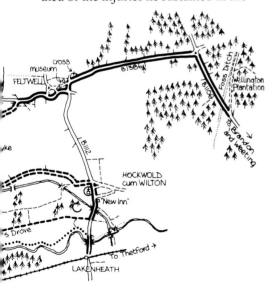

725873

203

Hockwold was on the route of the old pilgrims' way from Thorney Abbey to Walsingham, mentioned on p.199. But the religious significance of Hockwold can be traced to much earlier times. Anne Ross, the main authority on Celtic history and ritual, believes that a circular mask, which was excavated here, relates to a severed head cult; and that this pagan object was deliberately hidden in a pit during the coming of Christianity some time after the fourth century. She believes that this mask, and other ritual objects from the same villages, may have reference to a local god. Helen Clarke suggests that the five bronze diadems and twenty-three brooches which were found here, associated with a Romano-Celtic pagan temple, were buried to placate the gods and restore peace and prosperity.

From Lakenheath Station you can get a train east to Thetford or west to Ely. If you go to the west, you may be travelling above another legendary fen tunnel quoted in R.Rainbird Clarke's *In Breckland Wilds*. This tunnel is reported to have been used in the time of Hereward the Wake, and to have been very substantially made, having oak sides and roof. Above ground you will pass by Shippea Hill, south of Peacock's Farm, from which the first men to have left their traces in East Anglia went hunting.

Brandon Creek

Section 6

Important alignment points

Anstey Castle	167:403332
Ardeley	166:309272
Arkesden Church	154:482346
Ashgrove	154:382352
Barkway Church	154:384357
Barley Church	154:402385
Brent Pelham Church	167:434308
Cave Gate	166:389328
Cross Leys	154:414365
Heydon	154:432400
Hobs Aerie	154:485353
Little Hadham Church	167:445228
Meesden Church	167:439326
Reed Church	154:362358
Royston Crossroads	154:356407
Strethall Church	154:485398

Section 6: The Nuthampstead Zodiac

On earth as it is in heaven

O.S. maps 154, 166, 167

In this concluding section of the book, I am going to look in some detail at the terrestrial zodiac lying in the very south of East Anglia, at a place where three counties, Cambridgeshire, Essex and Hertfordshire, meet. It was first rediscovered by Nigel Pennick on October 18th, 1969, and I have used his maps and descriptions to work out the walks round the zodiacal figures. You can find them in a book he published jointly with Robert Lord, *Terrestrial Zodiacs in Britain* (1976). It includes maps for both the Nuthampstead zodiac and Robert Lord's Pendle zodiac, which lies across the Pennine Range and will be included in my book on the ley lines of Derbyshire. The book is available from the Institute of Geomantic Research, 142 Pheasant Rise, Bar Hill, Cambridge. For a discussion of the significance and interpretation of such zodiacs, see the general introduction to this book.

The Nuthampstead zodiac, which gets its name from the village nearest its centre, stretches across an unexpected area of rural landscape that lies between Royston, Baldock and Buntingford to the west and Bishop's Stortford to the east. It is a wooded, hilly region, with a feeling of remoteness totally alien to the London commuter belt which lies immediately to its south. Nigel Pennick points out that within 10 miles (16 km)

206

of its centre, appropriately named Cross Leys (a triangular patch of woodland, unfortunately strictly on private ground), the initiatory turf maze carved into the common at Saffron Walden and the Gog Magog figures of Wandlebury (see p.180) are sited.

He is also interested in the links which this area had with the Knights Templar, who were active here until the final suppression of the order by Pope Clement in March 1312, when the Knights were accused of renouncing Christ and spitting on the cross. For most people, their present-day association with the area extends no further than the Knights Templar restaurant in Baldock, but we shall find various hidden tokens of their presence as we walk around the zodiac.

It is possible that one of the order's headquarters was in the man-made cave at Royston. This excavation was discovered by some workmen in 1742, and immediately engaged the attention of the antiquarian Dr William Stukeley. The cave is bee-hive shaped, and is unique in this country, although there are several of the same pattern in Jerusalem, where the order of the Knights Templar was founded in 1119. The chalk cave has one extraordinary natural property. Whatever the outside temperature, the interior of the cave remains steady at 10°C. There is no arti-

3564

ficial heating or ventilating system, and the composition of the chalk makes drainage unnecessary. The carvings on the walls are still clearly decipherable, although the figures have lost the pigmentation which some authorities believe they originally had.

The Knights Templar belonged to an aristocratic lay order, whose members were feared by the clergy and common people alike, both on account of their great wealth and their supposed connection with witchcraft. The Knights were bound by codes of absolute secrecy, although it is known that their philosophy was based on the Cistercian rules of life compiled by St Bernard of Clairvaux. The order was so powerful that by a papal bull of Innocent II in 1139 it was enabled to set up its own places of prayer. The round church in Cambridge is probably one of the most famous of the Templar churches. There also used to be another round church to the east of this zodiac. In *The Newmarket, Bury, Thetford and Cromer Road* Charles Harper tells of a round church at Little Wenden, which was cleared away in 1662. That village no longer exists, the present Wendens Ambo containing both Little and Great Wenden. The Knights were allowed by the same Bull to administer their own churchyards and burial customs (see p.197); to appoint their own priests; and to enjoy with the Cistercians the privilege of being exempt from tithes.

Could it be, as Nigel Pennick suggests, that it was because the Knights Templar were so strong in this area that the lines denoting the figures of this zodiac have been preserved through the centuries? Alternatively, it could be that it was *because* the zodiacal figures were so firmly established here that the Knights Templar came to flourish in this region.

It is not possible to walk round each individual figure of the zodiac, although I intend to conclude the section with a walk round the westward-facing hound which, as at Glastonbury, guards the whole circle. For the main figures, I have worked out a route, following footpaths, which take you round the area of the zodiac.

Before you undertake these walks, it is best to spend a little time in the unlikely town of Royston, and to do so on a Saturday. The only time in the week, apart from Bank Holidays, that the cave is open is on a Saturday afternoon; and the excellent little museum is only open on Saturday mornings. You can, however, see the stone from which the town gets its name at any time. It is a glacial erratic, which was originally set to mark the place where the Icknield Way was crossed by Ermine Street. (now, more prosaically, where the southern part of the A10 and the A14 link with the A505). The stone has now been shifted slightly from its original site, to prevent obstruction to the traffic. In Saxon times, it probably supported a wooden cross.

I am going to take the walks round this zodiac properly anti-clockwise, which is the way that the zodiacal signs go round the year. I will start with Aries, the Ram, largely because the walks fit in better that way. For two reasons, I would

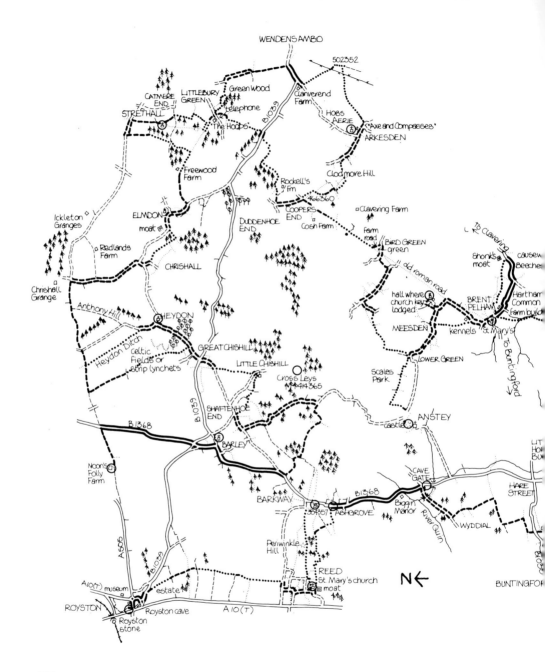

WENDENS AMBO

502352

CATMERE
END
STRETHALL

LITTLEBURY
GREEN

Green Wood

telephone

The Hoops

Clanverend
Farm

HOBS
AERIE

"Axe and Compasses"

ARKESDEN

Freewood
Farm

Rockell's
Fm

Clodmore Hill

466360

Clavering Farm

To Clavering

Ickleton
Granges

ELMDON
moat

DUDDENHOE
END

COOPERS
END

Cosh Farm

farm
road

BIRD GREEN
green

Shonks
moat

causew
Beeches

Redlands
Farm

CHRISHALL

old roman road

hall where
church key
lodged

BRENT
PELHAM

Hartham
Common
Farm build

Chrishall
Grange

Anthony Hill

HEYDON

MEESDEN

kennels

St Mary's

To Buntingford

Heydon Ditch

Celtic
fields or
strip lynchets

GREAT CHISHILL

LITTLE CHISHILL

Cross Leys
414365

Scales
Park

LOWER GREEN

B1039

SHAFTENHOE
END

ANSTEY

castle

LIT
HO
BU

B1368

BARLEY

Noon's
Folly
Farm

CAVE
GATE

HARE
STREET

BARKWAY

384357

ASHGROVE

Biggin
Manor

River Quin

WYDDIAL

A505

B1039

Periwinkle
Hill

REED

N

St. Mary's church
moat

BUNTINGFOR

A10(T) museum

estate

ROYSTON

Royston cave

A10(T)

Royston
stone

rather have begun with Pisces. The fishes of March are the natural start to the year in spring, and the fish symbol of the early Christians could also reflect the importance which Nigel Pennick believed the Knights Templar gave to this zodiac. However, to do so would mean doubling back on our tracks at an early stage in the walk. In any case, in both this zodiac and the one around Bury St Edmunds, the Ram is taken very much as a symbol of the Christian paschal lamb, lying with its feet folded beneath its body and its head turned to look backwards over its shoulder, ready

for the sacrifice which allowed the age of the fishes to begin.

The Nuthampstead Aries extends across Ermine Street, as it runs south from Royston. The heart of the effigy is at Barkway church, dedicated to St Mary Magdalene and standing on a site which has carried a Christian church since 1086, the Domesday date that keeps cropping up in the church history notes. Its rear leg is at Buckland on Ermine Street, where there is one of the

384357

358339

many East Anglian St Andrew's churches. For the connection of that saint with the Romano-Celtic religions, see the East Anglian Introduction and p.120. In the zodiac, the left haunch of the Christian lamb rests at Reed End to the south-east of Therfield.

I want to start the walk across the body of Aries by going from Reed, at the central, western edge of the creature's body, to Barkway in the east. To get to Reed from the centre of Royston (where the stone and the cave, wrongly marked on the O.S. map, are situated), follow the B1039 out of town until you reach the estate road which leads to the footpath to Reed.

The name 'Reed' may be associated with red, a colour which Alfred Watkins linked with pottery, and hence with prehistoric trade routes, and which in relation to the zodiac is the colour of Mars, the ruler of Aries, who once had a temple at Barkway. It is more likely, however, that as a place name Reed shares the same derivation as 'rod' and 'road'. Nigel Pennick has found an intricate grid lay-out based at Reed and parallel to Ermine Street, so perhaps the whole zodiac was extended from this point on the terrestrial graph. It is possibly relevant that there is also a village called Rede near the centre of the Bury St Edmunds zodiac; and another linked with the Pendle zodiac in Lancashire. Reed church, which is also dedicated to St Mary, stands at a bend in the lane beside a moat. From there you can take a footpath to Barkway, either going along the old drove route that runs under

3436

356407

363402

362358

209

Periwinkle Hill or skirting the southern edge of the woods, and so to the lane which brings you to Barkway church.

384357

If you choose the northern way, you will walk along the southern foot of the prehistoric mound of Periwinkle Hill. The five-petalled blue flowers of the periwinkle are sacred to the earth goddess. They are also a symbol of death, and Nigel Pennick tells us that in ancient times condemned criminals were garlanded with the plant. The walk nowadays is somewhat less impressive than the name, being overshadowed by the planes busy around the R.A.F. station at Barkway, and in any case it is no longer possible to climb over the slopes of the hill. I prefer the symbol of life that lies to the south. When you get clear of the woods you must follow the lane, for the footpath over the field to your left, although a public way, runs into a dead end at a private garden. After you have gone a little way along the lane, you can either turn left at the church or continue along the bridleway to Ashgrove. Ashgrove marks the lamb's right shoulder, and the tree for which it is named is the same as Yggdrassil, the Norse tree of life, sacred to Odin.

384353

The next figure in the zodiacal calendar is Taurus the Bull. This one is represented solely by its head and foot, and even these two features are not particularly satisfying. The top of the foot is at Biggin Manor. If you continue further south along the road from Ashgrove, you come to the outline of the Bull's head as soon as you have crossed the River Quin. His snout is at the next

387334

210

crossroads, known as Cave Gate. This was once believed to be the very entrance to Hell itself; and in all probability it was one end of an underground tunnel which runs from Anstey Castle to the north-east, a few hundred yards from the tip of the Bull's horn.

388328

Various legends are associated with the cave. It could have been a site blooded by the sacrifices of Mithraic rituals, although, if that was the case, one might have expected to have had the Bull more completely drawn. There is a seventeenth-century legend about a blind fiddler of Anstey, who dared to enter the cave and was never seen again, although his dog emerged singed and hairless. That fiddler may be the 'George' who lies safely buried in Anstey churchyard, but the story is one of several in which a fiddler goes to Hell through a hole in the earth. In Britain the stories extend to the Orkneys, where the tale is recalled by the Orcadian poet George Mackay Brown; and in East Anglia Nigel Pennick quotes instances at Granchester Manor, Cambridge, Binham Priory, Norfolk and Rushton Hall, Northamptonshire. All these stories must in some way be linked with the legends of both Orpheus and Persephone. It is fitting that there should be such a cave on the outline of a zodiacal figure which takes the calendar position of May, when the dark earth yields up the blossoms and fruits of summer.

It is fitting too that this figure of the springtime Bull should be flanked not by our own familiar twins of Gemini, but by the East Anglian devil, Wandil.

He is the spirit of destruction who steals the springtime, and whose eyes are the twin stars known to us as Castor and Pollux. This is the third figure of the **Gog Magog** trinity (see p.180) and, excepting that the Nuthampstead zodiacal giant is unarmed, he takes a similar shape to the one at Wandlebury. There is also a link with the limping giant who represents Gemini in the Bury St Edmunds zodiac, for this creature has no legs.

  These giants give us an excuse to consider the relation of the zodiac to the possibility of sentient beings in outer space. T.C.Lethbridge is among the writers who have tentatively put forward the theory that the great Neolithic enclosures, whose entrances are marked by wide causeways as well as henges and stone avenues, were originally constructed by, or as a signal to, beings who were looking at our world from the.outside. This idea is extended to the construction of terrestrial zodiacs in Anthony Robert's study of mythological and historical giants, *Sons of Thunder*. He claims that the giant effigies that make up the earth zodiacs 'can only be seen as an organic entity from height perspectives ranging between 30,000 feet (9144 m) and 5 miles (18 km)'.

There are many puzzles. Why is it that the figures in the zodiacs, like those carved in hillside chalk, are not simply gigantic in themselves, but are also popularly believed to have been created by giants? Why in almost every folklore do we find a time when giants inhabited the earth? And why are there so many myths of giants, like Wandil, being taken up into the sky? In some stories the stars, Castor and Pollux, are taken as being Wandil's eyes.

The Nuthampstead Wandil effigy lies to the north-east, reaching up to the Bull, with its two hands coming together between Biggin Manor and Cave Gate. Its head and body are at Wyddial, and the end of its torso at Bun- 3731 3629 tingford, where Ermine Street crosses the River Rib at Brick Bridge. From Cave Gate, you can follow the outline of the giant's right arm by taking the lane 380310 towards Wyddial and turning off along a bridleway, which goes south to Alswick 376296 Hall. From here you can start the walk across the next effigy, an enormous Lion, who, like the one at Glastonbury, seems to have completely swallowed the Crab.

This Lion stands erect looking towards the west, with the tumulus at Bummers 398286 Hill for his eye and the top of his head at 290405 Little Hormead. The B road from Hare Street to Braughing outlines his chest, 3922 his forefoot is at Standon, and his rear 4422 foot at Little Hadham about 2·5 miles (4 km) to the east along the A120, which for part of its route covers the Roman road of Stone Street.

To get to Bummers Hill tumulus from

Alswick Hall, take the path by the southern edge of a wood, crossing the road at Hare Street. You then cross the 39029 Quin by the road bridge. As soon as you have done that, you will find a path which leads you first by the Quin and then by its tributary to the tumulus standing close by the water. Continue south until your path is crossed by an 40028 east/west track, where you can either continue south for the lane to Braughing Friars, which defines the Lion's belly, or 4124 take the farm road to Cockhampstead 41925 Farm and join the path to Albury Hall and Clapgate. If you take the southern route to Braughing Friars, go through the village to the field path which passes the Lee Valley water tower (suitably 42424 situated over the Lion's bladder) and comes out near Albury church. From there you can either follow the path north to Furneux Pelham or take the lane to Clapgate.

If you are setting out now to look at some places on the next figure, Virgo, the goddess of harvest, the first alterna- tive is best. The path to Furneux Pelham crosses the one through the Albury Hall 43425 estate at the edge of a strip of woodland. From here you can zig-zag slightly head- ing for Patient End Farm. Continue 42827 north along the footpath past Furneux Pelham church to Brent Pelham. 43430

The footpath runs west of the lane enclosing Hartham Common on its western side, which also defines the Vir- gin's hood. She stands with her feet to the north-east, the edge of her hem lying at Hill Green, and the hem itself being 47832 defined by the tributary of the Stort

212

which runs through Stickling Green and Clavering Place.

The effigy is facing north-west, with Brent Pelham church a few yards from her face. In her hand she holds the traditional spica or corn dolly, which includes Meesden church.

9326

Brent Pelham church is dedicated to St Mary the Virgin. Although it is often kept locked, it is worth getting the key from the house next door; directions are given on the notice in the church porch. Inside the building, in the north wall, you will find Piers Shonkes' tomb. He was a giant dragon-slayer who is supposed to have lived in a house surrounded by a moat which still bears his name, and which lies just over a mile (1·6 km) to the east of the village on the road to Clavering.

His tomb is adorned with a Latin inscription (probably composed in the eighteenth century), which consists of two elegiac couplets in the style of Ovid. They put Shonkes in the usual tradition of dragon-slayers by comparing him with St George, and more originally with Cadmus, the legendary inventor of the alphabet, who killed the serpent which guarded the Castalian spring. There is a fairly free verse translation of the Latin on the tomb, but the prose version, which I have from Dr John Penman, who has helped me over this inscription, makes the matter clearer. It runs: 'Of Cadmus nothing remains except his fame, and greedy time devours the posthumous bones and tomb of St George; but safe in this wall is Shonkes the dragon-killer, put there in the Devil's despite.' This has the advantage of appearing to be an exact record of what happened.

The story of Piers Shonkes is an extraordinary mixture of old and new. His legendary feats surely belong to the realms of antiquity, and yet the date of his death is given as 1086 (see p.209). And for a man who was reputed to be 23 feet (7 m) tall in his lifetime, his grave is surprisingly normal in length. But the main point is its positioning, which the inscription hints at. The grave lies actually in the wall of the church, and they will tell you that it was placed there because this gallant giant, who rid Brent Pelham of demons, eventually killed the devil's favourite dragon. For that, Satan swore that although Piers might be safe while he lived, whether he was buried within or without the church, his soul would go to Hell. 'So we buried him in the wall,' the lady who was arranging the Whitsun flowers told me, as though the whole event had happened yesterday. In the devil's despite indeed.

There is, however, another version of how Piers came to lie in that place. It is said that, like Robin Hood and many other great heroes, when he knew he was dying he shot an arrow from his window, vowing he would be buried wherever it landed. The arrow is reported to have gone through the south wall of the church and lodged in the north. Now it seems to me that such arrow flights could well be connected with ley alignments. A quick glance at the map will show that there is no possible alignment from Shonk's Moat

213

going south/north through the church. He must have shot his arrow elsewhere, and its flight might reflect a south/north alignment running the whole extent of the zodiac from Little Hadham in the south to Heydon in the north. Brent Pelham is about half-way between the two.

This rather mixed memory of a ley alignment could be linked with the tales of Piers Shonkes' extraordinary height. Nigel Pennick has found that the prime number 23 commonly turns up in folk-lore; and in his book on the zodiac he quotes some research undertaken by Michael Behrend, who discovered that 23 and its multiples 46, 69 and 92 recur repeatedly in geomantic measurements in the area. So, it is possible that the height ascribed to the giant is part of a folk memory of the measurements that were noted when the land was surveyed as part of the construction of this zodiac.

I believe that Piers Shonkes was probably adopted by the early church in its fight against the 'dragon' of pagan ritual, which was no doubt most persistent in a place which carried the effigy of the earth goddess. Even after death the good giant retains a character fitting an up-holder of the moral establishment, for his ghost is said to have appeared in recent centuries to rebuke a man for theft. Indeed, the six rooms that formed a wing of Beeches House, which still stands by Shonk's Moat, had to be des-troyed so persistently did the giant's ghost appear.

Before you leave the church to look at Shonk's Moat and to visit Meesden, it is worth looking at one other tomb. This is a seventeenth-century brass dedicated to the two young wives of Francis Rowley, the first dying in 1625 and the second (aged twenty-seven) two years later.

'Thy sting oh death most sharply here appears, To take them both away in their prime of years,

– lamented their unhappy husband. So the two young women, who would have known Piers Shonkes' house (it was reported to be still standing, although derelict, in 1700) lie by the head of the earth goddess.

Outside the church you will find a puddingstone, built into the south corner of the tower. More of these stones form the base of the war memor-ial which stands at the road junction to the north-east of the village. Piers Shonkes' moat lies to the east of the vil-lage. To reach it, take the footpath past the farm buildings opposite the church. It goes east, running north of Beeches House, and across to the swamps of Shonk's Moat. When the path nears the road, you will find a causeway enabling you to reach the place where the old house must have stood.

To get to Meesden, you must retrace your steps, by road or field path, to Brent Pelham. Now take the road towards Anstey; when it forks the lane joins the old Roman road, which links the effigies of this zodiac, as the Fosse Way links those at Glastonbury. We shall return to it again on our way north to Scorpio.

The footpath for Meesden leaves the lane at a corner opposite the kennels, just before it straightens out along the course

214

of the Roman road. Meesden church is not easy to find. It stands on a wooded hillside to the east of the village.

The most immediately noticeable things about this church, which is also dedicated to St Mary, are its wooden tower and its porch of Tudor brickwork. But, as at Brent Pelham, its real interest lies inside the building, which again is usually kept locked. The keys are at the Hall, which is through a **wicket gate** at the south edge of the churchyard. There has been a church on this site since at least 1086 – the coincidence with the reputed year of Piers Shonkes' death is remarkable, especially as this year is referred to again in connection with the founding of the church of St Cecilia at Little Hadham by Leo's rear foot. But the oldest part of the building to be seen today is the twelfth-century nave; and the most interesting thing is the pavement of mediaeval glazed tiles, whose lines make up an intricate pattern in twelves and twenty-fours, which suggests a link with a zodiac.

meesden

Traditionally, the figure that should come after Virgo (the sign for the harvest) is Libra, the Scales. It is the sign that presides over the Jewish days of atonement, and is the right seasonal occasion for taking stock of the past year. So the figure should logically lie somewhat to the north of Clavering. Unfortunately, it doesn't. Where we would expect to find it, there is an extended Scorpio.

However, the Scorpion hasn't swallowed the Scales, as the Lion has incorporated the Crab. Libra still exists and, as at Glastonbury, the sign has the form of the Christian dove, holding the host in its mouth. I find it interesting that the only inanimate sign of the zodiac should be so translated (possibly a real substitution of the Old Testament by the New). Yet the Scales are not completely lost. On the stonework of the mediaeval tower on Glastonbury Tor, you will find the Scales of the Day of Judgement, and the Nuthampstead Dove lies over Scales Park. You must make up your own mind whether that name is coincidental. The Hertfordshire land originally belonged to a family of that name.

The tip of the Dove's right wing almost touches Anstey Castle, at the

215

centre of the zodiac, from which the underground tunnel runs to Cave Gate in Taurus (see p.210). To reach Anstey, you have to walk back to Meesden village, and on towards Lower Green. You can then follow the path through Scales Park, and along lanes going west to Anstey village and the castle.

Just beyond the castle is the church, dedicated to St George the dragon-slayer on the authority of its pre-Reformation tenor bell, which bears an invocation to that saint. There are still some traces of the original Norman building to be seen, but nothing remains of the Saxon church that once stood here. It is well worth a visit, though, for the thirteenth-century military graffiti on the chancel walls and for a pagan detail on one of the floor tiles in the choir; it depicts a foliate head with protruding tongue, adorned with clearly defined oak leaves.

To reach Scorpio by the old Roman road of Beard's Lane, you must unfortunately retrace your steps to Lower Green. Go north by the path that curves round to a similarly named hamlet outside the village of Langley.

Turn left into the village and then immediately head south to Bird Green. Take the farm road going north; this leads you to Beard's Lane, which follows the course of the Roman road. It soon degenerates into a very muddy, overgrown footpath, running through a scrubby wood. At a meeting of tracks you will find a tumulus, which is clearly visible, a steep mound obviously left unploughed, at the side of an arable field.

Past the tumulus Beard's Lane, which

still runs through a little wood, is much easier to walk along, although it is sad to see that the hedge which once marked its eastern edge has been slashed and burnt. The path leads into an unmade road, which still follows the course of the Roman road. At Cooper's End, a straggle of Army huts by a sharp bend in a metalled lane define the last segment of the Scorpion's tail. The animal stretches south almost to Stickling Green on the edge of the Virgo's hem. The effigy appears to be headless. Its right claw reaches round to the moat at Clavering Farm, and the left is defined by the lane that runs between Arkesden and Hobs Aerie. It is important that Arkesden church is on a hill to the east of the lane, for, as Nigel Pennick is at pains to make clear, no churches may be covered by the diabolical sign of Scorpio.

To reach Sagittarius, the largest figure in this zodiac, you can either go east across Scorpio to Arkesden, or define the end of the sting at Duddenhoe End. I will give both walks, starting with the one to the east, and in both cases ending up at Littlebury Green on the horse's rump. A word about the effigy of Sagittarius before we start. This is rather a comic figure, with no hint of the splendid archer/centaur offered by tradition. This outline shows a hooded human figure (whom Nigel Pennick equates with Helith, Helios or Hercules) falling off a scrawny, stumbling nag. The rider's hood reaches to Langley in the south; the horse's back is partly defined by the B road running from Great Chishill to Wendens Ambo, and its belly by the

4639
495360
465360

roads around the village of Elmdon. Its tail extends to Clanverend Farm.

For the first walk, follow the bridle-path that goes south-east from Cooper's End to join the lane to Arkesden. Go

MELBOURN

ICKLETON

Goffers Knoll

HEYDON

ELMDON

STRETHALL

GREAT CHISHILL

BARLEY

LITTLE CHISHILL

Cross Leys

NUTHAMSTEAD

The Hall

UPPER GREEN

ARKESDEN

ANSTEY

MEESDEN BURY

CLAVERING

BRENT PELHAM

priory

GREAT HORNMEAD BURY

BERDEN

Bummer Hill

STOCKING PELHAM

FURNEUX PELHAM

BRAUGHING

COCKHAMSTEAD

ALBURY

FARNHAM

ZODIAC based on Nigel Pennick's Map

straight through the village, and after you have passed the Axe and Compasses, a fashionable eating place for the office workers of Saffron Walden, take the lane that runs to the north-east towards Wendens Ambo (see p.207). This lane very soon becomes a field path. At 154:502352, turn north-west to Clanverend Farm. Then head east along the B road to Wendens Ambo, but before you reach the village go north along a lane which you leave by a foot-path on your left, north of a wood, to the lane which serves as the main street of the hamlet of Littlebury Green.

If you decided to go west at Cooper's End, you will take the lane towards Duddenhoe End, and then the bridlepath which skirts a wood, and heads down to the B road that defines the horse's back. When the road crosses a stream, you will have crossed from the animal's body to his tail. There is a right of way, although not much to indicate it, on the eastern bank of the stream. You can then go north-east over the hill to Littlebury Green.

To get to Strethall church from Littlebury Green, you must take the path that goes to the east of a house, formerly a pub, which still retains the name of The Hoops.

You come out into the lane of Catmere End, which although isolated, rural and muddy is also noisy, for it's an informal depot for large transport containers. Two ponds face you across the lane. Take the path, going north between the ponds, through some farm buildings, and then head downhill towards

495360

501364

496381

464367

484370

Strethall, which consists simply of the buildings you can see: the church, dedicated to St Mary the Virgin, the new farm building almost abutting on to it, and the rebuilt brick Hall.

When you get near the church, the path starts to climb quite steeply, and becomes a narrow lane between high banks, covered with violets in springtime. When I first came here, I met a loyal, local lady in the churchyard who told me it was the most beautiful place in England; and it is astonishingly quiet and lovely, untouched by the noise of either the Catmere End lorries or the new motorway workings for the M11. When Alfred Watkins' son, Allen, went there in the 1930s, he had an even more fruitful meeting, for he encountered a farm labourer, who said to him, 'Ah, you came by the Roman road. Now when I first came to these parts, the older folk said there did used to be an old Roman road straight from Strethall church here towards Cambridge. I've never seen it myself; but when the crop grows, you can see exactly where the old road went by the poorer crop; I've often seen than.' Alfred Watkins, who tells of this encounter in *Archaic Tracks around Cambridge* (1932), drew an alignment from Strethall church to Great Shelford church, and from there going through the west of Cambridge to Woodhouse Farm and thence to Belsar's Hill Camp to the south of Aldreth Causeway.

The church notes at Strethall will tell you that the church stands on the bend of a Roman road between Great Chesterford and Braughing, and that the first

218

Christian building on the site 'would most probably have been a wooden building put up by the local Saxon thane'. Parts of the present church, notably the chancel arch, date from the first stone church on the site, which was put up according to the Celtic plan of 'a small lofty nave with a miniature chancel' around 1000 AD.

From Strethall, which lies on the horse's rear leg, it is pleasant and easy to visit Chrishall, where his foreleg joins the back of the Goat's head. This Capricorn, who is facing west, is an ordinary creature, without the mythological fish tail. His stubbly goat tail is covered by the old lynchets of Coploe Hill to the north of Strethall, where the motorway runs now. His hind leg goes down to Ickleton.

To get to Chrishall, we go first to Elmdon, partly along a path that outlines the belly of the horse. From Strethall church carry on along the lane to the north. When you turn south after the metalled lane the track runs along the eastern and northern edges of some woodlands; the latter section is the outline of the horse's belly.

Go through Elmdon and take the footpath opposite Elmdonbury Moat. Following first the footpath and then the lanes, make your way to Chrishall Grange – the place of the Goat's front foot. There is no reason to follow the lane right through to the Grange. At 154:444424, you come to a crossing of the ways. The unmade field road on your left is one of the tracks of the Icknield Way (see Section 3). Follow this to reach the next figure of the effigy, an Eagle, who stands for Aquarius.

That needs some explanation. Nigel Pennick has this to say: 'In the Greek Zodiac, Aquarius was associated with the rising of the River Nile, the constellation being represented by Ganymede, the most beautiful boy born of mortal parents. Zeus, in the form of an eagle carried him off from Mount Ida, and made him cup-bearer to the gods. Thus the eagle is connected in classical mythology with the Aquarian figure of the British zodiac.' The association with a water carrier is continued in the dedication of Great Chishill church to St Swithin.

From the Icknield Way head south to Great Chishill. You can walk along 422419 Heydon's Ditch, haunted by headless warriors, fifty of whose bodies (headless) were actually excavated from the earthwork in 1927.

Alternatively, you can take the track at 414419 which becomes a field path climbing up the slope of a hill past some terraces of Celtic fields. The path brings you to an orchard and then skirts the 425397 western edge of the trees, outlining the Eagle's back.

The last effigy in this zodiac is Pisces, the Fishes. Although Nigel Pennick talks of two of them, there seem to me to be three distinct shapes on his map. They stand around the centre of the zodiac which is marked by the triangular woods of Cross Leys, whose apex is at 418373 414365. The church at Little Chishill is in the body of one of the smaller Fishes. The church can be reached by taking a footpath from the B1039 south to join a bridleway which leads you there directly. 421389

From the church, a field path goes to Shaftenhoe End, running just under a mile (1·6 km) to the north of Cross Leys, which is hidden from view by intervening woods.

The next Fish lies just to the east of Barkway and Newsells Park, which covers the head of Aries. The eye of the 402385 third and largest Fish is at Barley church; you can get there by the lanes from Shaftenhoe End. But if you want to visit the other Fish, and take a closer look at Cross Leys, keep going to the south- 404377 west until you find a turning on your left. This lane goes past Abbotsbury Moat, and then passes beside the south-western sides of the woody hills of Cross Leys. A track goes downhill across the fields on your right to Cokenach, where the remains of the Breton saint, Winwaloe, are supposed to 396362 lie. From here you can follow the road through Newsells Park to Barkway Hill. The minor road going north from here goes back to Shaftenhoe End; the B road goes into the village of Barley.

To get back to Royston, you can follow the B road north from Barley until the road is crossed by the wide track of 405416 the Icknield Way. Follow the track west past Noon's Folly Farm. It joins the A505 (Royston–Newmarket road) at a large lay-by, where you can frequently meet a tea van. You are now 1·5 miles (2·4 km) east of Royston.

Although we have now gone right round the zodiac, I want to look in detail

219

at one last figure: the westward-facing Guardian Hound, and to walk round it

3023 as far as possible. The Hound is leaping over the village of Benington, which lies to the east of Stevenage.

You can start the walk at Ardeley, along the lane that defines the Hound's ear. You can reach it by the lane or by footpaths from Hare Street on the B1037 from Stevenage. The most satisfactory

311286 way is to leave Hare Street by the lane which covers the Roman road running south-east to Cherry Green. When this lane branches into three footpaths, take the one on your right. It will bring you to a stream, and you can follow its

307277 northern bank until you reach the lane for Ardeley. The stream goes on across the lane, and defines the Hound's ear. There is now no path by the stream, but as you follow the lane into the village, you will be walking along the outline of the back of the ear. When you get to the

309272 village, turn right. The lane past the church of St Lawrence marks the base of the ear.

Take the footpath which curves north-west around Ardeley Moat, defining the jaw. The underside of the jaw is marked by some strips of woodland.

296272 You can cross through them, but then have to leave the effigy, going south to Walkern. You rejoin the effigy by turning left along the footpath which will

305266 bring you back to the woods.

The farm road of Walkern Bury Farm, which makes the outline of the Hound's chest, is not a right of way, so you must go through the wood until you get to its eastern edge, where you will find a path

220

to St John's Wood, which covers the

307256 effigy's heart. From here follow the road to Walkern. You rejoin the outline of the animal at 166:303260, where the farm road goes up to Walkern Bury Farm. You are now walking along the top of the Hound's foreleg, which extends to the banks of the River Bean, flowing to the east of Walkern.

The last witch trial in England was held in this village. The date was 1712, the accuser was the historian Sir Henry Chauncey of Ardeley Bury, and the accused was Jane Wenham. Although she was tortured, she was fortunately subsequently pardoned, but the incident underlines the terror which the orthodox establishment always has of ancient mysteries, perhaps especially so when, as in the case of this zodiac, a strong element of Christianity is mingled with the old beliefs.

There is no path beside the river, so you will have to go through the village,

288259 rejoining the river opposite the Stevenage turning. You meet it at a double bend, for it turns east here, outlining the underside of the Hound's leg and part of his body. Once you have crossed the first bridge over the river you have a choice of footpaths. The one on your left goes north of the river through the centre of the Hound's paw. It runs east

304257 to Bassus Green, and on towards Clay End. The path on your right goes to the south of the effigy. It crosses the river a second time, skirting the eastern edge of

297251 the woods, and finally joins the lane to Clay End.

From here, you can follow the actual

outline of the Hound almost completely. The lane goes south-east from Clay End past Holmes Farm and Walkern Park Farm defining the chest and belly. The track becomes a bridleway, still outlining the effigy. When it turns south, in a sharp bend, it marks the inner side of the hind leg. Follow the bridleway on towards Hebing End.

Head downhill to the River Old Bourne, and take the path along its western bank. You are now walking along the outside of the hind leg. Continue along the path past the river source to Rush Green, which marks the Hound's rump and the stump of his tail.

From here, you can continue north-east along the bridleway towards the Roman road (see p.220), but to walk along the outline of the Hound take the lane to Wood End. From Clay End until this point you have never deviated from the outline of the Hound, and you will continue to follow the outline until you reach our starting point at Ardeley, although the last section of the footpath around the back and neck is not quite so smooth.

From Wood End, take the minor road towards Parker's Green, and at the end of it turn right, doubling back on yourself. This path soon goes to the north, and then turns to the north-west making a proper delineation of the figure as far as the ear at Ardeley.

Because I have been greatly impressed by the way these figures, and indeed most of the alignments I have looked at in this book, are linked with Roman roads, I do suggest that you try to walk along the one to the north of this effigy. You can do so, by retracing your steps from Ardeley towards Hare Street, and then going south-west along the Roman road to Cherry Green. It is a matter of just over 3·5 miles (5·6 km), although you must be prepared to find that some stretches of it run across ploughland and you will have to establish your right of way without benefit of any public footpath signs.

If you feel you cannot face that, take the lane from Ardeley as far as the wide common land of Moor Green, which obviously once provided extensive grazing rights – for geese particularly, if the name of the village's pleasant pub is any indication. You will have to go a little out of your way if you want to visit The Goose, for the path to the Roman road is on your left, and goes via the grounds of Moor Hall. When you reach the Roman road head towards Hare Street.

324246

330237

337252

26255

322257

311286

356257

325267

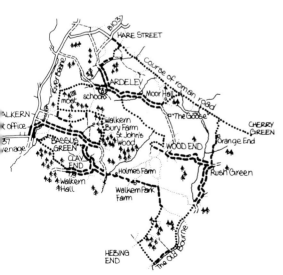

221

Walking in East Anglia

It will seem strange to anyone experienced in fell walking that I insist that a map and a compass are also essential in the heavily cultivated area of East Anglia. True, you will be in no actual physical danger here if you lose track of your whereabouts, but being able to pin-point your position exactly does help you to settle any rights of way disputes you may run into.

The owners of the rich agricultural land of Norfolk, Suffolk and the fens are very jealous of their territory, and on the whole they do not welcome walkers. So there are few public footpath signs, for most parish councils responsible for such way marks are made up of landowners. So you should be guided by the rights of way marked on the Ordnance Survey sheets; and when you are confronted with acres of ploughland, the dividing hedges having all been grubbed up, it is important to know where your path lies. At the same time, I would rather walk round the headland of a field, if it is at all possible, than trample on growing crops however illegally they have been planted. If you follow my example you will be trespassing; if you follow the letter of the law you will be destroying food. The choice is yours.

One other warning on rights of way: do not assume that the old concrete runways crossing the many disused airfields that you will come across are meant for the public. The whole matter of restoring access on the old paths that ran for centuries on land now occupied by the old airfields is still very confused and, wherever possible, I have tried to avoid them.

Another reason for taking a compass with you is for forest walking. The paths through the Forestry Commission's conifers are all numbered, but as they all look exactly the same to the newcomer, and as you will be mostly walking on the flat with few gradients to direct you, it is essential to have some means of knowing your whereabouts and direction.

It is best to keep dogs on leads: partly because it is very difficult to argue your case with a landowner while whistling your trespassing animal to heel or disentangling him from a fight with the farm dog; and partly because many of these walks go through nature reserves administered by various naturalist associations.

I have noted the areas which are particularly good for people who are interested in bird and plant life. The Breckland is an especially rich source of wild flowers, and happily visitors have at last begun to realize that they are for enjoying as they grow and not for picking.

There are some places, however, where you may feel tempted to interfere with the vegetation, and that is when a marked right of way has been allowed to get so overgrown that it is virtually

222

impassable – the old Roman road of Beard's Lane in the Nuthampstead zodiac is a sad example. In such a place you may have to cut your way through, but do it as neatly as possible – whatever the provocation, don't just tear at branches and undergrowth.

You are not likely to perish of exposure or starvation anywhere in East Anglia, but there are some areas where you could be walking for some six or seven miles without passing near a village and with no access to drinking water. I always believe in taking oranges on a walk, both as thirst quenchers and energy givers.

Many of these routes pass through lanes which make very pleasant cycling tracks. The bicycle is enjoying a great come-back in East Anglia, and several agencies in each area offer them for hire at reasonable cost.

East Anglia is rich in ancient churches, many dating from Saxon times, and frequently with more than one to a village. Several of these are now no longer in use and so are kept locked up. They are nearly all worth visiting, though, and the keys are usually easily obtainable from a nearby house, indicated by a note in the church porch. But this does mean that if you want to look inside one of the churches standing on a ley alignment, you will have to allow plenty of time for your visit.

Looking North-West

The royal roads of Britain, set out by the legendary Belinus and recorded by Geoffrey of Monmouth, are reported to have met by the western edge of the Icknield Way, where the Bedfordshire town of Dunstable now stands. Edward I found the place so holy, that he acted as though he considered it to be the spiritual centre of his kingdom. Here he set up a memorial to his dead queen, Eleanor, and decreed that people could claim sanctuary within the whole borough – as though the town were some vast cathedral.

It is from this unlikely conurbation, now almost completely merged with Luton, that I want to look north-west out of East Anglia towards the ley lines of the Peak District and the South Pennines. These northern ley lines relate to the northerly alignments from Stonehenge, as those in East Anglia relate to the ones running towards the sunrise.

Nowadays, northbound traffic finds it more significant that Dunstable lies close to the M1 than that its centre is marked by the crossing of the Icknield Way (following the chalk though to Wiltshire) and Watling Street (now the A5 going to Telford and North Wales). Nevertheless, in the nineteenth century Dunstable was one of the busiest coaching towns in the country, running regular and frequent services to Birmingham, Chester, Liverpool, Sheffield and Halifax. Luton only boasted one service, *The Peveril of the Peak*, a coach named partly in honour of Sir Walter Scott's novel of that name, and partly because it passed beneath the forbidding ruins of Peveril Castle in Castleton, Derbyshire, before terrorizing its passengers with the fearsome Winnats Pass. According to David H. Kennet, who gives an account of the coaching routes in *Portrait of Bedfordshire*, the Luton service was short-lived, although, for a while, it ran as far as Edinburgh and claimed to be able to get there in less than two days.

Coaching routes may not seem to have any immediate connection with ley lines, but I believe that we should follow Watkins' example by always taking trading routes into account, and then seeing how they fit with hypotheses about ley energy. Could it be that *The Peveril of the Peak* would have had a longer run if it had started out from the natural centre of Dunstable, as the other coaches did?

Long before the coaching days and the turnpike roads of the eighteenth century, when Watling Street was an almost impassable green lane, there was traffic between Dunstable and the Peak District – for Dunstable Priory owned lands around Elton, between Youlgreave and Bakewell. It is tempting to speculate that it was a fourteenth-century pilgrim connected with that priory who once owned the lead ampulla of our lady of Walsingham which was found in 1926 in a Derbyshire cottage garden at the foot of Stanton Moor. The ampulla is now on display in the little museum attached to Haddon Hall, just outside Bakewell in Derbyshire.

224

Thousands of years before Christianity, the route between East Anglia and the Peak District must have been frequented by traders. Today the recently ploughed fields of Elton Common, and the farm meadows around the stone circle of Arbor Low to the south, are filled with flints which very probably came from Grime's Graves; for Derbyshire, a county made up of limestone, shale and millstone grit, has no natural flints .

If you want to go to Dunstable before setting out on some of the Derbyshire ley line walks which I shall be outlining in my next book, go out to the downs, where you can watch the gliders and the hang-gliders, and visit the tumuli of the Five Knolls, standing to the west of the Icknield Way at 007210. These Bronze Age barrows were once part of a much more extensive group, and in more recent times the hillside was used as a place of execution and a centre for witchcraft. To offset that instance of the dark side of a ley lines crossing point, I should like to call on John of Dunstable, who died on Christmas Eve, 1453 leaving behind a great body of musical compositions, which are ironically more appreciated on the continent than in his native England. That does not detract from the notion that his creative energy may well have been enhanced by his birthplace.

Apart from the A5 covering Watling Street, there is one other modern road of interest to anyone connecting the alignments of East Anglia with those of the north-west of England. That is the Via Devana whose route we followed south-east from Wandlebury, which continues north-west out of Cambridge as the A604 to Huntingdon and Kettering, and once went on to Chester.

It is important because it focuses our attention on Cambridge. From the alignments discovered in Cambridge we shall probably be able to link the course of the ley lines running through East Anglia with those of the rest of the country. This has nothing inherently to do with the alignments themselves; it is because Watkins' only son Allen lived in Cambridge, and Nigel Pennick (whose researches I have constantly acknowledged in the course of this book) is currently based there. He is now organizing a group who are charting the projections from all the ley alignments in that city and the surrounding countryside. It is not cynical to observe that ley lines will always be thickest along the ground in the areas where the keenest and most energetic ley hunters work.

So we must look mainly in the Cambridge area for the long distance projections that link East Anglia to the main alignments drawn throughout the country from Stonehenge to Avebury. In *The Landscape Geometry of Southern Britain*, Michael Behrend gives three such lines running from Cambridge. The first goes from the north-east corner of King's College chapel *via* Olney church in north Buckinghamshire to the summit of Black Daren on Offa's Dyke. On the way it passes through Whiteleaved Oak (a hamlet standing at the junction of the counties of Hereford, Worcestershire and Gloucestershire) and the central

point of a decagon, of which the southern base is a line between Stonehenge and Glastonbury Abbey.

Behrend's second line runs from the Mare Way (see section 5, p.188) through Aylesbury and Nuneham Courtenay (just outside Oxford) by Avebury ring to the Lizard. The third, which starts from Soham church in Cambridgeshire, goes through the centre of Luton to Gallows Hill near Salisbury, which is a focal point for many of the geometric figures projected from Stonehenge.

So far nothing has been projected that links the East Anglian leys with those radiating from Arbor Low in Derbyshire, which some people take to be the true centre of the ley system in these islands. So here I would like to pause to consider how links could be made. There are three types of connection to be considered, and in each the vital places on the land are conspicuously marked, usually with some man-made feature dating from prehistoric times. Often the same feature (a cairn, barrow or standing stone) serves to mark all three types of connection. In such a case it will be a way mark for the traveller, an outlet for a channel of ley energy, and also a survey point, serving much the same function as our modern triangulation points.

I have already indicated some of the links which travellers, pilgrims and traders have made between East Anglia and the Peak District. I wish I could say something specific about the way the ley systems of the two areas connect, as I feel sure they do. It is as inconceivable to think of any network of ley lines existing completely on its own, as it is to imagine that the nervous system of your right hand is unrelated to that of your left foot.

Our knowledge of the anatomy of the ley system depends on the work of three interrelated disciplines. First, there are the surveys made by the dowsers and ley hunters who plot the course of the ley energy. Secondly, a strong contribution has been made by the academically respectable study of astro-archaelogy, which is concerned with the way that prehistoric sites are oriented towards aspects of the sun, moon and stars, and so towards each other. Finally, there has been a welcome development in traditional archaeology, which is now moving away from an almost total concentration on the dead and their grave goods and towards an appreciation of what the present landscape can tell us about the hundreds of generations of people who have made their living from it. I am confident that these three sources will enable us, in the next few years, to draw a convincing picture linking the ley systems throughout Britain.

Meanwhile, we are left with some, apparently, completely arbitrary geometric patterns on the land, which seem to point towards very early attempts to make sense of the terrain. Watkins realized the importance of the early surveyors, whom he called Dod-men. He was sure that they must have been treated with the same veneration as the astronomer priests if, indeed, the two functions were not carried out by the same people.

He believed that the Dod-men, with their two surveying staves, worked out the long straight tracks for the traders to follow. Since his time we have realized, from the geometric shapes discovered in the landscape, that a far more sophisticated operation was in progress; although, even in Watkins' time, the prehistory of land geometry had been observed.

In a letter of 26th July 1922, syndicated to three East Anglian newspapers in reply to a hostile review by W.G. Clarke of Watkins' *Early British Trackways*, Arthur Cross of Brisley commented that people should be looking for geometric shapes on the ground as well as for long straight lines. He did not actually make any geographical connections between the figures based on Stonehenge and those in East Anglia, but he compared the 'isosceles triangle of which Stonehenge and Avebury form the base and Silchester the apex' with those he had noted in Norfolk, which he claimed were based on the same measurement as that between Stonehenge and Avebury, i.e., 'approximately 18 miles or 20 Roman miles'. The Norfolk lines he noticed based on this measurement are those from Castle Acre to Brancester, from Norwich to Happisburgh, and from Tasburgh to Burgh Castle.

The measurements which the ley hunters are working on today are much more complex and precise, and they result in the discovery of involved, interlocking geometric figures stretching across the country. Projecting from the figures he has discovered around Cambridge, Michael Behrend shows how a line running from Adventurers' Fen through Thriplow church extends to the ley centre at Brisley in Surrey. It forms part of a geometric figure whose southernmost points lie beneath the English Channel. On that he bases his belief that the leys must have been marked out when that was still dry land, sometime between 7,000 and 6,000 BC, long before the building of the neolithic henges.

There is an obvious link, though as far as I am aware it has still been unexplored, between these geometric shapes and the triangles from which the earliest map-makers have worked out their projections. So far as I know nobody has yet tried to correlate the geometric figures marked by prehistoric sites with the projections from the various triangles plotted by successive generations of cartographers since the use of writing materials was invented.

We are left with the mystery of the zodiacs. The patterns that people now see as they pore over maps, discern from the ground or, more fortunately, observe from the air, appear to have been marked out in much later times, as the effigies all relate to those of classical mythology. Unlike the other types of projection that we have observed, which invariably interlink with other figures, the zodiacs, however close together they may be, rarely overlap. This was seen at the ones in Bury St Edmunds and Nuthampstead, and we shall see it again in the two zodiacs of the south Pennines based on Hebden Bridge and Pendle Hill.

Yet there is a pattern emerging in the siting of the zodiacs, and some people believe that when they have all been charted, they will all be found to stand in zones defined by lines radiating out from Arbor Low in Derbyshire. This circle of horizontal stones stands almost directly due north of Stonehenge; and forms the base of a local isosceles triangle whose other points are marked by a henge near Buxton to the west and one on Eyam Moor near Sheffield to the east. Another greater, but less well authenticated, triangle has Arbor Low at its apex while the base is drawn between St Michael's church at Ottery in Somerset and West Mersea in Essex.

If you are interested in the mathematical calculations on which all these projections are based you will certainly want to keep abreast of the new discoveries. I recommend *The Ley Hunter*, a magazine edited by Paul Devereux from P.O. Box 152, London N10 2EF. You should also consult *The Landscape Geometry of Southern Britain* which is available from the Institute of Geomantic Research at 142 Pheasant Rise, Bar Hill, Cambridge CB3 8SD. For a general account of the development of the theories behind these studies I can recommend John Michell's *A Little History of Astro-archaeology* and Nigel Pennick's *The Ancient Science of Geomancy*. And if, as I hope, you plan to follow me from East Anglia to Derbyshire and like to explore the rich variety of the links between places, you would do well to start off by looking at David H. Kennett's *Portrait of Bedfordshire*.

Bibliography

Ashbee, P. *The Ancient British* (Geo Abstracts, Norwich, 1978).

Barrett, W.H. *Tales from the Fens* ed. E. Porter (Routledge & Kegan Paul, London, 1963).

Bergier, J. *Mysteries of the Earth* (Futura, London, 1975).

Clarke, H. *East Anglia* (Heinemann Education, London, 1971).

Clarke, R. Rainbird. *East Anglia* (E.P. Publishing, Wakefield, 1971).

Clarke, R. Rainbird. *In Breckland Wilds* (E.P. Publishing, Wakefield, 1974).

Cook, O. *Breckland* (Robert Hale, London, 1956).

Cook, O. *Suffolk* (Paul Elek, London, 1948).

Dutt, W.A. *Highways and Byways of East Anglia* (Macmillan, London, 1902).

Dutt, W.A. *Norfolk* (Methuen, London, 1902).

Evans, G.E. *Pattern under the Plough* (Faber & Faber, London, 1971).

Field, J.E. *The Myth of the Pent Cuckoo* (Elliot Stock, London, 1913).

Fowler, J.P. ed. *Recent Work in Rural Archaeology* (Moonraker Press, Wiltshire, 1974).

Fox, C. *The Archaeology of the Cambridge Region* (C.U.P., 1923).

Gleadow, R. *The Origin of the Zodiac* (Jonathan Cape, London, 1968).

Graves, T. *Needles of Stone* (Turnstone Press, London, 1978).

Hippsley Cox R. *The Green Roads of England* (Methuen, London, 1914).

Lethbridge, T.C. *Gogmagog: the Buried Gods* (Routledge & Kegan Paul, London, 1975).

Lethbridge, T.C. *Witches* (Routledge & Kegan Paul, London, 1962).

Lord, R. & Pennick, N. *Terrestrial Zodiacs in Britain* (Institute of Geomantic Research, Cambridge, 1976).

Michell, J. *View over Atlantis* (Sphere, London, 1975).

Pennick, N. *Geomancy* (Cockaygne, Cambridge, 1973).

Robert, A. *Sons of Thunder* (Rider & Co., London, 1978).

Screeton, P. *Quicksilver Heritage* (Sphere, London, 1977).

Underwood, G. *Pattern of the Past* (Sphere, London, 1972).

Watkins, A. *Archaic Tracks around Cambridge* (Simpkin Marshall, London, 1932).

Watkins, A. *The Old Straight Track* (Sphere, London, 1974).

Index